# Liquid Criminology

This book explores the ways in which criminological methods can be imaginatively deployed and developed in a world increasingly characterized by the blurred nature of social reality. Whilst recognizing the importance of positivist approaches and research techniques, it advocates a commitment to understanding the ways in which those techniques can be used imaginatively, at times in combination with less conventional methods, discussing the questions concerning risk, ethics and access that arise as a result.

Giving voice to cutting-edge research practices both in terms of concepts and methods that shift the criminological focus towards the kind of imaginative work that comprised the foundations of the discipline, it calls into question the utility and credentials of mainstream work that fails to serve the discipline itself or the policy questions allied to it.

A call not to 'give up on numbers' but also not to be defined by statistics and the methods that produce them, *Liquid Criminology* sheds light on a way of doing research for criminology that is not only creative but also critical. As such, it will appeal to scholars of sociology, criminology and social policy with interests in research methods and design.

**Michael Hviid Jacobsen** is Professor of Sociology at Aalborg University, Denmark. He is the editor of *The Poetics of Crime* and co-editor of *The Sociology of Zygmunt Bauman, Encountering the Everyday, The Transformation of Modernity, Utopia: Social Theory and the Future* and *Imaginative Methodologies: The Poetic Imagination in the Social Sciences*.

**Sandra Walklate** is Eleanor Rathbone Chair of Sociology in the Department of Sociology, Social Policy and Criminology at the University of Liverpool, UK, and Adjunct Professor in the School of Justice, Queensland University of Technology, Australia. Her recent publications include *Victims: Trauma, Testimony, Justice* (with R. McGarry) and *The Contradictions of Terrorism* (with G. Mythen).

# Liquid Criminology

Doing imaginative criminological research

**Edited by Michael Hviid Jacobsen
and Sandra Walklate**

Routledge
Taylor & Francis Group

LONDON AND NEW YORK

First published 2017 by Routledge

2 Park Square, Milton Park, Abingdon, Oxfordshire OX14 4RN
52 Vanderbilt Avenue, New York, NY 10017

*Routledge is an imprint of the Taylor & Francis Group, an informa business*

First issued in paperback 2020

*British Library Cataloguing in Publication Data*
A catalogue record for this book is available from the British Library

*Library of Congress Cataloging in Publication Data*
A catalog record has been requested for this book

ISBN: 978-1-4724-5523-9 (hbk)
ISBN: 978-0-367-59638-5 (pbk)

Typeset in Times New Roman
by Swales & Willis Ltd, Exeter, Devon, UK

MIX
Paper from
responsible sources
FSC
www.fsc.org    FSC™ C013985

Printed in the United Kingdom
by Henry Ling Limited

# Contents

# Figures

# Contributors

**Matthew Bacon** is Lecturer in Criminology and a member of the Centre for Criminological Research at the University of Sheffield, UK. His research and publications have coalesced around policing, drug control policy and the informal economy. In addition to numerous articles and chapters, he is the author of *Taking Care of Business: Police Detectives, Drug Law Enforcement and Proactive Investigation* (2016).

**Pat Carlen**, Honorary Professor at Leicester University, UK, was recipient of the American Society of Criminology's Sellin-Glueck Prize for Outstanding International Contributions to Criminology in 1997, the British Society of Criminology's Award for Outstanding Achievement 2010 and an honorary Doctorate of Laws from Lincoln University 2011. A biographical chapter was published in *Fifty Key Thinkers in Criminology* (Routledge, 2010). A collection of her selected works, *A Criminological Imagination*, was published in Ashgate's Pioneers in Contemporary Criminology Series in 2010. Her next book is *Alternative Criminologies*, edited with Leandro Ayres Franca (forthcoming, 2016).

**Eamonn Carrabine** is Professor of Sociology at the University of Essex, UK. His books include: *Crime in Modern Britain* (co-authored, 2002), *Power, Discourse and Society: A Genealogy of the Strangeways Prison Riot* (2004) and *Crime, Culture and the Media* (2008), while his co-authored textbook *Criminology: A Sociological Introduction* is now in its third edition. He is currently writing a book on *Crime and Social Theory*, which will be published by Palgrave Macmillan, and was recently awarded a Leverhulme Trust Major Research Fellowship to research his project 'The Iconography of Punishment: From Renaissance to Modernity'.

**Kerry Carrington** is Head of School of Justice, Faculty of Law, Queensland University of Technology, Australia. She is an internationally leading expert in critical and feminist criminology and has published widely on the subject. Her books include: *Who Killed Leigh Leigh?* (1998), *Critical Criminology* (2002), *Policing the Rural Crisis* (2006), *Offending Youth* (2009) and *Feminism and Global Justice* (2015). She has been the recipient of several awards, including the Lifetime Achievement Award, (Division of Critical Criminology) American Society of Criminology and Distinguished Scholar (Division of Women and Crime), American Society of Criminology.

**Walter S. DeKeseredy** is Anna Deane Carlson Endowed Chair of Social Sciences, Director of the Research Center on Violence and Professor of Sociology at West Virginia University, US. He has published 20 books and over 160 scientific journal articles and book chapters on violence against women and other social problems. In 2008, the Institute on Violence, Abuse and Trauma gave him the Linda Saltzman Memorial Intimate Partner Violence Researcher Award. In 1995, he received the Critical Criminologist of the Year Award from the ASC's Division on Critical Criminology (DCC) and in 2008 the DCC gave him the Lifetime Achievement Award. In 2014, he received the Critical Criminal Justice Scholar Award from the Academy of Criminal Justice Sciences' Section on Critical Criminal Justice.

**Claire Ferguson** is a lecturer, researcher and consultant in forensic criminology at Queensland University of Technology, Australia. Her research surrounds offender evidence manipulation in violent crime. She offers assistance to law enforcement and contributes to training courses for professionals in the field. She is a board member of the *Journal of Forensic Social Sciences* (JFSS) and a member of the ASC's Homicide Research Working Group (HRWG).

**Jeff Ferrell** is Visiting Professor of Criminology at the University of Kent, UK, Professor of Sociology at Texas Christian University, US, and founding and current editor of the New York University Press book series *Alternative Criminology*. His books include *Crimes of Style* (1996), *Tearing Down the Streets* (2003), *Empire of Scrounge* (2005) and, with Keith Hayward and Jock Young, the first and second editions of *Cultural Criminology: An Invitation* (2008), winner of the 2009 Distinguished Book Award from the American Society of Criminology's Division of International Criminology. He is currently completing a book on drift and drifters.

**Kate Fitz-Gibbon** is a Senior Lecturer in Criminology in the School of Social Sciences at Monash University, Victoria, Australia, and Honorary Research Fellow in the School of Law and Social Justice, University of Liverpool, UK. Her research examines the adequacy of legal responses to violence against women and the impact of homicide law reform in Australia, the UK and the US. This research has been undertaken with a focus on constructions of gender, responsibility and justice. She has advised on homicide law reform reviews in several Australian jurisdictions. Her recent publications include *Homicide Law Reform, Gender and the Provocation Defence* (2014) and *Homicide Law Reform in Victoria: Retrospect and Prospects* (edited with Arie Freiberg, 2015).

**Barry Godfrey** is Professor and Faculty Lead for Research at the University of Liverpool, UK. He has authored or co-authored a number of books on the history of crime. His research interests include private policing, desistance, biographical historical methods, digital methodologies, longitudinal studies of sentencing, ethics and historical research, and changes to the operation of criminal justice over the nineteenth and twentieth centuries.

**Michael Hviid Jacobsen** is Professor of Sociology at the Department of Sociology and Social Work, Aalborg University, Denmark. His research is concerned with topics such as crime, utopia, ethics, death and dying, palliative care, qualitative methods and social theory. His recent publications include: *Utopia: Social Theory and the Future* (edited, 2012), *Deconstructing Death* (edited, 2013), *Imaginative Methodologies in the Social Sciences* (edited, 2014), *The Social Theory of Erving Goffman* (2014), *The Poetics of Crime* (edited, 2014), *Beyond Bauman* (edited, forthcoming), *Postmortal Society* (edited, forthcoming), *The Interactionist Imagination* (edited, forthcoming) and *Emotions and Everyday Life* (edited, forthcoming).

**Ashleigh Larkin** is a PhD student in the School of Justice, Faculty of Law, Queensland University of Technology, Australia. She is undertaking a study of girls' violence using innovative e-methodologies. The study combines e-methods with a survey of girls who have used or witnessed the Internet in the commission of violence against other girls.

**Ross McGarry** is Lecturer in Criminology in the Department of Sociology, Social Policy and Criminology at the University of Liverpool, UK. He has written widely in international journals on criminology, victimology and critical military studies, including *The British Journal of Criminology* and *Armed Forces and Society*. He is the co-editor (with Sandra Walklate) of *Criminology and War: Transgressing the Borders* (2015), the forthcoming *Palgrave Handbook on Criminology and War* and co-author with Sandra Walklate of *Victims: Trauma, Testimony and Justice* (2015). He is currently writing a monograph for the New Directions in Critical Criminology series for Routledge entitled *Criminology and the Military*.

**Maggie O'Neill** is Professor in Sociology and Criminology at the University of York, UK. Her research activity includes the development of social and feminist theory, a focus upon innovative biographical, cultural and participatory research methodologies, and the production of praxis – knowledge which addresses and intervenes in public policy. Her research activity has been instrumental in moving forward debates, dialogue and scholarship in three substantive areas: sex work and the commercial sex industry; forced migration and the asylum–migration nexus; and innovative participatory, biographical, performative and visual methodologies. Her recent publications include: *Advances in Biographical Methods: Creative Applications* (2014, with Brian Roberts and Andrew Sparkes), *Transgressive Imaginations* (2012, with Lizzie Seal) and *Asylum, Migration and Community* (2010). She is currently writing a book on walking method, *Walking Methods: Biographical Research on the Move* with Brian Roberts.

**Wayne A. Petherick** is a forensic criminologist and Associate Professor of Criminology at Bond University, Gold Coast, Australia. In addition to teaching and research, he works on cases from risk and threat assessment and management to stalking, sexual assault and homicide. He has lectured in Australia and the US on the areas of criminal motivations, forensic victimology, criminal profiling, applied crime analysis, stalking, sexual assault and homicide (including multiple homicide). Over the last 17 years in the tertiary education sector, he has authored or co-authored 60 textbooks, book chapters and journal publications, including *Forensic Criminology* (with Brent E. Turvey and Claire E. Ferguson, 2010). In his work, he has developed a unique approach to crime analysis called 'Applied Crime Analysis' to distinguish it from other types of analytic work, as described in *Applied Crime Analysis* (2015).

**Teela Sanders** is Professor in Criminology at the University of Leicester, UK. Her research focus is on the intersections between gender, regulation and the sex industry, with a focus on exploring hidden economies. She has an international profile as a leading expert in the studies of sex work building on research showcased in the monographs *Sex Work: A Risky Business* (2005) and *Paying for Pleasure: Men Who Buy Sex* (2008). Her recent publications include *Flexible Workers: Labour, Regulation and the Political Economy of the Stripping Industry in the UK* (2014). She has edited several collections, including the *Oxford Handbook of Sex Offences and Sex Offenders* (2016). Her current work focuses on the Internet and sex work in a large ESRC project (2015–18) with Jane Scoular entitled *Beyond the Gaze*.

**Sandra Walklate** is Eleanor Rathbone Chair of Sociology at the University of Liverpool, UK, and Adjunct Professor at Queensland University of Technology, Brisbane, Australia. Internationally recognised for her work in victimology and research on criminal victimization, her recent publications include: *Victims: Trauma, Testimony, Justice* (with Ross McGarry, 2015), *The Contradictions of Terrorism* (with Gabe Mythen, 2014) and *Criminology and War: Transgressing the Borders* (edited with Ross McGarry, 2015). She is currently Editor in Chief of the *British Journal of Criminology* and in 2014 was given the British Society of Criminology's Outstanding Achievement Award.

**Louise Westmarland** is Senior Lecturer in Criminology at the Open University. Her fields of interest include police culture, gender, homicide and ethics. She has recently completed a national study of police integrity and corruption. She has also carried out studies of police ethics in the US that involved shadowing homicide detectives as they conducted murder investigations and is a UK Home Office-accredited Domestic Homicide Review Chair.

# Preface and acknowledgements

This book is the tangible outcome of a conversation which took place at the University of Liverpool in December of 2014 – a conversation between two, at the time, complete strangers, and a conversation that actually was intended and expected to centre on other projects and purposes, but which incidentally also ended up materializing in this edited collection. Although this book was in this way the unintended consequence of other initiatives and intentions, we are delighted that we decided to pursue and complete the project. It has been an intriguing journey that has allowed us to toy with and develop our own understanding of criminology and its contemporary challenges. We do hope our readers will share our enthusiasm.

All books are either explicitly or implicitly indebted to and inspired by some-one other than the authors themselves, even though they often take all the credit as well as all the critique. This is perhaps particularly true when it comes to edited collections, as they are the obvious outcome of truly collaborative processes in which the editors serve the role of kick-starters and birth aides for ideas. We could therefore mention many sources of inspiration and gratitude behind this book. For the sake of brevity, however, we will refrain from such a speech of thanks and mention only those who have specifically contributed to the volume. Needless to say, we are obviously heavily indebted to the work of Zygmunt Bauman for his wonderful coining of the notion of 'liquid modernity' informing this book and its title. His critical understanding and way of practising sociology has served as an important source of inspiration for thinking about the discipline of criminology – its problems as well as its potentials. We are also grateful for the professional and always supportive collaboration with Ashgate Publishing and particularly with commissioning editor Neil Jordan. Moreover, we wish to thank all of our con-tributors who with their insights, experiences and perspectives have opened up the criminological imagination, thereby making this book possible.

Winter 2015/2016
*Michael Hviid Jacobsen*
Aalborg University

*Sandra Walklate*
University of Liverpool

# Introduction

## Introducing 'liquid criminology'

*Sandra Walklate and Michael Hviid Jacobsen*

### Why 'liquid criminology'?

For quite some time, the term 'liquid', both as a descriptor and a metaphor, has been associated primarily with the work of Zygmunt Bauman. It was invented by him at the turn of the millennium in the book *Liquid Modernity* in order to capture the new social landscape that confronted social researchers as well as ordinary people who, according to Bauman, had been used to navigating in a so-called 'solid modern' world. Its use is intended, in part, to capture the rapidly changing nature of the social world. In this worldview, not only have the foundations of social life become slippery and hard to grasp, the very things that people rely on are subject to constant re-configuration and re-negotiation. Such liquidity has become the default position for normal life. Now fluidity is the norm instead of solidity. As Bauman says:

> Liquid life is a precarious life, lived under conditions of constant uncertainty. The most acute and stubborn worries that haunt such a life are the fears of being caught napping, of failing to catch up with fast moving events, of being left behind, of over-looking 'use by' dates, of being saddled with possessions that are no longer desirable, of missing the moment that calls for a change of tack before crossing the point of no return. (Bauman 2005: 2)

If this view of the social world has legitimacy, and this collection starts from the position that is has, what implications does that have for doing research on the social world? Contrary to the situation in the discipline of sociology, and despite promotion of the notion by some of the stalwarts of the field (Ferrell, Hayward and Young 2008), the metaphor of liquidity has still not really caught on as a household concept within the field of criminology, although it has now been – with some time delay – widely accepted and adopted within many other neighbouring disciplines (see e.g. Jacobsen 2015). True, Bauman himself has not yet ventured into analysing the notion of 'liquidity' comprehensively or systematically to the topic of crime, although he has incidentally discussed and applied his general terminology to the topic of crime. He has also insisted that 'the new focus on crime and on dangers threatening the bodily safety of individuals and their property has been shown beyond reasonable doubt to be intimately related to the mood of precariousness' (Bauman 2007: 17; see also Daems and Robert

2007). Perhaps for Bauman's own lack of a systematic application of the meta-phor of 'liquid modernity' to the topic of crime, or perhaps for other reasons, the number of books, journal articles or research reports specifically owing to, draw-ing on, utilizing or playing with the notions of 'liquidity', 'liquid modernity' or 'liquid crime' is still not impressive (for a few exceptions, see e.g. Bolden 2012; Varney 2009; Zedner 2006), and the concept has so far not become a catchphrase for the discipline of criminology. However, the metaphor has not been entirely ignored. In criminology, this view of the social world has perhaps been most read-ily embraced in the work of Jock Young (1999, 2007, 2011). To Young, showing significant inspiration from Bauman's own analysis, the vertigo of such a liquid modern world is increasingly characterized by:

> broken narratives where economic and ontological insecurity abounds . . . [In such a world] the nature of crime and the response to it is far from mundane; that the actors are far from pallid creatures calculating the best manoeuvres through the social world in order to minimise risk and maximise contentment and that much of the dynamic behind crime is resentment and much of the response to it is vituperative. (Young 2007: 20)

In discussing the implications of such liquidity, Young (2007: 3) suggests that 'all of this creates great potentialities for human flexibility and reinvention. Yet it generates at the same time considerable ontological insecurity – precariousness of being'. This takes its toll on both social and individual processes, but, for the purposes of this edited collection, it also challenges criminology in how, as a dis-cipline, it can conduct its business.

Of course, it goes without saying that criminology is a space occupied by dif-ferent disciplines with different ways of doing criminological work tied together by the substantive topic of crime. It is an area of concern that has been historically preoccupied with the question of how to intervene in the crime problem in what-ever way that problem has been defined. It is, as David Downes (1988) observed some time ago, a 'rendezvous' subject. This much is self-evident from any crimi-nological textbook. However, despite the different voices that come together in this meeting place to speak about crime, the voices that predominate within it do not necessarily appreciate the contemporary liquid nature of social reality. There are still many positions and perspectives prevalent within criminology that linger in the terminology and understanding of a solid rather than a liquid modern world. Here the use of the notion of liquidity not only opens up the social world of crimi-nology to ingenious interpretation, but also invites disciplinary outsiders, heretic ideas and imaginative methodologies to participate in enhancing, developing and toying with our present understanding of crime (see e.g. Jacobsen 2014). As Mary Catherine Bateson (1989: 73) once observed: 'The most creative thinking occurs at the meeting places of disciplines . . . At the edges where the lines are blurred, it is easier to imagine that the world might be different.' Imagining such difference remains on the side-lines of much criminological endeavour. Of course, this obser-vation applies to many disciplinary areas, not just criminology, but in relation to the substantive issues that are the focal concern of criminology, it is an observation that is particularly pertinent. Indeed, the disciplinary 'ownership' of such topics like war, terrorism and security that recent world events have brought to the fore is becoming more blurred and the nature of those blurred boundaries has increasingly demanded the engagement of criminology in areas of concern once thought not to be within its ambit. Moreover, inter-disciplinary meeting places not only ask questions about how the world might be differently imagined, they also ask questions about how to engage with that world. How it is possible to explore and intervene in a world about which we share common concerns? This is the key question that underpins this collection. It is a question that asks us to consider what constitutes the criminological imagination under these liquid modern conditions and how it might be possible to operationalize that imagination. Consequently, this is not a conventional research methods book. Here we are not concerned with how *to do* research as an ideal practice or indeed how that reality might be practically engaged with in the course of doing research. Here we are rather concerned with embracing the concept of liquidity and engaging with it as an orientation towards what knowledge counts and how it might be possible to give voice to different ways of making knowledge count in the interests of those with whom we are engaged. Put simply, and following Young (2011), we are concerned to put the dominance of positivism within criminology in its place, both practically and metaphorically.

## Re-considering criminology in an age of liquidity

Much of Young's (2011: 80) attack on the so-called 'bogus of positivism' is directed towards the 'most influential criminology generated by the most atypical society' – that is, the kind of criminology that is dominant in North America. Young's particular preoccupations notwithstanding, there has been an increasing recognition that the discipline, and the policy agendas that derive from its concerns, are not currently best served by this 'the bogus of positivism'. Indeed, Jeff Ferrell has asserted this view much more strongly. He states:

> Criminology is today crippled by its own methodology, its potential for analysis and critique lost within a welter of survey forms, data sets, and statistical manipulations. Worse, criminology has given itself over to a fetishism of these methodologies. Methods such as these are not only widely and uncritically utilized by contemporary criminologists – they are detailed and reified to the point that, for many criminologists, they have now replaced crime and crime control as the *de facto* subject matter of the discipline. The crisis of criminology doubles back on itself; criminology first embraces methods wholly inadequate and inappropriate for the study of human affairs, and then makes these methods its message. (Ferrell 2009: 1)

Ferrell goes on to say that what criminology needs to do is to 'Kill method' and by this he means research methods informed by the presumptions of positivism. In a similar vein, Young (2011) offers a passionate critique of 'abstracted empiricism' and encourages us to re-visit the commitment of C. Wright Mills (1959) to 'socio-logical craftsmanship'. Remember how Mills specifically urged the sociologist (which also pertained to the criminologist) to stimulate his or her imagination by nurturing 'an attitude of playfulness toward the phrases and words which various issues are defined' (Mills 1959: 129) in order to avoid becoming one of those 'research technicians' who lack 'genuine intellectual puzzlement' and 'passionate curiosity' which eventually resulted in a 'deadly limitation of mind' (Mills 1959: 105). Of course, in urging us to re-visit the perspective of Mills, Young exhorts criminologists not to give up on 'number', but also not to be defined by them and the methods that produce them. As once suggested by Elliott Currie, we need 'a kind of sociological imagination that is able and willing to break free from old constraints and look at the problem of crime and punishment with fresh eyes' (Currie 2002: viii), but we also need a criminology that is willing and able to look beyond the methodological inhibitions of current criminological practice in order to explore new horizons.

It is now well recognized that Ferrell, Young and Currie (amongst many others) have been proponents of what has been termed 'cultural criminology' or at times also 'critical criminology'. This strand of criminology, when put in an international context, has remained marginal to much mainstream criminological work, yet the critique it offers of method is nonetheless profound and disturbing. It is profound because of the questions it asks not only about how criminological work is done, but also the policy agendas that can and do flow from that work. It is disturbing because of the increasing global reach of this 'bogus of positivism', as exemplified by its presence in the rising agendas of Asian and Chinese criminology. Set against the backdrop of liquidity, in which what is meant by crime, where and under what conditions is as subject to change as any other aspect of social life, criminology ignores this critique at its peril. In this collection, we are not exhorting the disci-pline to abandon number. However, in drawing this collection together, we are, by implication, asking for a different epistemological and methodological imagina-tion to unfold and take root. This demands more than the blurring of boundaries between disciplines; it demands that criminology takes a long hard look at itself and its ontological orientation.

Taking the questions raised by Ferrell and Young as our entry point, this edited collection adopts the view, expressed by Bauman (2001), that 'things are not necessarily what they seem to be' and that 'the world may be different from what it is'. Its central focus is to consider how criminological methods can be imaginatively deployed and developed in a world increasingly characterized by 'the blurred, devious, and ironic nature of social reality' (Young 2011: 224). The liquid nature of social reality lies behind this characterization: a social real-ity that cannot be readily captured by the bogus of positivism of which Young (2011) speaks. Perhaps more importantly, it is not just that the methods associ-ated with positivism are not equipped to capture this social reality, it is that reliance on them can distort that social reality. Put simply, the problem with number is also a problem of epistemology and methodology. This is an issue that requires further elucidation.

Further to the interventions of Young (2011), Raewyn Connell (2007) and Katja F. Aas (2012) have also offered some reflections on the nature of contemporary social scientific knowledge that also pose some fundamental questions for criminology, including questions relating to the epistemological, methodological and political implications of mainstream criminology (see also Barton et al. 2007). Connell (2007), for example, discussed the power and influence of what she calls 'Northern theorising'. Here she pays detailed attention to the way in which theoretical assumptions about globalization afford the conclusion that the processes of globalization take their toll on all of us, in the same way and to the same extent. Thus, the Westocentric bias of such theorizing becomes reified and not only blinkers but also blinds such theorizing to other ways of thinking. This has three consequences: other voices and visions of social processes are excluded, non-metropolitan experiences are erased, and the gathering of data from the 'periphery' becomes framed and informed by Northern concepts and methods (Connell 2007: 380). So these blinkers are not only conceptual blinkers, they also drive how the social sciences, including criminology, engage with social reality in practice: how they do their business. In a critique more focused on criminology, Aas observes:

> The global does therefore not present itself as a smooth, unified surface, a plane of immanence accessible through a zoom function, but rather as a dynamic multiplicity of surfaces and tectonic boundaries. It is in these meeting points and frictions between the global north and south, between licit and illicit worlds, that criminology has an opportunity to gain (and provide other social sciences with) invaluable insight into the nature of the contemporary world order. (Aas 2012: 14)

We would also add the following rider: only if there is the disciplinary imagination to practically engage with the world in ways that might capture and understanding these meeting points and frictions.

In line with this trajectory of thought, Boaventura de Sousa Santos (2014) recently called for 'a sociology of absences'. This sociology 'is a transgressive sociology because it violates the positivistic principle that consists of reducing reality to what exists and to what can be analysed with the methodological and analytical instruments of the conventional social sciences' (de Sousa Santos 2014: 172). Such a sociology, and here we are also taking this to apply to criminology, demands two imaginations: the epistemological and the democratic. These principles ask that we think about knowledge, and the knowledge production process, as diverse, complex and relational. Put simply, it implies challenging positivism and linearity, recognising difference and different ways in which it is possible to be productive, and understanding that 'what is the local is not reducible to the concept of hegemonic globalisation' (de Sousa Santos 2014: 179). If the implications of this sociology of absences are embraced, 'The future can thus be found at the crossroads of different knowledges and different technologies' (de Sousa Santos 2014: 200). This is, for instance, a matter of 'admitting that there is not one single linear road leading to knowledge about the social world and that detours, shortcuts, excursions, and roundtrips are an integral and imaginative part of the development of scientific knowledge' (Jacobsen et al. 2014:11). Taken together with the work of Connell (2007), Aas (2012) and de Sousa Santos (2014) amongst others, these views all add some considerable weight to the call made by Young (2011) of the need for criminology to re-think its engagement with the 'bogus of positivism' or, as he puts it, 'the nomothetic impulse [that] is at the heart of positivism: the search for generalizability which is independent of nation or locality' (Young 2011: 73). More than imaginative methods, it is at this juncture that questions of imaginative epistemologies become intertwined with those of geography and democracy.

The imaginations of which de Sousa Santos (2014) speaks – the epistemo-logical and the democratic – raise the spectre for criminology of Stanley Cohen's (1979) 'last seminar'. In other words, the tensions between who we study, why, with what outcome and what engagement have always been acutely felt by those criminologists of a more critical persuasion. These are far from new issues. However, in these liquid times, perhaps what is newer is to work with, and to create the space that liquidity affords, to not only re-visit the questions posed by Cohen's provocative essay, but also render them central to the criminological endeavour. In many ways, the adoption of different ways of thinking about how we know things (epistemology) of course seeps into different ways of practically engaging in that knowledge production process (democracy). Work emanating from feminism has long been an exemplar of this relationship. Indeed, in keeping with the feminist exemplar, the democratic principle implies that criminology not only centres the questions implied by Cohen (1979), it also implies a direct politi-cal challenge to the 'bogus of positivism'. This project can give space to drawing on different ways of doing criminology, as some of the chapters in this collection illustrate. It can also afford a space to different voices. By definition, it implies a critical resistance to the implicit occidental (and colonial) heritage that taints much contemporary criminological work.

If criminology is to make sense of the issues prescient across the globe, and in concert with Young (2011), it needs to loosen the conceptual and methodological shackles of the 'bogus of positivism'. The word 'shackles' is a deliberate refer-ence to slavery, but this slavery is induced by the 'most influential criminology generated by the most atypical society' (Young 2011: 80). For example, Sophie Body-Gendrot (2011) asks how different might the social sciences look and feel if writers and researchers in Africa, Asia and South America were afforded an equal platform to speak about world affairs in Anglophone books, websites and journals. These are good questions indeed and are equally pertinent to criminology. Thus, in recognizing these shackles, it becomes possible to address a major contradic-tion generated by the 'bogus of positivism'. This contradiction is a projection of American (liberal) values, particularly concerning individualism, on criminological endeavour everywhere. The embrace of positivism embeds these values within the discipline, contributes to the 'nomothetic impulse' (Young 2011: 79) and implies a denial of 'specificity' (Young 2011: 77). This liberal vision of knowledge and its production process not only denies culture, it also facilitates the comfortable and comforting liberal analyses of 'othering' and/or demonization found within criminology that are certainly prescient in contemporary thinking about violence, for example, though there are many others.

## About this book: intent and content

Contemporary liquid modern society is rapidly dismantling everything that previously passed or paraded as lasting, universal, unchanging and solid (Bauman 2007). At this juncture, it is timely to ask criminology to reflect on these changes, hence the title of this collection: *Liquid Criminology*. However, it is also important not to do away with positivism and its associated research techniques, but to reflect a commitment to understanding the ways in which those techniques can be and are being used imaginatively, as well as situating these more conventional methods alongside those not considered to be so conventional. Consequently, as indicated above, this edited collection is not a 'how to do' criminological research book, nor is it a book that is concerned with drawing the reader's attention to the 'realities' of criminological research. Both of these approaches are more than adequately covered in the existing literature. The contributions in this collection give voice to cutting-edge research practices both in terms of concepts and methods that shift the criminological focus away from being what C. Wright Mills termed 'cheerful robots' (Young 2011: 224) towards the kind of imaginative work that is indeed to be found in the origins of the discipline. In so doing, its purpose is to challenge the 'sad charade of science played out before us' (Young 2011: 225) and afford a way of doing research for criminology that is not only creative but also, by implication, critical.

Taking its title from the inspirational work of Zygmunt Bauman, this book is indebted to his critical sociological perspective as much as to the cultural and critical criminology of Jock Young, Jeff Ferrell and others. Despite their differences, they all share a common concern with opening the world up – to interpretation, to critical understanding, to diversity and to human action – in order to avoid the ossification of solid modernity. This is as much a welcome initiative as a daunting task. In discussing the contribution of Bauman's work to sociology, Michael Hviid Jacobsen (2013: 191) quotes Bauman and observes that his work sets out:

> a daunting task – 'to pierce the walls of the obvious and self-evident' – particularly because it is destined to provoke those who find comfort, status, and meaning in upholding the status quo and in defining 'the way things currently are'. Therefore it may pose a perilous endeavour to use means and methods usually seen as dangerous or inappropriate when doing sociology and when pointing to the hidden possibilities of the human world.

Here we might substitute sociology with criminology, and whatever disciplinary home someone as a criminologist occupies, the perilous endeavour remains the same. This collection is intended both to celebrate the work of those already engaged in this dangerous endeavour, to encourage those who are about to embark on thinking differently about the world and to challenge those who sit comfortably in the status quo.

This collection falls into three parts: using conventional methods imaginatively, developing imaginative methods and exploring the implications of the meta-methodological issues that arise when endeavouring to forge different imaginings of the criminological craft. No sections are mutually exclusive and all sections put to the fore, in different ways, the challenges encountered when thinking differently, critically and democratically about the research process.

Part I deals loosely with different ways of using conventional criminological methods imaginatively. Pat Carlen's chapter that opens this volume, 'Doing imaginative criminology', offers a timely reminder that whilst the issue with which this collection is concerned may have been marginalized, some of the questions posed here are certainly not new. Here Carlen outlines her personal practice of criminology as informed by three principles: a 'belief that everything that is could be different', a belief that 'it is more important to account for social phenomena than count them' and a belief that 'the concept of criminal justice must remain imaginary (that is, impossible of realization)' (see Carlen, Chapter 1 in this volume). As she points out, this kind of criminological imagination has been central to critical criminology for some time. It is a criminology that is both transgressive and transformative. It constantly offers different ways of doing justice. This chapter offers a concrete articulation of the aforementioned 'sociology of absences' of which de Sousa Santos (2014) speaks and outlines the practical spirit against which the contributions that follow might be understood.

In Chapter 2, Walter S. DeKeseredy develops this critical imagination. In this discussion DeKeseredy charts the growth and influence of the National Criminal Victimization Survey method as a reflection of the dominance of the 'bogus of positivism' commented on by Young (2011). Indeed, particularly in the US, as he argues, the bulk of crime surveys are conducted by orthodox scholars who are caught up in using 'cutting-edge' statistical procedures to produce results that have few, if any, meaningful policy consequences other than reinforcing the inequitable status quo. However, he goes on to develop the view that survey work should be abandoned altogether. Set against the backdrop of creative surveys informed by feminism, this chapter shows how the empirical, theoretical and political concerns of critical criminologists can be effectively addressed by adhering to some of the canons of mainstream survey research. It particularly celebrates the feminist woman abuse surveys and those of small-scale, local projects specifically designed to discern how broader social forces shape crime and societal reactions to it in poor inner-city communities. This imaginative use of the survey method more readily captures both the voices and the social reality of those largely erased by the bogus of positivism.

Continuing the spirit of capturing the voices that some conventional criminological work erases, in Chapter 3, Louise Westmarland reveals the challenges posed when engaged in ethnographic work that demands imaginative understanding and analysis of the stories revealed. Here she draws on data gathered as part of ethnography observing a specialist homicide detective unit in the US. In this context, the local populace, including close friends and relatives of the homicide victims, were generally unwilling to talk to the police and detectives were observed using a number of seemingly unethical means to obtain evidence and confessions. The way in which she dealt with and made sense of these observations and the officers' own stories about their working lives is central to this discussion. As a result, she reveals the complexities of ethnography that are 'real life' in some senses, yet stage-managed and transient in others. Out of this complexity, there emerges a nuanced understanding of these police officers whose moral code, which may on occasion result in unethical practices, nonetheless served the families and victims with which they were concerned, posing a provocative challenge to conventional understandings of 'cop culture'. In engaging in this ethnography, Westmarland learned much about the nature of forensic evidence.

In Chapter 4, Wayne Petherick and Claire Ferguson take us on a journey in thinking critically about forensic psychology. This chapter not only affords an opportunity to appreciate the diverse nature of criminological voices, it also serves usefully to remind us that criminologists engage with and are committed to justice in a range of different ways. The chapter asks us to think further about what can be learnt from practitioners. It discusses the processes of applied crime analysis and draw parallels between this process and the general criminological research process. It makes the case that whilst criminological research mostly applies to the generation of nomothetic knowledge, applied crime analysis relates mostly to idiographic study in order to answer investigative and legal questions. Much can be learned from the latter form of study and critically applied to the former, resulting in the consequent enrichment of both.

In Part II of this collection, the contributors consider the ways in which different kinds of data can be revealing for the criminological imagination: imaginative methods. The potential for research employing mixed methods is being increasingly recognized, and in Chapter 5, Maggie O'Neill develops a critical recovery of the histories and lives of certain marginalized people using inter-textual research to represent the complexity of their lived lives. She makes the case that inter-textual and imaginative methodologies are a response to the fragmentation, plurality and utter complexity of the reduction of these lives as oppressed/marginalized/exploited. Mixing participatory, performative, visual and arts-based research methods, defined as 'ethno-mimesis' and undertaken in participation with the usual 'subjects' of research, she highlights the contradictions of oppression and the complexity of contemporary bureaucratic society. She argues that the imaginative mixing of methods may also help criminologists to produce critical reflexive texts that address social harm, foster social justice and move towards a radical democratic imaginary.

Accessing the complexity of people's lives is also taken up by Ross McGarry in Chapter 6. His focus of concern is the value of biographical data for victimology. Despite this early pioneering role of biographical work in shaping criminological theory, such work has remained marginal to both criminological and victimological endeavours. McGarry suggests that this is curious omission, given that Mills (1959) places the uses of biography and history side-by-side as creative and methodological tools to explain the ways in which we understand the world. McGarry explores a number of critical questions about the practical application of the biographical method when used to study both offenders and victims. This exploration highlights the value of using biographical data for the development of contemporary criminological theory that can both complement and challenge traditional research methods employed within orthodox areas of the discipline. This affords a different route into accessing people's voices and the complexity of their lives. That complexity is given an added dimension in the powerful presence of the visual in setting the scene for engagement with crime.

Eamonn Carrabine picks up this theme in Chapter 7. Recognizing that there is no single, shared view on how images should be used or to what ends they might be put, Carrabine makes the case that the field of visual methodology is now the site of innovative inter-disciplinary scholarship and offers a telling indication of the increasingly prominent place images occupy in contemporary life. The breadth and diversity of the presence of the visual image both challenges and opens up new possibilities for criminology, and these are discussed in this chapter. In discussing this material, Carrabine describes a way of doing criminology that is not only creative, but also critical. Like McGarry, he takes a lead from Mills (1959) and his scathing assessment of mid-century American sociology, which, for him, ignored the major issues of the day – how a post-war corporate economy was corroding social structures and generating profound inequalities. Instead, the profession was content to produce timid, conservative, inaccessible work that lacked any sense of the big picture or the transformative politics required to change the social order for the better. Today mainstream sociology is even more thoroughly mired in the trough identified by Mills. In this regard, Carrabine argues that in doing visual criminology, the discipline can both be re-centred and re-sensitized through an appreciation of the politics of representation.

Not only are images about crime all around us on contemporary society, so is data. In Chapter 8, Barry Godfrey explores the power and the impact of the increasingly widespread and available digital data for the crime historian. Here he argues that online digitized data has the power to transform crime historical research. Its scale and the speed with which it can be accessed engender new forms of crime history which have the capacity to shift its theory and practice with a rapidity hitherto not encountered. These processes also constitute a democratization of data since they permit all viewers to interpret the data for themselves, and re-interpret what the academic experts have posited. Godfrey suggests that these processes raise some interesting ethical questions for those historians who have used the biographical method to analyse, re-cast and 'rescue' ruined lives. This ultimately poses questions for how these new digital entrepreneurs protect the interests of those offenders and ex-offenders (or their descendants) who appear on the various websites that now make such data available. These questions afford an important link with the final part of this book.

Part III of the volume is concerned with the craft and challenges of an imaginative liquid criminology. Each of the chapters in this part illustrates how criminological research is continuously fraught – and perhaps in liquid modernity increasingly so – with meta-methodological considerations and concerns that highlight the necessity for a conscientious methodological craft. In Chapter 9,

Matthew Bacon and Teela Sanders consider the contemporary ethical dilemmas faced by those concerned with doing criminology. The chapter starts with the recognition that criminologists inevitably work with participants who are considered 'risky' because of a combination of their behaviour, assigned criminogenic characteristics or the environment in which they 'work'. In an era in which Research Ethics Committees and review processes are an embedded and compulsory aspect of contemporary university-led research, the authors problematize the concept of 'risky research' and seek to identify a baseline of acceptable risk. They do this by interrogating the institutional framework which determines what and who is 'risky' based on everyday experiences of ethnographic social investigation. They explore the discrepancies between institutional expectations of how risk will be raised in certain research contexts, and the realities of when and how risk occurs and importantly how it is managed. In developing an understanding of ethics as constantly in the making, they develop the case that whether a risk should be tolerated depends partly on why people are prepared to take it. They stress the importance of researchers' capacity for 'in situ' ethical decision making that often runs counter to institutionally framed understandings of ethics.

Similarly, Kate Fitz-Gibbon in Chapter 10 points to the ongoing negotiation required with gatekeepers, and criminal justice professionals in particular, in order to gain access to do research. Here she treats us to a nuanced analysis of the importance of research that goes beyond making claims about how the law should operate and justice should be achieved, to understanding how this actually occurs in practice. Penetrating the barriers between those researching and those operating within the law can be arduous and complex, and this chapter examines the use of qualitative research interviews with members of the criminal justice system as one way of doing this. It offers a detailed consideration of the issues surrounding gaining access to those within the system alongside the value of research that does so and emphasizes the importance of managing and maintaining research partnerships in this process. Both Chapters 9 and 10 allude to some political aspects of the research process that have undergone and continue to undergo change, and thus need constant negotiation.

In Chapter 11, Kerry Carrington and Ashleigh Larkin set these politics within a wider appreciation of disciplinary politics which neatly returns us to the question of the bogus of positivism and the marginalization of more critical criminological voices. Carrington and Larkin examine the politics of doing criminological research within the changing make-up of social and cyber spaces. They argue that choice of method is a practical and not a political choice, and is shaped by the questions being investigated. They use case studies to illustrate the ways in which research approaches and methods have become less dogmatic, more liquid, more practical, more democratized and more transnational. They go on to explore the contradiction that while globalization produces inequalities and enhances the opportunities for transnational crimes, and new crimes like sexting and cyber-stalking, the technologies of globalization have opened up many new opportunities for transnational feminist intersectional studies of crime and social control. Here they conceive of intersectionality as a political praxis and a corrective methodological to the masculinist, Anglophone and metropolitan biases of more traditional criminological research. Such work gives voice to those often at the margins of mainstream criminological work, both geographically and conceptually.

Completing this section is a conclusion in which we as editors of this volume re-visit the notion of 'liquid criminology' and seek to dot the i's and cross the t's of what we consider to be some of the main potentials and major pitfalls of such a criminological endeavour. We pay particular consideration to the topics of politics and poetics in this endeavour to re-imagine criminology in times of liquidity by summarizing what we believe to be some of the obstacles as well as some of the possible pathways to such a criminological re-orientation.

Finally, Jeff Ferrell offers a provocative postscript to this collection. Here he encourages us to throw off the shackles of modernist method and dig up the positivist foundations on which they were built and imagine method as more a fluid process of engagement with a world that is itself increasingly ill-defined and adrift – to see method, that is, as more a tentative orientation than a set of technical certainties. In burying criminological method, he suggests we can also give it new life. In this new life, criminological method is mobilized, animated by openness and innovation, and attuned to features of liquid social life. On the basis of this collection, we might also say that this criminology will be attuned to its critical history, a commitment to social justice and the desire to render its own existence obsolete.

So we invite you to explore this collection as a journey into the imagination. We ask you to consider how might the world be different? How might criminology be different? How might criminology engage in research that gives voice to those silenced as a result of the dominance of Westocentric thinking about the nature of social reality? We believe this is a timely journey to undertake.

## References

Aas, Katja F. (2012) '"The Earth is But One But the World is Not": Criminological Theory and its Geopolitical Divisions'. *Theoretical Criminology*, 16(1): 5–20.

Barton, Alana, Karen Corteen, David Scott and Dave Whyte (eds) (2007) *Expanding the Criminological Imagination: Critical Readings in Criminology*. Cullompton: Willan Publishing.

Bateson, Mary Catherine (1989) *Composing a Life*. London: Grove Press.

Bauman, Zygmunt (2000) *Liquid Modernity*. Cambridge: Polity Press.

——. (2001) *The Individualized Society*. Cambridge: Polity Press.

——. (2005) *Liquid Life*. Cambridge: Polity Press.

——. (2007) *Liquid Times – Living in an Age of Uncertainty*. Cambridge: Polity Press.

Body-Gendrot, Sophie (2011) *Globalisation, Fear and Insecurity: The Challenges for Cities*. Basingstoke: Palgrave Macmillan.

Bolden, Christian L. (2012) 'Liquid Soldiers: Fluidity and Gang Membership'. *Deviant Behavior*, 33(3): 207–22.

Cohen, Stanley (1979) 'The Last Seminar'. *Sociological Review*, 27(1): 5–20.

Connell, Raewyn (2007) 'The Northern Theory of Globalization'. *Sociological Theory*, 25(4): 368–85.

Currie, Elliot (2002) 'Preface', in Kerry Carrington and Russell Hogg (eds), *Critical Criminology: Issues, Debates, Challenges*. Cullompton: Willan Publishing, pp. vii–x.

Daems, Tom and Luc Robert (2007) 'Crime and Insecurity in Liquid Modern Times: An Interview with Zygmunt Bauman'. *Contemporary Justice Review*, 10(1): 87–100.

De Sousa Santos, Boaventura (2014) *Epistemologies of the South: Justice against Epistemicide*. Boulder, CO: Paradigm Publishers.

Downes, David (1988) 'The Sociology of Crime and Social Control in Britain 1960–87', in Paul Rock (ed.), *A History of British Criminology*. Oxford: Oxford University Press, pp. 20–34.

Ferrell, Jeff (2009) 'Kill Method: A Provocation'. *Journal of Theoretical and Philosophical Criminology*, 1(1): 1–22.

Ferrell, Jeff, Keith Hayward and Jock Young (2008) *Cultural Criminology: An Invitation*. London: Sage Publications.

Jacobsen, Michael Hviid (2013) '"Metaphormosis": On the Metaphoricity of Zymunt Bauman's Social Theory', in Mark Davis (ed.), *Liquid Sociology: Metaphor in Zygmunt Bauman's Analysis of Modernity*. Farnham: Ashgate, pp. 191–218.

——. (2015) 'Introduktion: Velkommen til den flydende moderne verden – Zygmunt Baumans samfundskritiske samtidsdiagnose [Introduction: Welcome to the Brave New Liquid World – Zygmunt Bauman's Critical Diagnosis of the Times]', in Zygmunt Bauman (ed.), *Fagre flydende verden [Brave New World of Liquidity]*. Copenhagen: Hans Reitzels Forlag, pp. 7–52.

——. (ed.) (2014) *The Poetics of Crime*. Farnham: Ashgate.

Jacobsen, Michael Hviid, Michael S. Drake, Kieran Keohane and Anders Petersen (2014) 'Introduction: Imaginative Methodologies: Creativity, Poetics and Challenges to Conventional Social Science', in Michael Hviid Jacobsen, Michael S. Drake, Kieran Keohane and Anders Petersen (eds), *Imaginative Methodologies in the Social Sciences*. Farnham: Ashgate, pp. 1–22.

Mills, Charles Wright (1959) *The Sociological Imagination*. New York: Oxford University Press.

Varney, Denise (2009) 'Radical Disengagement and Liquid Lives: Criminology by Arena Theatre Company'. *Australasian Drama Studies*, 54: 125–41.

Young, Jock (1999) *The Exclusive Society*. London: Sage Publications.

——. (2007) *The Vertigo of Late Modernity*. London: Sage Publications.

——. (2011) *The Criminological Imagination*. Cambridge: Polity Press.

Zedner, Lucia (2006) 'Liquid Security: Managing the Market for Crime Control'. *Criminology and Criminal Justice*, 6(3): 267–88.

# Part I

# Using conventional methods imaginatively

# 1    Doing imaginative criminology

*Pat Carlen*

## Introduction

It is nearly 50 years since I first read C. Wright Mills' *Sociological Imagination.*
I read it before I began my sociology studies at London University, and though
I did not fully understand it (at that time, indeed, I had never even heard of the
sociological debates referred to), I do remember consciously taking away one
thing from that seminal work. I gleaned that sociology is about making connections between seemingly disparate historical and present-day social phenomena in
order to produce new knowledge of the relationships between them. And also that,
because all disciplines, models, paradigms, definitions and statistics necessarily
delimit meanings and lead to ideological closure, it is desirable, in order to create
new knowledge, constantly to deny the already-known by crossing disciplines,
puncturing models, denying paradigms, questioning definitions and going behind
the statistics to get some inkling of why they take the form they do. Of course, I
didn't put it like that at the time. Rather, in 1967, I fitted Mills into a worldview
that I already espoused – and without realising that I had just read one of the greatest books in sociology.

In 1910, in *Howard's End*, the English novelist E. M. Forster used the epi-
gram 'only connect' to capture his novel's philosophical vision that, in order
to understand how other people can have very different worldviews from ourselves, we need to appreciate the differing geographical and historical conditions
in which their rationalities and sensibilities have been fashioned, and to read
their biographies within the elemental emotional, cultural, ideological, political
and historical components which, in different combinations, render each of us
unique. Again, Forster in his book – he was primarily concerned with reconcil-
ing pairs of opposites – did not put it quite like that in 1910, and nor did I when
I read *Howard's End* in 1957. But by 1968, when I began my sociology degree,
I was already imbued with a vague sense that new knowledge is generated from
a *bricolage* of concepts and conceits that thinkers put together when the already-
known forms of knowing do not seem quite adequate to investigation of the
topic in question. This, I later came to understand, is the same process (though
from innumerable disciplinary or artistic perspectives and achieved with varying
degrees of competence, talent or artistry) that allows physical scientists, social

scientists and artists of various kinds to imagine new possibilities for glimpsing the presently unknown, hearing the presently unheard, feeling the presently unfelt, thinking the presently unthinkable and, if they are of radical political persuasion, speaking the presently unspeakable.

Lacking belief in any compelling disciplinary focus, I have never had a strong (or exclusive) commitment to any 'position' in sociology. Questions as to whether anyone is a positivist, a functionalist, a symbolic interactionist – or any of the more modern 'brands' of sociologist, e.g. public, postmodernist or whatever – just leave me cold. 'If that is so', I hear you saying, 'Why use the terms "sociologist", or "criminologist" at all? What is "sociological" about "sociology" – and, more to the point here, what is "imaginative" about "imaginative criminology"?' In reply, I will outline what I see to be the 'promise' of 'imaginative criminology' and then what I understand to be its 'craft'. Meanwhile, two definitions: 'sociological criminologist' in this chapter refers to any academic whose fundamental rules of engagement with crime issues stem from academic perspectives relating to the social meanings of social phenomena, while 'imaginative criminology' refers to attempts to make new connections between the diverse conditions of existence of contemporary crime and justice.

## The promise of imaginative criminology

It seems to me that most people ruminate on society and crime, and develop coherent explanations of different social and crime phenomena. From such a perspective, therefore, it might be argued that there are many different sociologies and many different criminologies (see Carlen 2011). Police officers and magistrates, for instance, frequently hold very cogent views about the causes of different types of crime and the making of different types of criminals. Politicians and churches, and a range of others, likewise argue for crime policies based on their own particular ethical or political beliefs about, say, human nature or the complementary social responsibilities of individual and state. Therefore, to the extent that many perspectives and interests are brought to bear on answers to questions of crime and justice, academic criminology is just one criminology among many.

Yet academic criminology has a distinctiveness of its own. It is characterized by its professional commitment to scientific and ethical protocols which must always be capable of explication and assessment by other academic criminologists and their various publics. Its aim is to provide new knowledge of the meanings of crime in society. In furtherance of that aim, criminology's practitioners may work from a variety of perspectives and with a variety of aims – statistical, theoretical or empirical/investigative – and some of that work will replicate the already-known in attempts to check and/or build on previous work. The most original, however, will be imaginative insofar as statisticians, theorists and social investigators will puzzle over new ways of working, of seeing new connections and of informing their analyses with concepts, metaphors and methods taken sometimes from perspectives which might previously have been considered to be totally eccentric to the topic under investigation (see Cain (1989) on 'transgressive criminology' and Young (2011) on 'transformative criminology'). This is how all scientific progress is made. However, when I refer to 'imaginative criminology', I am not referring to this more general use. My usage is more specific.

Despite Émile Durkheim's (1895/1938) imaginative and radical demonstration that crime in society is 'normal' (statistically speaking, that is), lawbreaking has always been seen as a social problem, and law and order issues have repeatedly been amongst the prime concerns of governments seeking legitimacy and/or re-election. It is not surprising therefore that, in the early days of criminology, a professional administrative criminology developed which, rather than posing new questions and looking for new answers about the causes of crime, took its questions (and funding) from governments whose own agendas were not directed at open investigation, but at 'managing' law and order. The questions asked and the permissible knowledge range within which answers might be given were limited by policy interests more concerned with gaining descriptive knowledge about criminals and lawbreaking for the purposes of prevention and intervention than they were with examining critical issues about the meanings of crime in society and why crime issues take the form they do.

Administrative criminology persists to the present day (see Young (2011) for a searing critique of its more bizarre varieties) and, because of university pressures on academics to gain funds, it is practised occasionally even by criminologists who at other times engage in the more imaginative criminology that allows them to use their scientific arts both to experiment with innovative ways of knowing and to produce new knowledge (see Carlen 2012). When I use the term 'imaginative criminology', therefore, I am not using it in recognition that 'imagination' is used by all scientists and artists. Indeed, elsewhere (Carlen 2011) I have referred to criminology as a *scientific art* in general recognition that *all* scientific breakthroughs (including some made in the pursuit of an administrative criminology agenda) employ imagination at some stage in the production of new knowledge. In this chapter, however, the term 'imaginative criminology' is used to refer specifically to a criminology which, in eschewing the pre-given knowledge parameters of administrative criminology, consciously seeks to destroy the ideological (already-known) conditions of its existence. Its aim is not only to produce something new, but also to imagine new and more just forms of social justice.

Insofar as imaginative criminology eschews administrative criminology's quest for evidence of the already-known in favour of imagining the new, it is one manifestation of a broader critical criminology. Unlike administrative criminology, which involves a reflexive journey into an official past, imaginative criminology embarks on an uncharted voyage into an unofficial future. But, more than that, the promise of imaginative criminology is that it is well-designed to be a bridge between critical criminology and a critical politics of criminal justice policy. For imaginative criminology, in the second and very specific sense that is being used here, does not pretend to exclude politics from critique (Carlen 2012). Though it might be possible to use administrative criminology's evidence-based approach in part-support of a critical politics of criminal justice, an evidence-based approach is, in itself, inadequate as a guide to social change. This is because while 'evidence', as I have already pointed out, is necessarily about what has been done in the past, the imagined principles of a new criminal justice are about how we might want to live in the future. The promise of imaginative criminology, therefore, is that by deconstructing the minutiae of already-known criminal justice issues, it can sort through the debris of old ways of thinking about criminal justice and then, from that very debris, fashion new desires and locate new possibilities for a more just criminal justice – subject always, of course, to the political conditions of the time. That for me is the promise of imaginative criminology. Its promise is multifaceted and unlimited. Likewise, its practice.

By definition, there can be no rules for doing imaginative criminology, although as, also by definition, it is in part answerable to an intellectual discipline, it is, at times, likely to engage with ethical and methodological imperatives shared with other types of academic criminology. C. Wright Mills himself (1959) referred to the *craft* of sociology. I will, in the rest of this chapter, outline the practice of an imaginative criminology in the service of a critical politics for more just, more equal and more humane criminal justice. Before I make this attempt, two disclaimers. First, I cannot imagine anything more inappropriate to write about than to attempt a description of 'doing imaginative criminology'. Creative work cannot be subpoenaed and fenced-in with protocols. Second, I am supremely conscious of the irony of discussing imaginative criminology in the prosaic terms employed in this chapter. Therefore, I salve my conscience by inviting readers who would like to experience what is actually imaginative about imaginative criminology to read Jock Young's *The Vertigo of Late Modernity* (2007) and *The Criminological Imagination* (2011) – together with the other imaginative works which I list in the chapter's final section.

## The practice of imaginative criminology

In 2010, I outlined a personal practice of criminology as being based on three working beliefs:

> First, an ontological belief about the social world: that everything that is could be different. Second, a belief about the task of social science; that it is more important to account for social phenomena than it is to count them. And third, a belief about the task of [academic] criminology: that as the concept of criminal justice must remain imaginary (that is, impossible of realization) in societies based on unequal and exploitative social relations, one rationale for investigating the meanings of contemporary lawbreaking and the social responses to it is to imagine the conditions for them being otherwise. For me, the project of a criminological imagination is forever to demonstrate that contemporary penal justice is both just and unjust, both possible and impossible, and with conditions of existence that have infinite possibilities for change. (Carlen 2010: 1)

I summed up my favoured mode of operation as involving:

> A method of qualitative critique or argument which, like a kaleidoscope, first partially describes and theoretically deconstructs events and discourses

and then, equally partially, reconstructs and re-inscribes them in alternative discourses, the aim being to create something new. The moment when an analysis is recognized (or not recognized) as *possible* knowledge is the moment of knowledge/ideology; when an alternative analysis is legitimated as *desirable* knowledge it is the moment of politics/ideology. (Carlen 2010: 1)

More practically and prosaically, such a mode of operation:

1   begins with a common-sense question about what is being observed, read or thought about. For instance: 'How can anyone make sense of what is going on in one of London's magistrates' courts where formality is often undermined by poor acoustics, defendants and witnesses who do not understand the court rules and professionals all working under different auspices themselves?' (see Carlen 1976; 2010);

2   tries to see the scene, hear the discourse or read the text via a particular theoretical perspective, as well as according to its own logic – or the logic of the interviewees in the case of interviews. When one perspective fails to shed any light on what is happening, other perspectives are tried, and if none of them works, the question is changed and maybe, too, the mode of knowing. Perhaps a metaphor sheds light on what has previously been so puzzling; maybe there is a sudden awareness of a glaring absence in the text or that the logic of people's explanations is absurd insofar as they are formally contradictory or substantively incredible; or sometimes it is a line from a play, a theme from a novel, some well-worn folk cliché or the lyric of a pop song that is inspirational. And, occasionally, it is a throwaway line by another academic or a new understanding of someone else's arguments. There is no hurrying this stage; it takes as long as it takes and just involves thinking, thinking, thinking . . . until;

3   there is a realization that the whole thought process began in the wrong place and with the wrong questions. Some bits of the investigated phenomenon then seem to fit together to form new questions. But other bits of the puzzle become even more puzzling and don't fit anywhere. And so the process of deconstruction, reconstruction and deconstruction continues, taking one to places one never expected to be – and also leading the imaginative investigator up quite a few dead ends. Though remember, a cul de sac for one investigator may well be the beginning of something new for a subsequent one and should not be tidied away in the service of a solution, a logic or a proof. Rather than being seen as a dead end, it should be left as a loose end. Nonetheless, and as I have argued previously, although an imaginative criminology should never lead to an ideological closure suggesting that all that is to be known about a crime or justice issue is now and forever always and already known, an imaginative criminologist should also be able (if he/she so wishes) to imagine how elements of the imaginary of today's criminal justice might, if imagined differently, give birth to new and more democratic conceptions of criminal justice (Carlen 2008; 2016).

I will illustrate this process of construction and deconstruction of the imaginary in service of a critical politics of criminal justice by outlining what I retrospectively imagine were the analytic moves made in two recent papers: the first is titled 'Imaginary Penalities and Risk-Crazed Governance' (in Carlen 2008), hereafter referred to as 'Imaginary Penalities'; the second, 'Against Rehabilitation: For Reparative Justice' (Carlen 2013) is hereafter referred to as 'Against Rehabilitation'. Much of what follows, therefore, is necessarily adapted from these two papers. The overall objective is to indicate how, through a series of analytic manoeuvres, I moved from two rather mundane research questions about the practice of rehabilitation to endpoints in two very different places: imaginary penalities and reparative justice.

## Doing imaginative criminology: a glimpse of 'imaginary penalities'

The concept of imaginary penalities originated in a study of a women's prison in Australia which, for the purposes of anonymity, I called Optima. I had initially asked permission to undertake research there because I had read on the relevant Corrections website that Optima had been designed with the aim of running therapeutic programmes for sentenced women with a view to their re-integration into the community. However, when I began the research a year after the prison had been opened, no rehabilitation courses were running. The prison staff nonetheless continued to act *as if* they were working in a therapeutic prison designed for re-integration via programming and appropriate back-up outside, even though everyone interviewed said they were very aware that the prison's whole concept of re-integration was (what I was later to call) 'imaginary'. It was imaginary insofar as it was posited upon: imaginary prisoners (they were short-term remand rather than sentenced); imaginary programmes (they were not running because unsentenced prisoners cannot be advised to undertake rehabilitative programmes); and imaginary 'back-up' in the 'community' (neither 'back-up' nor 'community' existed). But it was an imaginary penalty that was having material effects: it was incurring financial costs and maybe its continuing claims to being a rehabilitative institution were also influencing sentencing. Additionally, by perpetuating a belief in the promises and possibilities of in-prison rehabilitation, it was providing a rationale for the existence and perpetuation of short-term imprisonment and, concomitantly, more prisons.

I realized that the original objective of researching rehabilitative programmes was impossible. I was more intrigued, in any case, by the staff's insistence that although the rehabilitative ideal was neither being realized nor even pursued, they had to act as if it were. How could prison personnel tell me that all the re-integrative objectives of the prison were impossible to achieve and yet, at the same time, continue to design rehabilitative programmes for official approval? Certainly their view of the likely outcome of this 'as if' activity was not that of constructivist psychology, that trying out different realities might help realize them. The staff had no doubt that because of the rehabilitation deficit outside the prison, there was no chance of the rehabilitative objectives being met. Yet their pessimism could not be explained by any lack of ideological commitment to the institutional objectives either. All staff had been selected for their commitment to rehabilitation. But once they realized that, owing to conditions completely beyond their control, Optima's re-integrative objectives were impossible, staff had replaced them with more limited and realizable goals of their own. Instead of assessing their work according to achievement of the official rehabilitative criteria, they saw themselves as being successful if the inmates behaved well while in prison.

Another thing which intrigued me was that the staff could be so explicit when *talking* about the imaginary nature of the prison's formal rehabilitative objectives while at the same time *acting* as if they fully believed in their reality. So I posed two questions while reading and re-reading the interview transcripts: what kind of analytic work might the staff themselves be doing in order to accommodate these opposed occupational realities within a coherent occupational worldview? What knowledge did they have to suppress, and why?

The explanation I came up with was that the organizational consciousness of the staff had been constituted within the space between the material structural conditions constitutive of the rehabilitation deficit (i.e. the excluded Other of the rehabilitation discourse) and the organizational discourse of audit and appraisal which demanded that the excluded Other be both recognized and denied. In other words, if it had been officially and explicitly recognized that the change in Optima's use had made the organizational goal of 'rehabilitation' irrelevant, the staff would not have been constrained to act an imaginary role as rehabilitation therapists. They could have conducted themselves as prison officers. Alternatively, they could have acted *as if* they were doing rehabilitation work within the prison without ever recognizing the existence of the excluded Other conditions which constantly negated any possibilities for the rehabilitation of women upon release. But because of the lack of official recognition that rehabilitation was no longer possible, the prison's organizational demands of audit and appraisal of the prison as a therapeutic establishment remained couched in the language of rehabilitation. Accordingly, when called to account in terms of prison audit and personal appraisal, the staff had to resurrect an Other which, though it had had been excluded from the prison's official discourse, they themselves had to invoke as justifications for the actual non-pursuit of the organization's proclaimed objectives. This Other was, as already indicated, comprised of the following knowledge: that there were no rehabilitative facilities outside the prison; that assessing the levels of re-integration was well-nigh impossible as there was no provision for the careers of ex-prisoners to be tracked unless they were brought back into the criminal justice system; and that the deep-rooted outside-prison problems of many of the women were not going to be dispelled by a short spell in prison (rather, they were likely to be increased and/or aggravated). At the same time, for the purposes of getting on with their day-to-day work, the staff had to suppress that Other knowledge and act 'as if' these material problems did not exist. Though believing themselves to be justified in replacing unrealistic rehabilitative objectives with more achievable institutional objectives of their own, faced with programme accreditation, programme evaluation, personal appraisals and other managerialist techniques of audit, quality control and a search for reflexive evidence of 'what works', Optima staff had to take both the formal objectives of rehabilitation and the Other which had both engendered them and rendered them unachievable back into the official evaluative frame. And *then* they had to confront the fact that if the conditions necessary to rehabilitation had actually existed in 'the community', the prisoners with whose rehabilitation they were now charged would most probably not have been sent to prison in the first place.

In working out the mechanics of the discursive moves made by the staff at Optima, I developed the concept of imaginary penalities to explain *how* they could so knowingly acquiesce in the absurd and thereby contribute to an imaginary penality which in turn had real effects. These prison staff were not dupes of official ideological spin. Nor did they try to dupe me. Rather, they made an assessment of the competing and contradictory conditions of their professional lives and created a narrative which allowed them to sum up the competing interpellatory discourses within which their professional identities were continually fractured and reassembled. They were as aware as I was that in order to do so, they were having to exclude mention of some very significant factors conditioning their working lives and, furthermore, that it was this excluded Other which made the contradictions between their actions and their discourse take the form they did. When these exclusions were forced upon them in terms which they could not ignore, e.g. programme evaluation or an interview situation, they had to construct yet newer narratives to suggest that compliance was being achieved – though in novel ways and under exceptional conditions. On these occasions the previous exclusions from the discourse were reinstated and new exclusions were made.

The development of the concept of imaginary penalities raised two further questions for me. I had answered (for the time being) the *what* and the *how* questions, but there still remained the *why* and the *so what*. *Why* did the staff at Optima acquiesce in the absurd? *What* is the significance of imaginary penalities for critical criminal justice politics?

Thomas Mathiesen (2004) has argued that, once rhetoric has become an effective reality, people are silently silenced by the implication that to protest would attract public derision for stating the obvious. However, the staff at Optima suggested that, given their backgrounds in rehabilitation and programming philosophies, they also wanted to keep the rehabilitative space open, even though they were aware that in doing so, they were colluding in the false belief that social issues could be addressed by penal means. In reply to my querying the absurdity of the prison's imaginary practices, they asked: 'What is the alternative?' They thought that if the prison's rehabilitative philosophy were to be abandoned, the result would be a harsher regime. There was no official space wherein they could put forward alternatives. Thus, although Ian Loader (2006) has given a rather negative assessment of the likelihood of criminal justice professionals ever again having as much influence on penal policies as they did in the US, the UK and some other countries during the twentieth century, my awareness of professionals' twenty-first-century embodied knowledge of imaginary penalities suggests to me that Loïc Wacquant (2008: 285) is correct in arguing that professionals should be supported in attempts to regain a greater influence in penal policy debates. There is a need for as many alternative voices as possible, and especially those of criminal justice professionals currently being silently silenced into acting *as if* imaginary penalities can deliver justice. Which leads me to the second question: why do imaginary penalities matter?

Imaginary penalities are assemblages of ideological practices. But what is distinct about them is that they are practices which are presented as having no moral dimension (i.e. as being facts of life). The conditions of existence of imaginary penalities, moreover, are not always the same. However, in recent prisons policy and in many different countries, their main conditions of existence have been similar: on the one hand, an increasing promotion of risk discourse by governments aiming to induce popular demand for stiff penalties; on the other, a routine use of regulatory/disciplinary audit to limit the power of professionals to intervene in penal debate by putting forward opposing viewpoints. In response to crime and rising prison populations, the pragmatic policy maker's priority that 'something must be done about it' has been replaced by the pragmatic politician's priority that 'something must be *seen* to be done about it'. That 'something' is an imaginary penalty.

The main policy implication drawn from the identification of imaginary penalities in the case of rehabilitative imprisonment is that the positivistic auditing of organizational practices in terms of goal fulfilment should be replaced with accounting procedures which allow penal personnel to debate ever-changing possibilities of both goal relevance and goal fulfilment, and that more discretion should be given to professionals. The main analytic/political inference drawn was that although all of us who discourse on crime and punishment are (wittingly or unwittingly) complicit in the making of imaginary penalities, the preconditions and effects of the imaginary can be exposed to critique, and the imaginary itself contested, first, by investigating what is excluded from its discourse, and then by analysis and exposure of the means by which the exclusion is effected. For the same knowledges that are incorporated into imaginary penalities are also those which, re-imagined differently, might one day give birth to new, more democratic and more socially enhancing knowledge of the meanings of crime and justice in grossly unequal societies.

## Doing imaginative criminology: a glimpse of reparative justice

Unlike the 'Imaginary Penalities' piece, 'Against Rehabilitation' was not based upon interviews. I started to assemble what I already knew about rehabilitation for ex-prisoners after being invited to give the opening address at an international conference on rehabilitation. While campaigning against women's imprisonment, I had previously been involved with many rehabilitative projects and had never questioned the taken-for-granted assumption that 'rehabilitation is a good thing'. 'A Century of Rehabilitation' was the subject assigned to me, and therefore I began to read books about rehabilitation since the mid-1800s. I read and re-read the texts, but did not see anything exceptional in them, except that rehabilitation seemed to come in many varieties, few of which appeared to be successful in helping people to become law-abiding – until I realized that there was an absence in the discourse. What all rehabilitation talk had in common was that it always presumed a working-class or non-working criminal who, prior to his/her law-breaking or imprisonment, had been integrated into society – but always at a fairly disadvantaged level. It struck me then, for the first time, that rehabilitation has always been imagined as a working-class phenomenon. What I had to locate and explain was not a contradiction, but several absences: Who is to be rehabilitated to What? In other words, who is the subject of rehabilitation and what is its context? Locating the two absences of the who and the what, moreover, raised yet a third question about the why: why are rehabilitative measures in terms of changing *corporate* cognitions and attitudes not seen as being as necessary, desirable and possible as changing the cognitions and attitudes of poorer lawbreakers? In constructing an answer, I imagined a reparative justice which might strive to repair the breach between social and criminal justice: first, by recognizing that unequal access to social goods is matched by unequal access to criminal justice; and, second, by struggling to ensure that the same penal principles of reparation for lawbreaking be applied across all classes.

So, the first absence in rehabilitation discourse is its subject. *Who* is to be rehabilitated? Rehabilitation programmes in capitalist societies have tended to be reserved for poorer prisoners found guilty of crimes against property and for prisoners released after serving long sentences for non-business-related crimes. They have not usually been designed for corporate criminals, however long their records of recidivism. But, given the dominance of theories that causally relate some types of crime to adverse social circumstances, it could be argued that it is understandable that remedial social support should have been reserved for offenders most in need. Agreed. And where such support has been available, there is evidence that it has been strategic in enabling ex-offenders to remain law-abiding. However, historically, such support has seldom been wholeheartedly given by governments. Now, in the second decade of the twenty-first century, rehabilitation has become a major victim of national austerity programmes occasioned by economic recession. As a result, prison populations have continued to expand as non-custodial rehabilitation projects have been axed by governments that, powerless to curb global corporate greed or international malfeasance (such as war-mongering and media corruption), have recouped their debts and losses where they can – in the public sector of their national jurisdictions. The ensuing cuts in public expenditure have fallen most heavily upon the most vulnerable citizens and especially upon those vilified as being the least deserving and receiving welfare benefits of any kind whatsoever. *These* are also the perennial *subjects* of both non-custodial and custodial rehabilitation.

The second, and related, anomaly in rehabilitation discourse is in relation to its social and political context. Rehabilitation to *what*? With the recent erosion of welfare in many countries, the poverty of more minor lawbreakers has no longer been seen as qualifying them for state-supported rehabilitative measures. Rather, poverty is nowadays seen as a positive risk factor predictive of future lawbreaking and requiring either disciplinary imprisonment to make poorer lawbreakers come to terms with poverty, low wages or unemployment or, if they are foreign nationals, repressive incarceration or deportation to reduce their risk. Thus, today, as in the past, it is recognized that when the majority of lawbreakers have nothing to be reha-bilitated to, it is more politic to pay greater attention to their risk potential than to their rehabilitative requirements, and to keep them in their place, either by laws controlling mendicancy or (at times when pacification via welfare is thought to be impolitic) by poverty, unemployment, repression, border controls and deportation. By contrast, many white-collar and corporate criminals are too embedded in, and/ or too geographically dislocated from, local jurisdictions for prosecution to be pos-sible. When successful prosecution does occur, rehabilitative measures in terms of changing corporate cognitions are not usually seen as being necessary, desirable or possible. But why? And this was the third absence in the rehabilitation texts: the lack of any explanation as to the absent Other lawbreakers.

Rehabilitation is not seen as being necessary for corporate and other white-collar criminals because their punishments seldom *de*-habilitate them in either material or status terms. Nor is rehabilitation considered to be desirable in terms of turning corporate offenders away from wrongdoing. Corporate lawbreaking is such a celebration of capitalist societies' subterranean values and its miscreants so embedded in their constitutive economic and political systems that, on those infrequent occasions when corporate offenders are brought to trial, they, unlike their poorer brothers and sisters in crime, are seldom assessed as people whose cognitions require changing. Instead, after being fined or serving a short prison sentence, they are either quietly reinstated in their former positions or paid off with substantial sums of money. More practically, governments are reluctant to see corporate criminals in court at all, as there is always the fear that adverse pub-licity will result in public agitation for more corporate regulation, a destabilising of markets or an exodus of corporate capital to more sympathetic jurisdictions.

Finally, rehabilitation is not seen as being possible because corporate and other powerful criminals nowadays have such unprecedented access to worldwide com-munications, global travel and hospitality that they can ensure they are sufficiently dislocated from their national jurisdictions to make bringing individual suspects to trial impossible and certainly to render laughable any talk of attempting to change their future behaviour by rehabilitative reprogramming. So much for the myth of equality before the law. After a century of rehabilitation policy and prac-tice, rehabilitation's main achievement has been to ensure that poor lawbreakers are kept in *their* place – and richer lawbreakers in *theirs*. What kind of reparative criminal justice might be imagined to remedy this inequality before the law?

When I began thinking about the absences in rehabilitation discourse, I had no expectation that a symmetrical comparison could be made between penal responses to the rich and the poor. Like most people, I already knew that there is an asymmetry between the penal response to street crime and the penal response to suite crime (Levi 1986/2013). However, until I began to write about rehabilita-tion, I did not realize how difficult it is to talk about a penal imaginary that has given birth to a discursive absence – the absence of the powerful criminal from rehabilitation discourse – especially when it is a systemic absence and not merely a temporary design fault! It was through explicating and confronting this absence that I came to recognise rehabilitationism's non-relevance to the rich and injustice to the poor, and this, in turn, prompted me to move from a concern with the concept of rehabilitation to a concern with a concept of state and citizen reparations which would require that the fundamental logic of criminal justice itself be informed by a jurisprudence of social justice as inequality reduction (see Carlen (2013) for a detailing of the concept of 'reparative justice').

There! That was the road I went down. That was how an invitation to talk about the history of rehabilitation started me out on a journey which began with reading about innumerable rehabilitation projects in anticipation of merely charting their different rationales, ideologies and methods. It was only slowly that I became aware of the absence from the texts of any mention of corporate or political criminals. In the search for the missing subjects and contexts of these texts, I was led to revisit works on corporate crime (notably Levi 1986/2013) and to raise questions about the reasons for these inequalities in the responses to crime – but always in the context of my own ethical/political beliefs about the desirability of justice as fairness and the politics of social inequality. Then, finally, I considered the implications for criminal justice and attempted to sketch out some arguments about how the missing Others (corporate and political criminals) of the rehabilitation texts could be brought back into a conception of reparative justice which would frame more egalitarian responses to lawbreaking.

## The tradition of imaginative criminology

Imaginative criminology is a transgressive and transformative criminology that constantly produces new possibilities for a more humane and egalitarian criminal justice. It has always been central to critical thought about crime and justice, law and order. Concepts such as class, racism and gender, which are nowadays fully embedded in criminological studies, were all imported into criminological perspectives by theorists who located absences in criminological discourse and have ever since imagined how the discourse could be Other wise. Every year, newer criminological 'brands' – such as cultural and visual criminologies – invite us to share newly imagined visions of criminal realities, and all innovative criminology owes its existence to those who have imagined the hitherto un-thought of. As Jock Young (2011: 175–218) has so comprehensively illustrated, the criminological imagination has been integral to critical criminology in the US, the UK, Australasia and elsewhere. Indeed, Young's own book *The Vertigo of Late Modernity* (2007) is one of the best recent examples of an imaginative criminology. Others, for me, would include: Kelly Hannah Moffat's *Punishment in Disguise* (2001), Stanley Cohen's *States of Denial* (2002), Elliott Currie's *The Road to Whatever* (2004), Thomas Mathiesen's *Silently Silenced* (2004), Loïc Wacquant's *Punishing the Poor* (2004), Megan Comfort's *Doing Time Together* (2008), Pat O'Malley's *The Currency of Justice* (2008), Steve

Hall, Simon Winlow and Craig Ancrum's *Criminal Identities and Consumer Culture* (2008), Eamonn Carrabine's 'Visual Criminologies' (2012), as well as Lois Presser and Sveinung Sandberg's *Narrative Criminologies* (2015). If one began with the early ethnographic work on crime in the US and the UK and then extended the list to include all critical social analysts – anywhere in the world – who have imagined and continue to imagine anew the meanings of crime in society, the list would be never-ending. But end I must.

## References

Cain, Maureen (1989) 'Introduction: Feminists Transgress Criminology', in Maureen Cain (ed.), *Growing Up Good: Policing the Behaviour of Girls in Europe*. London: Sage Publications, pp. 1–18.

Carlen, Pat (1976) *Magistrates' Justice*. Oxford: Martin Robertson.

——. (ed.) (2008) *Imaginary Penalities*. Cullompton: Willan Publishing.

——. (2010) *A Criminological Imagination: Essays on Justice, Punishment, Discourse*. Farnham: Ashgate.

——. (2011) 'Against Evangelism in Academic Criminology. For Criminology as a Scientific Art', in Mary Bosworth and Carolyn Hoyle (eds), *What is Criminology?* Oxford: Oxford University Press, pp. 95–110.

——. (2012) 'Criminological Knowledge: Doing Critique; Doing Politics', in Steve Hall and Simon Winlow (eds), *New Directions in Criminological Theory*. London: Routledge, pp. 17–29.

——. (2013) 'Against Rehabilitation: For Reparative Justice', in Kerry Carrington, Matthew Ball, Erin O'Brien and Juan Tauri (eds), *Crime, Justice and Social Democracy*. Basingstoke: Palgrave Macmillan, pp. 89–104.

——. (2016) 'Alternative Criminologies', in Leandro Franco Ayres and Pat Carlen (eds), *Alternative Criminologies*. Curitiba: iEA Editora.

Carrabine, Eamonn (2012) 'Just Images: Aesthetics, Ethics and Visual Criminology'. *British Journal of Criminology*, 2(3): 463–89.

Cohen, Stanley (2001) *States of Denial: Knowing about Atrocities and Suffering*. Cambridge: Polity Press.

Comfort, Megan (2008) *Doing Time Together: Love and Family in the Shadow of the Prison*. Chicago: University of Chicago Press.

Currie, Elliott (2004) *The Road to Whatever*. New York: Henry Holt, Owl Books.

Durkheim, Émile (1895/1938) *The Rules of Sociological Method*. Chicago: University of Chicago Press.

Forster, Edward Morgan (1901) *Howard's End*. London: Edward Arnold.

Hannah-Moffat, Kelly (2001) *Punishment in Disguise*. Toronto: University of Toronto Press.

Hall, Steve, Simon Winlow and Craig Ancrum (2008) *Criminal Identities and Consumer Culture: Crime, Exclusion and the New Culture of Narcissism*. Cullompton: Willan Publishing.

Levi, Michael (1986/2013) *Regulating Fraud: White-Collar Crime and the Criminal Process*. London: Routledge.

Loader, Ian (2006) 'Fall of the "Platonic Guardians": Liberalism, Criminology and Political Responses to Crime in England and Wales'. *British Journal of Criminology*, 46(4): 561–86.

Mathiesen, Thomas (2004) *Silently Silenced: Essays on the Creation of Acquiescence in Modern Society*. Winchester: Waterside: Press.

Mills, Charles Wright (1959) *The Sociological Imagination*. Oxford: Oxford University Press.

O'Malley, Pat (2008) *The Currency of Justice: Fines and Damages in Consumer Society*. Abingdon: Routledge/Cavendish.

Presser, Lois and Sveinung Sandberg (2015) *Narrative Criminology: Understanding Stories of Crime*. New York: New York University Press.

Young, Jock (2007) *The Vertigo of Late Modernity*. London: Sage Publications.

——. (2011) *The Criminological Imagination*. Cambridge: Polity Press.

Wacquant, Loïc (2008) *Punishing the Poor: The New Government of Social Insecurity*. Durham, NC: Duke University Press.

# 2 Using crime surveys as tools of critical insight and progressive change[1]

*Walter S. DeKeseredy*

## Introduction

Like all of the previous National Deviancy Conferences, the 2014 event at Teesside University generated much progressive thought and debate. However, conspicuously absent from this gathering of energetic scholars were these pioneers in critical criminology who died over the past several years: William Chambliss, Stanley Cohen, Stuart Hall, Barbara Hudson, Geoffrey Pearson, Mike Presdee, Julia Schwendinger, Ian Taylor, Paul Walton and Jock Young. Had they been there, though, they would have undoubtedly been delighted to attend intellectual sessions devoid of what Young (2011) refers to as 'datasaurs'. Also coined by him as 'Empiricus Abstractus', the datasaur:

> is a creature with a very small head, a long neck, a huge belly and a little tail. His head has only a smattering of theory, he knows that he must move constantly but is not sure where he is going, he rarely looks at any detail of the actual terrain on which he travels, his neck peers upwards as he moves from grant to grant, from database to database, his belly is huge and distended with the intricate intestine of regression analysis, he eats ravenously but rarely thinks about the actual process of statistical digestion, his tail is small, slight and inconclusive. (Young 2011: 15)

American criminology in particular is riddled with datasaurs and the crime survey, especially the National Crime Victimization Survey (NCVS), is one tool that these positivists frequently use in the 'data generating process' (Hope 2007; Nelson, Wooditch and Gabbidon 2014). From a critical criminological standpoint, most of what the survey work orthodox researchers do is tantamount to 'so what? Criminology' or 'voodoo criminology' (Currie 2007; Young 2004). In other words, they conduct a-theoretical, quantitative research on relatively minor issues and present the findings in an unintelligible fashion (DeKeseredy 2011a). While claiming that their empirical offerings are done in the spirit of seeking truth or establishing facts, there are, in this current era characterized by the corporatization of universities/colleges, career-oriented reasons for becoming a datasaur, which some observers claim are more powerful determinants (DeKeseredy 2012).

Many datasaurs analyse NCVS statistics, as well as other secondary data resources (e.g. Uniform Crime Reports). A large amount of the secondary data they published from 2000 until 2010 appeared in highly ranked, mainstream journals such as *Criminology, Criminology and Public Policy* and *Justice Quarterly*. During this stretch, roughly 15 per cent of the articles included in these journals relied on data older than ten years and only 10 per cent of them identified this as a limitation (Nelson et al. 2014). What accounts for this? Nelson and his colleagues provide three answers to this question. First, gathering primary data generally requires financial assistance from grant agencies. Added to this challenge is that writing grant proposals is time-consuming and the odds of success are limited, especially in a neo-liberal political climate hostile to the social sciences (DeKeseredy 2013). Thus, junior scholars have scant time to publish material that is tenure-worthy. Second, to get tenure, many early scholars and more established ones seeking promotion are required to publish in the above journals. Since these outlets routinely accept articles that present old quantitative data, there is little, if any, incentive to do primary research. Inflated tenure expectations is another reason identified by Matthew S. Nelson et al.:

> secondary data analysis has likely increased publication standards for tenure in criminology and criminal justice, especially at research-oriented universities (Orrick and Weir, 2011). Whereas in the past, a modest stream of solid publications might have been tenure-worthy, we speculate that because of the increasing use of secondary data analysis, the number of publications required for tenure has also become a more pronounced consideration in the tenure and promotion process. (Nelson et al. 2014: 30)

Nelson et al.'s research prompts us to question whether much of criminology is 'out-of-date'. Clearly, in America, it has sharply moved towards more quantitative research (while dismissing or marginalizing qualitative research) and there is growing evidence that some researchers will never collect original data in their entire career. Massive federal, state, provincial and local-level government cutbacks also play a major role in the decline of original research (DeKeseredy 2013). No wonder, then, that the overuse and sometimes misuse of survey data influences the bulk of the critical criminological community to be sceptical or outright dismissive of their legitimacy (Kraska and Neuman 2011).

Even so, regardless of one's theoretical, empirical or political orientation, it is always necessary to remember that any research method is a tool that can be used in a variety of ways. Think of something as simple as a shovel. It can help build a prison or a battered women's shelter. Critical criminologists prefer constructing the latter. Similarly, as a tool, a survey can be used in imaginative ways to enhance progressive, theoretically informed understandings of social problems and to aid the development of policies aimed at alleviating much pain and suffering. The main of objective of this chapter is to support this claim. There is a reality that must be addressed by critical criminologists who see no value in surveys. In the words of Peter B. Kraska and W. Lawrence Neuman:

The fact is that all crime and justice researchers work in some way with numbers. There is no getting around it. As social scientists, we possess a skeptical appreciation for crime and justice statistics, and how they are collected and analyzed. Quantitative analysis is the mainstay of both basic and applied research in criminology and criminal justice. One would have little more than a pedestrian point of view about the core questions of the field without referencing quantitative research. (Kraska and Neuman 2008: 342–3)

## The strengths and limitations of mainstream survey research

Crime surveys have a long history and the two most common types are self-report studies and victimization surveys (Mosher 2013). The former ask respondents to report the crimes they committed, while the latter generally ask a large number of people if they have been crime victims and summarizes the types of crime they report, the characteristics of those crimes, the effect of the crimes on the victims, and whether the crimes were reported to the police. Both variants were born in the US, but are certainly not limited to this country. For example, victimization surveys are routinely conducted around the world, with the International Crime Victimization Survey (ICVS) being the most widely known in mainstream academic circles (van Kesteren, van Dijk and Mayhew 2014). Data gleaned by the Crime Survey for England and Wales (the new name for the British Crime Survey) are also read and cited globally, but the survey that is arguably used the most for secondary data analysis is the NCVS.

Prior to describing the major problems with mainstream surveys and then making the case for critical or imaginative ones, it is first necessary to identify the main positive features of crime surveys. First, they reveal that much more crime occurs than was uncovered by, reported to and recorded by the police (Mosher, Miethe and Hart 2011). Second, depending on the questions included, they enable researchers to test entire theories or hypotheses derived from various theoretical perspectives, and a large amount of sound policy evaluation research is based on surveys (Kraska and Neuman 2011). Third, while it is naive to assume that accurate statistics derived from large- or small-scale representative sample surveys generally motivate government agencies to devote more resources to developing effective prevention and control strategies, 'the principal questions that organize policy efforts are ultimately quantitative – how many are there, who are they, where are they, how bad are the consequences, how much will it cost?' (Bart et al. 1989: 433).

There are some cases in which crime survey data have actually influenced governments to take progressive steps to reduce much pain and suffering endured by socially and economically excluded populations. Consider Gurcharn Basran, Charan Gill and Brian D. MacLean's (1995) Canadian local survey of corporate violence against Punjabi farm workers and their children. This study persuaded Kwantlen Polytechnic University and the government of British Columbia to provide suitable and affordable childcare for Punjabi farm workers.

Additional strengths of surveys include efficiency, generalizability to large populations and versatility (Bachman and Schutt 2007). Nonetheless, all crime surveys, regardless of the theories or politics that inform their development and administration, share pitfalls that are difficult to overcome and are not likely to be eliminated in the near future. For example, ethical survey researchers always guarantee their respondents anonymity. Still, there are a wide variety of reasons why both victims and offenders might not disclose incidents. These 'age-old problems' include embarrassment, fear of reprisal, 'forward and backward telescoping', deception and memory error (DeKeseredy and Schwartz 1998; Kennedy and Dutton 1989; Smith 1987, 1994). Others suggest that under-reporting can come from the reluctance or inability to recall traumatic incidents and the belief that some crimes are too trivial or inconsequential to be worth mentioning (DeKeseredy and Rennison 2013a; Smith 1994; Straus, Gelles and Steinmetz 1981).

Today, the most popular means of collecting survey data are telephone interviews, email surveys and web surveys (Bachman and Schutt 2007; Kraska and Neuman 2011). A significant shortcoming of these methods is that many people do not have access to telephones or the Internet. Homeless people are prime examples and so are scores of individuals institutionalized in penal or psychiatric settings. In addition to excluding these and other special populations (people who cannot read and those with hearing and speech disabilities), most surveys do not capture the life experiences of populations who do not understand the official language of the country in which the survey is conducted. Related to this problem is the fact that many recent immigrants from dictatorships or police states not only have language barriers, but also do not believe researchers' assurances of confidentiality (DeKeseredy and MacLeod 1997; Koss 1993; Schwartz 2000).

Another problem with all surveys is that they cannot provide rich information on complex behaviours, emotions and social processes associated with crime because self-administered questionnaires and telephone surveys only ask a brief set of questions about specific events (DeKeseredy and MacLeod 1997; Kotze and Temple 2014). More criticisms of surveys could easily be provided, but the most important point to consider here is that 'no survey fully satisfies the theoretical ideals of scientific inquiry' (Babbie 1973: 3) and, as David A. Hay (1993: 63) observes, 'all surveys represent a compromise between the deal and what is really possible'. Following Earl Babbie, he also reminds us that there is no such thing as a perfect survey, but that good ones can be done.

As a critical criminologist, my definition of a good survey is one that moves beyond those that use narrow, legalistic definitions of crime and that only attempt to capture the experiences of 'identifiable' or 'ideal' victims (Carrabine et al. 2009; Walklate 1989). A recent example of such a problematic survey is the ICVS, a study deemed by some to be 'without a doubt the most advanced survey instrument for measuring the extent, nature, and responses to conventional crime across different societies' (van Dijk and Shaw 2009: 261). Typically used to help justify the claim that crime has dropped around the world, it primarily measures what Jan van Dijk (2008), one the principle investigators of the ICVS, defines as 'common crimes' (e.g. burglary, theft of personal property or theft of a bicycle) and thus numerous offences that cause a substantial amount of social harm, physical pain and that have major mental health consequences are typically not counted, such as the creation of cyber-criminal markets and the 'real-world' harm done to women by their male intimate partners who view pornography (Hobbs 1998; Kotze and Temple 2014; Pakes 2012).

Self-report surveys, too, are typically guilty of the above problem. Most measure delinquent activities by high school students and tend to focus on relatively minor offences, such as using drugs or alcohol (Mosher 2013). Yet there are exceptions. Some self-report surveys have focused on the abuse of women in university/ college dating and other intimate contexts (e.g. DeKeseredy and Schwartz 1998; Straus and Gelles 1986), the illegal conduct of convicted offenders (Petersilia, Greenwood and Lavin 1977; Tremblay and Morselli 2000; Visher 1986) and drug use among arrestees (Taylor and Bennett 1999). Nonetheless, since the bulk of self-report surveys target youth, it is quite fair to say that the largest gap in our knowledge remains self-reported adult crime.

Some defenders of the positivist status quo assert that orthodox academic criminologists and some government agencies occasionally conduct surveys that measure certain crimes of major concern to critical criminologists. One case in point is the US National Violence Against Women Survey (Tjaden and Thoennes 2000). At first glance, this study appears to be a progressive response to feminist calls for taking private gendered violence seriously. Actually, it is little more than a neo-liberal government's attempts to appropriate or co-opt the feminist movement against violence against women (Bumiller 2008; DeKeseredy and Schwartz 2015). For example, it does not examine how broader social forces such as patriarchy contribute to gender violence. Moreover, it defines sexual and physical violence in narrow legalistic terms and hence uncovered a very low annual rate of intimate male-to-female physical assault (1.3 per cent) than do independent surveys, which normally elicit 12-month rates of 11 per cent or higher (DeKeseredy and Schwartz 2013).

More recent North American government public health surveys also elicit very low annual rates of physical and sexual violence against women. For instance, the Centers for Disease Control's (CDC) National Intimate Partner and Sexual Violence Survey only uncovered a 12-month rate of four per cent, and this figure includes violence by a same-sex partner (Black et al. 2011). In addition, the CDC's Behavioral Risk Factor Surveillance System survey of women living in 23 states and two territories only generated an annual sexual violence rate of 3.5 per cent (Black et al. 2014).

Victimization and self-report surveys are also guilty of primarily testing mainstream theories, such as John Hagan's (1989) power-control theory, Lawrence E. Cohen and Marcus Felson's (1979) routine activities theory, and Travis Hirschi's (1969) social control theory. Among the few exceptions to the rule are surveys that test hypotheses derived from feminist and male peer support perspectives (Block and DeKeseredy 2007; DeKeseredy and Schwartz 1998; Smith 1990), victimization surveys heavily guided by left realism, and Jock Young's (1999) theoretical work on social and economic exclusion (Crawford et al. 1990; DeKeseredy et al. 2003; Jones, MacLean and Young 1986). The dearth of critical criminological theory testing using survey methods is partially explained by the fact that most critical criminologists prefer to use qualitative methods, including iconography, biography, narrative, deconstruction and ethnography (DeKeseredy 2011a; Lynch, Michalowski and Groves 2000).

Again, surveys are expensive and often require government sponsorship, which is another reason for the dearth of critical theory testing. Many, if not most, critical criminologists are opposed to all forms of state-sponsored surveys, even when they are guided by progressive insights. Some define this work as simply social control science that takes two forms: 'it is related either to defense against potential external enemies, or the development of techniques for the pacification, manipulation and control of the indigenous population' (Rose and Rose 1976: 14–15). Such claims are frequently (and rightfully so) made by indigenous critical criminologists (e.g. Tauri 2013).

Most state-funded orthodox surveys *do* contribute to the maintenance of what Malcolm M. Feely and Jonathan Simon (1992) refer to as the 'new penology' (Savelsberg, King and Cleveland 2002). Nevertheless, a select few critical criminologists, such as me, receive funding for their surveys and produce results that challenge the inequitable political economic status quo. As stated before, some surveys occasionally make a difference. For example, left realists' British local crime surveys and Basran, Gill and MacLean's (1995) survey of Punjabi farm workers were definitely not means of strengthening inequality so that people can continue working under capitalism; rather, they are examples of empirically informed 'realistic solutions to distorted social conditions' (Devine and Wright 1993: 189). The same can be said about surveys guided by feminist thought.

In addition to conducting state-funded research specifically designed to identify people who suffer in silence and to promote social democracy, some critical criminologists serve as consultants to state agencies that conduct their own surveys, such as the US Department of Justice. Does this mean that their empirical guidance and their research are simply means of buttressing an oppressive regime? Have they simply been co-opted by the ruling class? Contrary to what Ian Taylor (1992) has argued, progressive survey researchers do not see criminal justice agencies as simply 'more or less autonomous' and they are deeply concerned about their work being used to further victimize disenfranchised people. Nonetheless, John Lea and Jock Young (1984: 103), among others, sensitize us to the reality that although any capitalist, racist and patriarchal state represents the interests of the powerful, 'gains can be wrung from it; reforms, however difficult are possible and, in fact, relate to the state as in essence a site of contradicting interests'.

As a close feminist friend and colleague who chooses to remain anonymous once said to me when I expressed reluctance to review a set of research proposals submitted to a state agency: 'It is important that progressives serve on government grant peer review panels to help prevent the bulk of the funds going to right-wing research.' Periodically, this goal is achieved and, in fact, some critical criminologists have helped facilitate government surveys of woman abuse and other social problems. Three scholars that immediately come to mind are the late Michael D. Smith, Russell Dobash and Rebecca Dobash. These feminists served as consultants to Statistics Canada during its development of the Canadian National

Violence Against Women Survey (VAWS) (see Johnson 1996). This study benefited greatly from these academics' suggestions and it turned out to be much better than it otherwise would have been if left solely in the hands of government researchers. In fact, the VAWS yielded much higher rates of violence and abuse than earlier surveys designed to measure either crime or family conflict (Dobash and Dobash 1995). In addition, the impact of the groundbreaking developments made in this survey is still felt today (DeKeseredy and Dragiewicz 2014). The VAWS has been replicated in national studies in countries such as Australia, Finland and Iceland (Walby and Myhill 2001), and in regional studies such as the Chicago Women's Health Risk Study (Block 2000).

Even so, critics like Stuart Henry (1999) contend that the efforts and the consultative work done by progressive survey researchers only serve to strengthen 'capitalist exploitative reality'. My response, and that of some left realists (e.g. DeKeseredy, Alvi and Schwartz 2006), is that by not viewing the state as a site of struggle and by not conducting surveys of crimes experienced by socially and economically excluded social groups, critical criminologists minimize the seriousness of harms done to them and ignore the state's potential to help solve problems that plague 'the truly disadvantaged' (Wilson 1987).

It is not the intent here to be totally dismissive of what progressive critics of survey research have to say. Critical survey researchers should always be vigilant about co-optation and the dangers of turning into 'cheerful robots' of the state. Following the radical sociologist of his time, C. Wright Mills (1959), and the dearly departed Jock Young (2011: 224), it is essential to take what is 'useful from method' and to craft a quantitative 'humanistic criminology'. How to achieve this goal using survey research is the subject of the next section of this chapter.

## Using surveys to buttress the critical criminological imagination

In *The Criminological Imagination*, Jock Young (2011: 224) does not wholly reject quantitative research. On the contrary, he asserts that 'a humanistic criminology needs numbers just as it is not restrained and defined by them'. Moreover, let us not forget that he was heavily involved in British left-realist local survey work and is co-author of *The Islington Crime Survey* (ICS) and the *Second Islington Crime Survey* (Crawford et al. 1990; Jones et al. 1986). It should also be noted that ICS ranked near the top of the list of the most widely cited critical criminological books in the 1990s (Wright and Friedrichs 1998).

What exactly are the types of numbers required by a critical, humanistic criminology? Put simply, they are statistics that offer 'the counter-voice to neoliberalism and conservatism' (Young 2011: 217). In addition, they are, to again quote Young, not purposively 'chosen . . . to fit the favoured model and the model is finessed and meticulously adjusted to fit the data' (Young 2011: 16). And they are numbers generated by surveys that define and categorize crime publicly, 'not as officially processed through official categories' (MacLean 1991: 230).

There are some important steps in conducting imaginative surveys. Obviously, the first is to select a topic (Kraska and Neuman 2011). No matter what researchers want to examine, to develop questions that adequately address the complexities of crime experiences and/or societal reactions to them, the next step is to include a 'preparatory component of qualitative investigation' (MacLean 1996: 92). This involves in-depth interviews and conversations with members of the community in which the survey will be administered. For example, prior to crafting the instrument used in DeKeseredy et al.'s (2003) study of poverty and crime in six Canadian public housing communities, the research team talked at great length with staff at a local community health centre, public housing residents, youths who participated in health centre activities, local merchants, and local probation officers. Further, valuable information about the housing estates was obtained by working with community health centre staff to develop a programme to train members of the local community to prevent substance abuse in their neighbourhoods, schools, workplaces and other areas.

Not only did community members support the study and appreciate that their concerns were taken seriously, but they also sensitized the research team to key issues not addressed in the extant literature on inner-city poverty and crime. To be sure, feminist scholars have demonstrated for years that non-academic members of the community in which a study is done 'can help researchers formulate sophisticated and intellectually rich questions' (Schechter 1988: 311). Plus, preparatory work helps establish a positive 'relationship between the researcher and the researched' (Hoyle 2007: 148).

One member of DeKeseredy et al.'s research team devoted a substantial amount of time and effort to the above training programme. He further contributed to the preparatory component of the study by spending long hours 'hanging around' the housing estates and their immediate surroundings talking to people and observing street life. As is the case with most researchers, DeKeseredy et al. sought the assistance of academics, including Dr William Julius Wilson's research assistant, who sent the research team open-ended and closed-ended surveys used in the Chicago Urban Poverty and Family Life Study (see Wilson 1996). The end result was a local survey tailored specifically to examine the concrete problems experienced by poor urban public housing residents. The survey also captured data on issues that were then either completely ignored or trivialized by official statistics and mainstream government surveys, such as violence against women and public racial/sexual harassment in poor Canadian public housing communities.

Over the past 33 years, we have witnessed great advances in crime survey research, due in large part to the efforts of feminist researchers. Further, many feminists today recognize that their empirical concerns can be effectively addressed by adhering to the 'canons of established science' (Smith 1994: 123). Certainly, there is much to gain from feminist insights when drafting violence against women questionnaires. For example, many feminists offer broad definitions of abuse that include psychological abuse, coercive control and other hurtful non-physical acts. Surveys that examine these behaviours, as well as acts of physical and sexual violence, avoid the pitfall of creating a 'hierarchy of abuse based on seriousness' (Kelly 1987). In addition, broad definitions coincide with many women's real-life experiences and minimize the problem of under-reporting by uncovering high levels of injurious events than government agency victimization surveys that use narrow legalistic definitions of male-to-female violence (DeKeseredy 2000, 2011b; Smith 1994).

Feminist scholars also alert us to the importance of not relying only on closed-ended questions. The woman abuse survey literature reveals that add-ing supplementary open-ended questions about certain harms give respondents more opportunities to disclose events and build researcher–respondent rapport (DeKeseredy and Rennison 2013a), which is a central goal of feminist scholar-ship. According to Michael D. Smith:

> For one thing, an open format may reduce the threat of a question on vio-lence, because it allows the respondent to qualify her response, to express exact shades of meaning, rather than forcing her to choose from a number of possibly threatening alternatives. For another, open questions may reduce the power imbalance inherent in the interviewer situation (the relation-ship between researcher and researched parallels the hierarchical nature of traditional male-female relationships) because open questions encourage interaction and collaboration between interviewer and respondent . . . The less threatening the question and the more equal the power relationship, the greater the probability of rapport and, in turn, of eliciting an honest answer to a sensitive question. (Smith 1994: 115)

Note, too, that Smith (1987) added supplementary questions to his Toronto woman abuse survey and found that some silent or forgetful female survivors ($N = 60$) changed their answers when asked again in different words by a telephone interviewer. Belated responses increased the overall violence prevalence rate by approximately 10 per cent, and 21 belated disclosures increased the severe violence prevalence rate. Smith defined prevalence as the percentage of women who reported ever having been physically abused.

Supplementary open-ended and closed-ended questions also enhance the quality of self-report crime surveys, but they are rarely used in such studies. One salient excep-tion is the following question included at the end of the male questionnaire developed for the Canadian national survey of woman abuse in university/college dating:

> We really appreciate the time you have taken to complete this survey. And we'd like to assure you that everything you have told us will remain *strictly confidential*.

> We realize that the topics covered in this survey are sensitive and that many men are reluctant to talk about their own dating experiences. But we're also a bit worried that we haven't asked the right questions.

> So now that you have had a chance to think about the topics, have you had any (any other) experiences in which you physically and/or sexually harmed your dating partners and/or girlfriends while you attended college or university. Please provide this information in the spaces below.

There are a series of standard technical procedures that come after crafting a questionnaire, including pretesting the survey, getting a sampling frame, recording the data and analysing the statistics. Indeed, the process is complex, time-consuming, and requires careful organization and record-keeping (Kraska and Neuman 2011). Not to labour the point, but survey work is also expensive. It is simple to say that critical criminological surveys must be independent and should be funded in partnership with various levels of government (MacLean 1996). This is much easier said than done. It is, to say the least, a major challenge to get any type of funding for progressive crime research in this current neo-liberal era. For instance, close to the time of writing this chapter, the Canadian federal government was involved in a full-frontal attack on science in general and criminology in particular. Prime Minister Stephen Harper labelled criminologists 'ivory tower experts' who are part of society's crime problem. He also said that criminologists 'are not criminals themselves, but who are always making excuses for them, and when they aren't making excuses, they are denying that crime is even a problem' (cited in Heath 2013: 1).

Canadian conservative politicians' disdain for the social sciences is not only channelled through assaults on universities' ability to maintain their infrastructure and to hire full-time faculty (DeKeseredy 2013). In addition, research funding and government support for scholarly journals have been slashed. Note that a few years after Harper was first elected Prime Minister, the Social Science and Humanities Research Council of Canada (SSHRC), which is the main funder of social scientific criminological research, prioritized business-related doctoral studies (DeKeseredy and Schwartz 2010; Fenwick 2009). This helped Harper win his war against criminologists and hence, as is the case in other nations, 'academic criminology appears to becoming more marginalized and irrelevant' (Matthews 2009: 341). The same can be said about the gathering of original, progressive survey data.

What, then, is to be done? Some major problems associated with secondary data analysis were identified earlier in this chapter. Do progressives interested in working with secondary survey data have no choice but to go to 'the dark side' or abandon their empirical, theoretical and political interests altogether? The answer is no. True, historically, the NCVS was used mainly by orthodox criminologists, but there are some recent examples of imaginative work done by feminist scholars. Take into account that I was part of a research team that used aggregate NCVS data either from 1992 to 2005 and from 1992 to 2009 to examine:

- urban, suburban, and rural intimate relationship status variations in violence against women (Rennison, DeKeseredy and Dragiewicz 2013);
- urban, suburban, and rural differences in racial/ethnic variations in violence against women (DeKeseredy, Dragiewicz and Rennison 2012);
- urban, suburban, and rural variations in separation/divorce assault (DeKeseredy and Rennison 2013b; Rennison, DeKeseredy and Dragiewicz 2012); and
- dominant situational contexts of reporting of violence against women to police across rural, suburban, and urban areas (Rennison, Dragiewicz and DeKeseredy 2013).

Collectively, the results of these studies and the qualitative and quantitative work done by colleagues in Australia (Carrington and Phillips 2006; Neame and Heenan 2004; Wendt 2009) show that rural women are at higher risk of experiencing male intimate violence than women in more densely populated areas. The key risk factors identified in the extant literature include patriarchal male peer support, geographical isolation, the 'old boy network' consisting of criminal justice officials, inadequate public transportation, community norms prohibiting survivors from publicly revealing their experiences and from seeking social support, and barriers to service (DeKeseredy 2015; DeKeseredy and Schwartz 2009; Donnermeyer and DeKeseredy 2014; Logan et al. 2005).

What also makes the above studies unique is that much of the emphasis in rural criminology is on testing place-based theories (e.g. social disorganization theory), which is understandable given the obvious geographical aspects of rural and remote areas (Donnermeyer and DeKeseredy 2014). Even so, many other possibly useful theories are ignored, especially critical perspectives. Walter S. DeKeseredy, Callie M. Rennison and Molly Dragiewicz's secondary analysis of NCVS data was crafted in part to address this problem and their work reveals that feminist perspectives on certain types of rural crime have much explanatory value.

Though not widely known, used or discussed in scholarly publications, the NCVS includes 'incident narratives', which are open-ended responses to a final question at the end of the survey that asks participants to report what happened to them. Albeit qualitative in nature, the narratives are not the actual victims' verbatim accounts, but rather statements transcribed by NCVS interviewers (Jaquier, Johnson and Fisher 2011). Moreover, the narratives lack rich contextual detail about events leading up to an assault or after an attack, and it is hard to determine from reading them why incidents were not reported to the police. Nevertheless, Karen G. Weiss' (2009, 2011) analyses of NCVS incident narratives reveal that they can generate some fruitful information on sexual assault, including survivors' excuses and justifications for unwanted sexual contact and coercion. Hopefully, more critical criminologists will follow in her footsteps and uncover data that enhance a critical understanding of other major social problems.

Numerous secondary data resources, including the Crime Survey for England and Wales, can be used for progressive, imaginative purposes. However, those who do employ them 'should do so with good reason, rather than just solely due to convenience' (Nelson et al. 2014: 31). Relying heavily on old data sets strips our discipline of the criminological imagination and thus, following Nelson et al.'s advice, scholars should be praised instead of punished for conducting exploratory pilot surveys. However, much time and effort committed by a large cadre of criminologists is needed to change an academic culture that rewards the 'piecemeal publication' of the results of secondary data analysis (Gartner, Osgood and Baumer 2012).

## Conclusion

The imaginative use of crime surveys is by no means restricted to the above suggestions. Undoubtedly, many readers can probably think of more. Whether we like them or not, surveys are here to stay and thus it is time for more critical criminologists to use them creatively and to avoid simply producing 'oppositional rhetoric' about orthodox studies and about mainstream criminology in general (Carlen 2011). Moreover, critical criminologists who use surveys should not have to justify their existence to other progressive scholars because their quantitative work has much to offer and opens new avenues of empirical and theoretical inquiry. For instance, if it wasn't for left realist local crime surveys, explanations for inner-city crime would be totally dominated by routine activities and place-based theories of intra-class and intra-racial victimization. Similarly, the aforementioned rural research treats gender as much more than a variable to be treated lightly in abstracted empiricist venture.

At any rate, no matter how critical criminologists use surveys and what they study, these progressive scholars should always follow C. Wright Mills' sage advice:

Be a good craftsman: Avoid any rigid set of procedures. Above all, seek to develop and to use the sociological imagination. Avoid the fetishism of method and technique. Urge the rehabilitation of the unpretentious intellectual craftsman, and try to become such a craftsman yourself. Let every man be his own methodologist; let every man be his own theorist; let theory and method again become part of the practice of a craft. (Mills 1959: 225)

Mills was not a feminist and many scholars have criticized his use of malestream language and his 'missing the boat on gender' (Burawoy 2008: 368). Such criticism is fair and warranted. Nevertheless, if there ever was a need to answer the above call, especially in America, it is now. As Jock Young (2011: viii) puts it, 'abstracted empiricism has expanded on a level that would surely astonished Mills himself'.

Consistent with Claire M. Renzetti's (2013) cautionary note about her recommendations for future feminist criminological work, I, too, must admit that my suggestions for using surveys imaginatively reflect a few of my own personal priorities, some of which progressive readers will agree with and some that they may reject. This is to be expected since critical criminology involves using a diverse range of methods and theories. Repeatedly stated by Steve Hall, Simon Winlow and others who attended the 2014 National Deviancy Conference, critical criminology needs to move forward and constructive debates from within progressive circles are necessary for advancement. On the other hand, reflexivity and debates should not be limited to critical understandings of crime, law, and social control. Pat Carlen reminds us that criminology as a whole:

should be: open; constantly recognizing, questioning, and, if necessary, destroying the conditions of its own existence; and neither 'trimming' its questions to make them politically correct or expedient, nor 'clubbing' – that is, pulling its punches – either to conform to contemporary academic fashions or political prejudices, or in response to disciplinary bullying by either political or academic powers that be. (Carlen 2011: 97)

## Note

1 I would like to thank Molly Dragiewicz, Amanda Hall-Sanchez, Michael Hviid Jacobsen, Justin Kotze, Peter B. Kraska, Callie M. Rennison, Martin D. Schwartz, David Temple and Sandra Walklate for their assistance and comments.

## References

Babbie, Earl (1973) *Survey Research Methods*. Belmont, CA: Wadsworth Publishing.

Bachman, Ronet D. and Russell K. Schutt (2007) *The Practice of Research in Criminology and Criminal Justice*. Thousand Oaks, CA: Sage Publications.

Bart, Pauline B., Patricia Y. Miller, Eileen Moran and Elizabeth A. Stanko (1989) 'Guest Editors' Introduction'. *Gender & Society*, 3: 431–6.

Basran, Gurcharn S., Charan Gill and Brian D. MacLean (1995) *Farm Workers and Their Children*. Vancouver: Collective Press.

Black, Michele C., Kathleen C. Basile, Matthew J. Breiding and George W. Ryan (2014) 'Prevalence of Sexual Violence against Women in 23 States and Two U.S. Territories, BRFSS 2005'. *Violence Against Women*, 20: 485–99.

Black, Michele C., Kathleen C. Basile, Matthew J. Breiding, Sharon G. Smith, Mikel L. Walters, Melissa T. Merrick, Jieru Chen and Mark R. Stevens (2011) *The National Intimate Partner and Sexual Violence Survey (NIVS) 2010 Summary Report*. Atlanta, GA: National Center for Injury Prevention and Control, Centers for Disease Control and Prevention.

Block, Carolyn R. (2000) *Chicago Women's Health Risk Study, Risk of Serious Injury or Death in Intimate Violence: A Collaborative Research Project*. Washington DC: US Department of Justice.

Block, Carolyn R. and Walter S. DeKeseredy (2007) 'Forced Sex & Leaving Intimate Relationships: Results of the Chicago Women's Health Risk Study'. *Women's Health & Urban Life*, 6: 6–23.

Bumiller, Kristin (2008) *In an Abusive State: How Neo-liberalism Appropriated the Feminist Movement against Sexual Violence*. Durham, NC: Duke University Press.

Burawoy, Michael (2008) 'Open Letter to C. Wright Mills'. *Antipode*, 40: 365–75.

Carlen, Pat (2011) 'Against Evangelism in Academic Criminology: For Criminology as a Scientific Art', in Mary Bosworth and Carolyn Hoyle (eds), *What is Criminology?* Oxford: Oxford University Press, pp. 95–109.

Carrabine, Eamonn, Pamela Cox, Maggy Lee, Ken Plummer and Nigel South (2009) *Criminology: A Sociological Introduction*. London: Routledge.

Carrington, Kerry and Janet Phillips (2006) *Domestic Violence in Australia: An Overview of the Issues*. Canberra: Parliament of Australia.

Cohen, Lawrence E. and Marcus Felson (1979) 'Social Change and Crime Rate Trends: A Routine Activities Approach'. *American Sociological Review*, 44: 588–608.

Crawford, Adam, Trevor Jones, Tom Woodhouse and Jock Young (1990) *Second Islington Crime Survey*. Middlesex: Centre for Criminology, Middlesex Polytechnic.

Currie, Elliott (2007) 'Against Marginality: Arguments for a Public Criminology'. *Theoretical Criminology*, 11: 175–90.

DeKeseredy, Walter S. (2000) 'Current Controversies in Defining Nonlethal Violence against Women in Heterosexual Relationships: Empirical Implications'. *Violence Against Women*, 6: 728–46.

——. (2011a) *Contemporary Critical Criminology*. London: Routledge.

——. (2011b) 'Feminist Contributions to Understanding Woman Abuse: Myths, Controversies and Realities'. *Aggression and Violent Behavior*, 16: 297–302.

——. (2012) 'The Current Condition of Criminological Theory in North America', in Steve Hall and Simon Winlow (eds), *New Directions in Criminological Theory*. London: Routledge, pp. 66–79.

——. (2013) 'Crime, Justice, and Inequality: Oh Canada, Where Art Thou?' *International Journal for Crime, Justice and Social Democracy*, 2: 15–26.

——. (2015) 'New Directions in Feminist Understandings of Rural Crime and Social Control'. *Journal of Rural Studies*, 39: 180–7.

DeKeseredy, Walter S. and Linda MacLeod (1997) *Woman Abuse: A Sociological Story*. Toronto: Harcourt Brace.

——. (2009) *Dangerous Exits: Escaping Abusive Relationships in Rural America*. New Brunswick, NJ: Rutgers University Press.

——. (2010) 'Friedman Economic Policies, Social Exclusion and Crime: Toward a Gendered Left Realist Subcultural Theory'. *Crime, Law and Social Change*, 54: 159–70.

——. (2013) *Male Peer Support and Violence against Women: The History and Verification of a Theory*. Boston, MA: Northeastern University Press.

——. (2015) 'The Mismeasure of Violence against Women: The Contribution of Government Survey Research in an Era of Neo-liberalism'. Paper presented at the annual meetings of the Academy of Criminal Justice Sciences, Orlando, FL.

DeKeseredy, Walter S. and Molly Dragiewicz (2014) 'Woman Abuse in Canada: Sociological Reflections on the Past, Suggestions for the Future'. *Violence Against Women*, 20: 228–44.

DeKeseredy, Walter S. and Callie M. Rennison (2013a) 'New Directions in the Social Scientific Study of Separation/Divorce Assault', in Kelly Richards and Juan M. Tauri (eds), *Crime, Justice and Social Democracy: Proceedings of the 2nd International Conference, 2013, Volume 1*. Brisbane: Crime and Justice Research Centre, Faculty of Law, Queensland University of Technology, pp. 47–57.

——. (2013b) 'Comparing Female Victims of Male Perpetrated Separation/Divorce Assault across Geographical Regions: Results from the National Crime Victimization Survey'. *International Journal for Crime, Justice and Social Democracy*, 2: 65–81.

DeKeseredy, Walter S. and Martin D. Schwartz (1998) *Woman Abuse on Campus: Results from the Canadian National Survey*. Thousand Oaks, CA: Sage Publications.

DeKeseredy, Walter S., Shahid Alvi and Martin D. Schwartz (2006) 'Left Realism Revisited', in Walter S. DeKeseredy and Barbara Perry (eds), *Advancing Critical Criminology: Theory and Application*. Lanham, MD: Lexington, pp. 19–42.

DeKeseredy, Walter S., Molly Dragiewicz and Callie M. Rennison (2012) 'Racial/Ethnic Variations in Violence against Women: Urban, Suburban, and Rural Differences'. *International Journal of Rural Criminology*, 1: 184–202.

DeKeseredy, Walter S., Shadid Alvi, Martin D. Schwartz and Andreas Tomaszewski (2003) *Under Siege: Poverty and Crime in a Public Housing Community*. Lanham, MD: Lexington.

Devine, Joel A. and James D. Wright (1993) *The Greatest of Evils: Urban Poverty and the American Underclass*. New York: Aldine de Gruyter.

Dobash, Russell P. and R. Emerson Dobash (1995) 'Reflections on Findings from the Violence Against Women Survey'. *Canadian Journal of Criminology*, 37: 457–84.

Donnermeyer, Joseph F. and Walter S. DeKeseredy (2014) *Rural Criminology*. London: Routledge.

Feely, Malcolm M. and Jonathan Simon (1992) 'The New Penology: Notes on the Emerging Strategy of Corrections and its Implications'. *Criminology*, 30: 449–74.

Fenwick, Scott (2009) 'Business Focused Fix for SSHRC'. *The Gateway*, 9: 1.

Gartner, Rosemary D., Wayne Osgood and Eric Baumer (2012) 'Salami-Slicing, Peek-a-Boo, and LPUS: Addressing the Problem of Piecemeal Publication'. *The Criminologist*, 37: 23–5.

Hagan, John (1989) *Structural Criminology*. New Brunswick, NJ: Rutgers University Press.

Hay, David A. (1993) 'Methodological Review of "The Incidence and Prevalence of Woman Abuse in Canadian University and College Dating Relationships: Preliminary Results from a National Survey" by Walter S. DeKeseredy and Katharine Kelly'. *Journal of Human Justice*, 4: 53–66.

Heath, Joseph (2013) 'In Defence of Sociology'. *Ottawa Citizen*, available at: http://spon. ca/in-defence-of-sociology/2013/05/01.

Henry, Stuart (1999) 'Is Left Realism a Useful Theory for Addressing the Problems of Crime? No', in John R. Fuller and Eric W. Hickey (eds), *Controversial Issues in Criminology*. Boston, MA: Allyn & Bacon, pp. 134–7.

Hirschi, Travis (1969) *Causes of Delinquency*. Berkeley, CA: University of California Press.

Hobbs, Dick (1998) 'Going Down the Glocal: The Local Context of Organised Crime'. *The Howard Journal*, 37: 407–22.

Hope, Tim J. (2007) 'Theory and Method: The Social Epidemiology of Crime Victims', in Sandra Walklate (ed.), *Handbook of Victims and Victimology*. London: Routledge, pp. 60–90.

Hoyle, Carolyn (2007) 'Feminism, Victimology and Domestic Violence', in Sandra Walklate (ed.), *Handbook of Victims and Victimology*. London: Routledge, pp. 146–74.

Jaquier, Véronique, Holly Johnson and Bonnie S. Fisher (2011) 'Research Methods, Measures and Ethics', in Claire M. Renzetti, Jeffrey L. Edleson and Raquel K. Bergen (eds), *Sourcebook on Violence against Women*. Thousand Oaks, CA: Sage Publications, pp. 23–45.

Johnson, Holly (1996) *Dangerous Domains: Violence against Women in Canada*. Toronto: Nelson.

Jones, Trevor, Brian D. MacLean and Jock Young (1986) *The Islington Crime Survey: Crime, Victimization and Policing in Inner-City London*. Brookfield, VT: Gower.

Kelly, Liz (1987) 'The Continuum of Sexual Violence', in Jalna Hanmer and Mary Maynard (eds), *Women, Violence and Social Control*. Atlantic Highlands, NJ: Humanities Press International, pp. 46–60.

Kennedy, Leslie W. and Donald G. Dutton (1989) 'The Incidence of Wife Assault in Alberta'. *Canadian Journal of Behavioral Science*, 21: 40–54.

Koss, Mary P. (1993) 'Detecting the Scope of Rape: A Review of Prevalence Research Methods'. *Journal of Interpersonal Violence*, 8: 198–222.

Kotze, Justin and David Temple (2014) 'Analysing the "Crime Decline": News from Nowhere'. Paper presented at the 2014 National Deviancy Conference, Teesside University.

Kraska, Peter B. and W. Lawrence Neuman (2008) *Criminal Justice and Criminology Research Methods*. Boston, MA: Pearson.

——. (2011) *Criminal Justice and Criminology Research Methods*, 2nd edn. Boston, MA: Pearson.

Lea, John and Jock Young (1984) *What is To Be Done about Law and Order?* New York: Penguin.

Logan, T. K, Lucy Evans, Erin Stevenson and Carol E. Jordan (2005) 'Barriers to Services for Rural and Urban Survivors of Rape'. *Journal of Interpersonal Violence*, 20: 591–616.

Lynch, Michael J., Raymond J. Michalowski and W. Byron Groves (2000) *The New Primer in Radical Criminology: Critical Perspectives on Crime, Power and Identity*. Monsey, NJ: Criminal Justice Press.

MacLean, Brian D. (1991) 'In Partial Defense of Socialist Realism: Some Theoretical and Methodological Concerns of the Local Crime Survey'. *Crime, Law and Social Change*, 15: 213–54.

——. (1996) 'A Program of Local Crime-Survey Research for Canada', in Brian D. MacLean (ed.), *Crime and Society: Readings in Critical Criminology*. Toronto: Copp Clark, pp. 73–105.

Matthews, Roger (2009) 'Beyond "So What?" Criminology: Rediscovering Realism'. *Theoretical Criminology*, 13: 341–62.

Mills, Charles Wright (1959) *The Sociological Imagination*. New York: Oxford University Press.

Mosher, Clayton (2013) 'The Myth of Accurate Crime Measurement', in Robert M. Bohm and Jeffery T. Walker (eds), *Demystifying Crime & Criminal Justice*. New York: Oxford University Press, pp. 3–12.

Mosher, Clayton, Terance Miethe and Timothy Hart (2011) *The Mismeasure of Crime*. Thousand Oaks, CA: Sage Publications.

Neame, Alexandra and Melanie Heenan (2004) *Responding to Sexual Assault in Rural Communities*. Melbourne: Australian Institute of Family Studies.

Nelson, Matthew S., Alese Wooditch and Shaun L. Gabbidon (2014) 'Is Criminology Out-of-Date? A Research Note on the Use of Common Types of Crime Data'. *Journal of Criminal Justice Education*, 25: 16–33.

Orrick, Erin A. and Henriikka Weir (2011) 'The Most Prolific Sole and Lead Authors in Elite Criminology and Criminal Justice Journals, 2000–2009'. *Journal of Criminal Justice Education*, 22: 24–42.

Pakes, Francis J. (2012) 'Comparative Criminology', in David S. Clark (ed.), *Comparative Law and Society*. Cheltenham: Edward Elgar, pp. 61–76.

Petersilia, Joan R., Peter W. Greenwood and Marvin Lavin (1977) *Criminal Careers of Habitual Felons*. Department of Justice Report R-2144 DOJ. Santa Monica, CA: Rand Corporation.

Rennison, Callie M., Walter S. DeKeseredy and Molly Dragiewicz (2012) 'Urban, Suburban and Rural Variations in Separation/Divorce Rape/Sexual Assault: Results from the National Crime Victimization Survey'. *Feminist Criminology*, 7: 282–97.

——. (2013) 'Intimate Relationship Status Variations in Violence against Women: Urban, Suburban, and Rural Differences'. *Violence Against Women*, 19: 1312–30.

Rennison, Callie M., Molly Dragiewicz and Walter S. DeKeseredy (2013) 'Context Matters: Violence against Women and Reporting to Police in Rural, Suburban and Urban Areas'. *American Journal of Criminal Justice*, 38: 141–59.

Renzetti, Claire M. (2013) *Feminist Criminology*. London: Routledge.

Rose, Hilary and Steven Rose (1976) *The Political Economy of Science: Ideology of/in the Natural Sciences*. London: Macmillan.

Savelsberg, Joachim J., Ryan King and Laura Cleveland (2002) 'Politicized Scholarship: Science on Crime and the State'. *Social Problems*, 49: 327–48.

Schechter, Susan (1988) 'Building Bridges between Activists, Professionals and Researchers', in Kersti Yllo and Michele Bograd (eds), *Feminist Perspectives on Wife Abuse*. Beverly Hills, CA: Sage Publications, pp. 299–312.

Schwartz, Martin D. (2000) 'Methodological Issues in the Use of Survey Data for Measuring and Characterizing Violence against Women'. *Violence Against Women*, 6: 815–38.

Smith, Michael D. (1987) 'The Incidence and Prevalence of Woman Abuse in Toronto'. *Violence and Victims*, vol. 2, pp. 173–87.

——. (1990) 'Patriarchal Ideology and Wife Beating: A Test of a Feminist Hypothesis'. *Violence and Victims*, 5: 257–73.

——. (1994) 'Enhancing the Quality of Survey Data on Violence against Women: A Feminist Approach'. *Gender & Society*, 18: 109–27.

Straus, Murray A. and Richard J. Gelles (1986) 'Societal Change and Change in Family Violence from 1975 to 1985 as Revealed by Two National Surveys'. *Journal of Marriage and the Family*, 48: 465–79.

Straus, Murray A., Richard J. Gelles and Suzanne K. Steinmetz (1981) *Behind Closed Doors: Violence in the American Family*. New York: Anchor Books.

Tauri, Juan M. (2013) 'Indigenous Critique of Authoritarian Criminology', in Kerry Carrington, Matthew Ball, Erin O'Brien and Juan M. Tauri (eds), *Crime, Justice and Social Democracy: International Perspectives*. New York: Palgrave Macmillan, pp. 217–33.

Taylor, Bruce and Trevor Bennett (1999) *Comparing Drug Use Rates of Detained Arrestees in the United States and England*. Washington DC: National Institute of Justice.

Taylor, Ian (1992) 'Left Realist Criminology and the Free Market Experiment in Britain', in Jock Young and Roger Matthews (eds), *Rethinking Criminology: The Realist Debate*. London: Sage Publications, pp. 95–122.

Tjaden, Patricia and Nancy Thoennes (2000) *Extent, Nature, and Consequences of Intimate Partner Violence*. Washington DC: National Institute of Justice.

Tremblay, Pierre and Carlo Morselli (2000) 'Patterns in Criminal Achievement: Wilson and Abrahamse Revisited'. *Criminology*, 38: 633–59.

Van Dijk, Jan (2008) *The World of Crime: Breaking the Silence on Problems of Security, Justice, and Development across the World*. Thousand Oaks, CA: Sage Publications.

Van Dijk, Jan and Mark Shaw (2009) 'The International Crime Victim Survey: Impact and Future Policy', in John Winterdyk, Philip L. Reichel and Harry R. Dammer (eds), *A Guided Reader to Research in Comparative Criminology/Criminal Justice*. Bochum: Universitatsverlag Brockmeyer, pp. 261–73.

Van Kesteren, John, Jan van Dijk and Pat Mayhew (2014) 'The International Crime Victims Surveys: A Retrospective'. *International Review of Victimology*, 20: 49–69.

Visher, Christy A. (1986) 'The Rand Institute Survey: A Reanalysis', in Alfred Blumstein, Jacqueline Cohen, Jeffrey A. Roth and Christy A. Visher (eds), *Careers and Career Criminals*. Washington DC: National Academy Press, pp. 161–211.

Walby, Sylvia and Andrew Myhill (2001) 'New Survey Methodologies in Researching Violence against Women'. *British Journal of Criminology*, 41: 502–22.

Walklate, Sandra (1989) *Victimology: The Victim and the Criminal Justice Process*. London: Unwin Hyman.

Weiss, Karen G. (2009) 'Boys Will Be Boys and Other Gendered Accounts: An Exploration of Victims' Excuses and Justifications for Unwanted Sexual Contact and Coercion'. *Violence Against Women*, 15: 810–34.

——. (2011) 'Neutralizing Sexual Victimization: A Typology of Victims' Non-reporting Accounts'. *Theoretical Criminology*, 15: 445–67.

Wendt, Sarah (2009) *Domestic Violence in Rural Australia*. Annandale: Federation Press.

Wilson, William J. (1987) *The Truly Disadvantaged: The Inner-City, the Underclass and Public Policy*. Chicago: University of Chicago Press.

——. (1996) *When Work Disappears: The World of the New Urban Poor*. New York: Knopf.

Wright, Richard A. and David O. Friedrichs (1998) 'The Most-Cited Scholars and Works in Critical Criminology'. *Journal of Criminal Justice Education*, 9: 95–121.

Young, Jock (1999) *The Exclusive Society*. London: Sage Publications.

——. (2004) 'Voodoo Criminology and the Numbers Game', in Jeff Ferrell, Keith Hayward, Wayne Morrison and Mike Presdee (eds), *Cultural Criminology Unleashed*. London: GlassHouse Press, pp. 13–28.

——. (2011) *The Criminological Imagination*. Cambridge: Polity Press.

# 3 'Snitches get stitches'?

## Telling tales on homicide detectives

*Louise Westmarland*

### Introduction to the killing fields of downtown DC

As research topics in criminology go, murder is a tough one. It occurs with some frequency but little regularity, making it difficult to predict where and when it will take place. Murder scenes are often 'closed' to outside view as the integrity of evidence at the scene could be compromised, especially as forensic techniques become more capable of detecting minute traces. The problem for researchers is to find a ready supply of suspicious deaths and a receptive gatekeeper. As the excerpt from the *Washington Post* article presented below suggests, in some cities, at least the first part of this requirement is fulfilled. This chapter reflects on a study of homicide detectives working in a small corner or 'District' of the US capital where murder is a regular occurrence. With around 500 deaths per year across the city, mostly in the African-American ghettos, this was a 'land of the dead', cynically dubbed 'the killing fields' by the homicide squad detectives:

> A night and early morning of gunfire in the area left five people dead and four wounded, including a teenage student found shot to death in a stolen car. Shortly before 11 pm Saturday, District police were called to the first crime scene. Officers found a car that had crashed into a tree. Inside officers found a girl, 16, collapsed in the front passenger seat. Minutes after arriving at the first scene police found two male teenagers in an adjoining parking lot. One youth, 15, had been shot in the leg and arm, the other, 18, had been shot in the leg. In a shooting a mile away that District police thought might be related, officers were called about a half-hour later and found a man who had been shot in the leg.
>
> The violence continued about 2.30 am when police were called to investigate a shooting about five miles from the previous one. There, officers found one man dead with at least one gunshot wound to the upper body. Police said they found a second man who had been shot in the shoulder. About 5.20 am near the District line, police responded to a call about a shooting. Two men were found collapsed inside of a Jeep Wrangler. The driver and passenger were struck by gunfire, officers said, apparently as they travelled along the street, causing the vehicle to go out of control, hit a car and stop on a side-walk. The driver was pronounced dead at the scene and the passenger died

at a hospital. Officers were called at 7.30 am to investigate gunfire. In the back of a vehicle, they found a man who had been shot. He was pronounced dead at the scene, authorities said. A police spokeswoman said investigators knew of no suspects or motives in the shootings. She said police are investigating possible links among the shootings. (Clarence Williams and David. S. Fallis, *Washington Post* staff writers, Monday 27 September 2004, pp. B1–B2, abridged)

The study of DC murder investigations which is described here was initially designed to explore the morals and ethics of homicide detectives. As murder is usually viewed to be the most serious crime of all, it carries with it the most pressure to solve, and seemed to be a useful place to examine 'professional ethics' or 'morals in action'. The idea behind the study sprung from Martin Innes' (2003) contention that homicide teams use personal ethics to project 'moral careers' onto suspects and victims they encounter. According to Innes, the detectives he studied drew upon their own morals and beliefs to help them decide who is a 'worthy victim' – a 'good wife and mother' for example, or as Innes argues, that 'honest, decent people's' murders may be given a higher priority. It follows therefore that some of the victims 'had it coming' and whereas some perpetrators came from 'nice families', others were just 'scumbags'.

Whilst these might seem to be perfectly normal reactions to people everyone encounters in daily life, for the study of homicide detectives, it is especially interesting because, as Innes argues, they are using these moral judgements to frame their investigations. He uses examples of politicians, children and 'other public interest figures' to explain how murder investigations are graded for importance. As he shows, using detailed analysis, the way in which murder is investigated depends to some extent upon the detectives' beliefs about the 'morality' of the participants. In a broadly similar way this chapter reflects on a study of a small group of American homicide detectives who were observed as part of an ethnographic study. They were working in a specialist squad concerned only with murders and serious woundings. As they were located in a large, ethnically diverse city, the squad were faced with a significant number of homicides of around ten cases each per year and a population who were generally unwilling to 'snitch'. Detectives were attempting to solve murders without access to very useful evidence or help from the local population, who regularly told the police that 'snitches get stitches and I ain't saying shi-it' (Westmarland 2013). The study was ethnographic in that it aimed to understand the occupational culture and 'worldview' of the police and the people they encountered in their daily lives. It was an attempt to follow in the footsteps of many classic studies of the police, which often illuminate 'backstage' misdemeanours.

## Common cultures?

Police occupational, canteen or 'cop' culture is often said to have common characteristics which may vary and mutate depending upon the situation.

Manifestations of these differences might be seen in the difference between the operational culture of traffic cops and detectives, for example, or domestic violence and firearms units (see Westmarland 2008, Chapter 11). Essentially police culture is difficult to define and time-consuming to research because it requires a certain closeness that is difficult to develop until trust and confidence from both sides has been established.

One of the most famous early police ethnographers from the 1960s, Jerome H. Skolnick, argued that although police culture varies from place to place and has changed over time, it has certain universal stable and lasting features and a recognizable 'working personality' (Skolnick 2005: 264). Robert Reiner (2000) and more recently other scholars (see, for example, Cockcroft 2013; Loftus 2009) have argued that there are some enduring characteristics of police culture of which Reiner identifies seven:

- a sense of mission;
- suspicion;
- isolation/solidarity;
- conservatism;
- machismo;
- pragmatism;
- racial prejudice.

Reiner argues that although a great deal of police work is carried out alone or in pairs, there must be 'acceptance of the rank-and-file definition' of the way it is conducted by the group. As such although individual styles of policing might vary, it 'reflects and perpetuates the power differences within the social structure it polices' and is generally based upon danger, authority, including the potential for force, and the need to produce results (Reiner 2000: 88–9, quoted in Westmarland 2008).

One of the ways in which police officers are said to deal with the need to produce results is to bend the rules. Sometimes called 'noble cause corruption', as suggested by Carl B. Klockars in the 1980s, officers might come up against the 'Dirty Harry Problem', from the film of that name. This is where, for example, officers 'know' that a suspect is guilty, but have no legitimate or legal means of proving it. The 'noble cause' part of the term suggests that they are not bending the rules for personal gain, but to protect or avenge society in some way. For example, Richard A. Leo says that American detectives do not see themselves as breaking any laws or 'engaging in any morally questionable behavior', yet their methods are 'based on thoroughgoing manipulation and deception' and are treated as a 'game' whereby the detective can use any means and then 'absolve himself of any doubts he may have about the ethics of the means through which he elicits incriminating statements' (Leo 2008: 24, quoted in Westmarland 2013).

In the discussion which follows, from the detectives' perspective, these pressures to commit 'noble cause corruption' are examined as 'acceptable' means to achieve their ends. In effect, they do not seem to have any rules, or few are evident.

Their occupational culture, personal morals and professional ethics are analysed and the pressure from the researcher's point of view to collude is examined.

## Getting up close to murder

The main reason to conduct an ethnography of the police is to try to 'see it how it is' at first hand, unadulterated by second-hand opinions framed by senior officers concerned with the organization's reputation. The researcher can see what happens, record how the police react under stress and provide a version of reality for the reader. These accounts can include the personal sentiments of the researcher; emotions such as fear, disgust, humour and sadness. Emotions may be recorded as the researcher begins to feel as if they are part of the group, scene or events. Some police ethnographies rely upon access to more unusual and potentially emotional scenes than others. The 'dirty work' described by Laura Huey and Ryan Broll (2015) includes 'physically dirty' situations, such as searching for 'objectionable' materials (for example, blood and body parts), as well as 'social dirt', which refers to coming into contact with people who have 'stigmatised identities, such as drug addicts, sex trade workers and ex-convicts' (Huey and Broll 2015: 238). 'Taking part' in a group endeavour with research participants can sometimes involve more close contact than others. Dick Hobbs described that after a night out with the CID, he was torn between writing up and 'bringing up' the previous night's experiences (Hobbs 1989), and Simon Winlow has argued that to maintain his cover as a nightclub bouncer, he had to accept stolen goods on occasions (Westmarland 2011: 136). In previous ethnographies I have recounted hiding behind trees at firearms stake-outs, driving police cars and accidently catching escapees (Westmarland 2001).

One argument is that to research the police in all their glory is to feel and experience their lives, yet in order to conduct academic research, distance is required. What would be the point of doing police ethnography, people might ask, other than to expose their sexist, racist and unethical behaviour – but once they have shared their worst deeds, hopes and fears with you, is it ethical to betray their trust? This process of trust begins with spending time with the participants and sharing emotional experiences. Not many academic studies begin with a bath full of dirty clothes under which is hidden a doll, purporting to be a dead baby. The doll is covered in fake blood and there are 'clues' in the pile of clothing such as a cord from a dressing gown and a bloodied knife. Nearby, on the floor under a towel, is a gun and splotches of more fake blood. As I am part of a team who are learning to make observations about crime scenes, we carefully replace the 'baby' and start drawing a plan of the bathroom, mapping the gun, blood and any other pieces of evidence we might be expected to have noticed.

This was because I was being inducted into the US homicide investigative system before commencing the main part of the fieldwork by taking part in a practical forensics course. At the time, it felt like a week wasted that could have been used more fruitfully on the 'real' ethnography, but it was a useful introduction, not only to the terminology of forensic evidence, but also to the type of people who would be at the crime scene. Forensic evidence is regarded by the police as an increasingly important part of solving, proving and backing up what is supposed to have happened at a murder scene, especially where few witnesses are prepared to 'snitch'. The credibility of a course certificate and the ability to at least understand some of the processes and language was useful, affording a little bit of 'insider' knowledge to an 'outsider' at the real murder scenes.

Once the main study commenced, I was working early evening and night shifts with a group of six detectives, accompanying one of two key officers who were assigned to 'look after' me. As explained above, the aim of the study was to observe detectives' behaviours in order to see whether they assigned 'moral careers' to victims and suspects. Initially this was explained to the various gate-keepers who asked as being about 'decision-making processes', making it seem more of a resource allocation issue than one of moral judgement. When asked in more detail what the study was about, I would say it was looking at how deci-sions about which lines of enquiry to follow are made and which homicides are 'prioritized'. Once they got to know me better, I would explain that murders in England are graded for importance, and some are given more detectives to work on the case. This meant little to the US detectives, who normally had three 'live' cases to investigate simultaneously, with around ten cases each per year, whereas in the UK, a 'Grade A' murder could have up to 38 detectives working together on one case (Innes 2003: 90–1).

As the police are good at detecting motives and understanding people, they soon realized that the study was about their ethics and how they decided who was or was not guilty, and who was a 'deserving' victim and who 'had it coming'. They were, in line with Robert Reiner's categories of defining characteristics of police culture (Reiner 2010), suitably cynical about the cases they were allocated. They would receive these on a random basis, taking it in turns to be 'man up', and had an annual clear-up target of three per year from around ten allocations in total. So if a 'self-solver' came in and the next detective in turn received it, they would make remarks about 'getting themselves a bone', but if a 'whodunit' case came in with few clues, they would groan and complain about not being able to achieve their clear-up target.

It seemed in fact that their cynicism knew no bounds and that they were willing to do almost anything to solve their cases; for example, the first homicide call on the initial night of the fieldwork was a multiple shooting of three young black men on the front porch of a house in the most deprived area of the city. One man, not much more than a boy, died at the scene and two others received life-threatening injuries. It was initially reported to the police as they arrived that both young male black victims were going to lose their legs. The man who died had a large hole in the lower half of his spine, the fatal injury which he sustained, it later transpired, whilst running away from his assailants. Great hilarity was caused when police officers attending the scene were told by one of the ambulance crew that one of the gunshot victims had been answering their questions about potential assailants until they tried to move him and 'one leg went east, and one west, that was the end of the conversation!'.

At this first case, once the dead and wounded had been rushed off to hospital, evidence at the scene consisted of 57 spent shotgun cartridges scattered across a small residential street, in front of a house next door to a nursery school. In addition to the three adult victims, a baby of six months almost became the fourth as a bullet casing from one of the shots fired was found in the mattress of his travel cot. He had been lying in the cot just inside the door of a house where the victims of the shooting had been sitting on the porch throughout the incident.

At the scene, the lead detective, whom I was accompanying, interrogated the local detective who had got there before us, asking 'Who done it?':

> *Local Detective*: One of the victims said it was someone called Carl from Howard's Farm in a maroon-coloured Honda.
>
> *Lead Homicide Detective*: (aside, sarcastically) Well, I believe *that*.

Being the height of summer in a city with a serious smog problem, the air was very hot and humid, with one of the detectives remaking: 'Hell, if I lived down here [in the 'ghetto'] *I'd* feel like killing someone.' As we discussed the case sitting together in his car to use the air conditioning to cool down, he explained that the local people were 'knuckleheads' who would 'rather lie than tell the truth' and would 'probably not know the difference'.

After considering the options for a while in the car, we walked over to the house where the victims had been shot whilst sitting on the front porch earlier that evening in order to interrogate the tenant of the house. She was a young black woman with a number of small children around her, including the six-month-old baby she was holding on her knee, which had just missed receiving one of the bullets:

> *Lead Detective:* Now, I know there's a gun in this house somewhere and I want you to level with me because if you lie to me and I find a gun you'll be in serious trouble.
>
> *Woman:* I ain't got no gun. I got my children here and I'm on a Section 17 already.
>
> *Lead Detective:* Well, I'm applying for a search warrant and if I find a gun, I'm telling you . . .

This warning was delivered by the detective standing over the woman who was nursing her baby protectively on the sofa. He was wagging his finger at her to emphasize that she would be in serious trouble if she did not tell him where the gun was hidden. Outside the house, the detective complained bitterly that he knows 'there's a gun in there somewhere', but he needs to wait to get the warrant to search it. He says he knows the woman is lying, but wouldn't help him, even though one victim of the shooting was her brother, the other was her lover, and her baby was very nearly killed in the crossfire. The investigation, including the coding of all the bullets and casings and holes in the walls and doors and windows, went on until 2 am and a search warrant was enforced at that point, with no gun being found.

## Hanging out waiting for someone to die

As explained earlier, the origins of this study was Martin Innes' theory (2003) that homicide detectives create a 'moral career' for suspects and victims, and use this to decide upon the seriousness of the crime, the resources to be deployed and the approach to be taken. In effect, the study set out to look at which murders are seen as 'serious' and worthy of effort, and which are less important, and whether this was based on some aspect of race, colour, sex or class. In order to develop the ideas, the aim was to observe as many cases of homicide investigation as possible to see whether police officers seemed to be making moral judgements in the ways Innes described. The problem was that hanging around waiting for a murder to happen in the UK is time-consuming and unproductive. With the average number of murders in England and Wales standing at about 500 per year, in an average-sized town of 250,000, there may only be one murder a year, so observing an investigation at first hand would be a difficult logistic exercise.

In fact, in Washington DC, it would be a very quiet night if at least one if not two life-threatening incidents did not occur. The officers working in a separate unit dealing only with homicide and serious woundings in a large and violent city were a source of almost constant and varied action. As the press report at the beginning of this chapter shows, one night shift could involve calls to numerous murders and shooting incidents, meaning that a significant amount of data could be collected in a short period. These detectives were also interesting in terms of police cultures because their elite status and enthusiasm for the type of work they were doing meant they had developed into an unusually close-knit group. As pressure to clear cases led to cooperation and shared celebrations at the conclusion to successful clear-ups, detectives were used to helping each other and sharing information on cases, strengthening mutual bonds.

One of the reasons they had to cooperate so closely was the lack of help from witnesses. US detectives use methods that would be against the law and codes of practice in British policing. At one point during the study, a 'guilty' suspect was refusing to admit his part in a homicide. As the following field notes illustrate, 'ethics' seem less important than being able to solve the case:

> We are sitting in a side room watching the suspect Billy being interviewed via the video link. Billy is having none of it. He wasn't there, it wasn't him – he knows nothing – 'straight up'. Big Bird (one of the sergeants) enters the room, announces himself to the video recorder and pulls out a long strip of paper with numbers written on it. The detective tells the suspect 'we have all your cell phone calls for the past 24 hours. We know you are involved, now tell us the truth'. Billy confesses he had the gun. Afterwards, at the celebratory drink, the detectives laughed at the idea that they could get these details so quickly, and it had in fact been a list of the detective's own phone calls.

These sort of tactics, seemingly reminiscent of detective behaviour on screen or in real life at least 20 years ago, before the introduction of the Police and Criminal

Evidence Act (PACE) or even during the 1970s under the 'Judges' Rules', would not generally be risked today in the UK. They certainly could not be used in court as part of the prosecution case, as video evidence would preclude their admission. This is one aspect, but what about the detectives' feelings about using these tactics when asked about telling lies to get confessions? Their general reaction was 'These aren't lies! We're just acting!', taking an 'all's fair in love and war' approach. In some senses it was a 'war', as they were attempting to win their cases and suspects had (according to the detectives) 'forfeited their rights' by being involved in certain activities. When I asked about the ethics of this sort of approach, one of the detectives responded, aghast: 'Ethics? This is a *murder* inquiry!'

Another set of field notes, given below, illustrate the sort of area in which the police station was located and the detectives' perceptions of the dangerous locale:

> As a group of white officers operating in a largely black, socially deprived African-American part of the city, the detectives are sensitive to issues of race and ethnicity. They told me never to use the petrol station opposite the squad office and on one occasion, when I was about to go to the post office in the next block, two officers insisted on driving me there and both brought their guns, joking that they were the 'letter posting armed guard'. As a white, female, 'innocent abroad' they viewed me as being at risk in an all-black neighbourhood, and in discussing the make-up of their squad in terms of who might be asked to join them when a colleague was about to leave, one officer remarked: 'The problem is, we've got too many white males already.'

> Everyone is now aware that I'm interested in ethics and decision making and the way resources are allocated. Tonight I accompanied officers who attended a fatal double shooting in a car; a few minutes later they arrested a man who was found nearby with a gun in his pocket trailing blood across the housing estate from gunshot wounds to his leg; we then heard over the radio a report of a middle-aged couple shot dead in their car a mile away by a black assailant in an argument over a parking space; next, we went to the back of a nearby apartment block where an African-American man involved in shooting was lying dead with a hole through his chest, his friend having been taken to hospital with serious gunshot wounds. The detectives referred to these latter two as 'innocent' victims as they seemed to have been having sex with a prostitute when robbers approached and shot them. The detective I was accompanying said to me: 'You see how it's all black on black? You think we're racist, but this is how it is.' (Field notes abridged from Westmarland 2013)

During the course of the fieldwork, numerous suspects were arrested and there were few references to the law, the suspects' rights or any sort of ethical issue. Although the suspects' Miranda rights would be read to them, they did not seem to be 'streetwise' in the sense that would be apparent to a researcher in the UK. In the US, none of the suspects was witnessed asking for a lawyer even though they were accused of murder. At a celebratory drink in a local bar, officers laughed when they explained that one suspect thought he was coming in (voluntarily), with his mother, and was subsequently arrested for murder. Later, as the officer recounted the story of the arrest to his colleagues, he said: 'His mom was like "No, no" and crying.'

## Is the police cultural world really as it seems to be?

From the evidence presented so far in this chapter and more extensively in the paper more fully describing the study (Westmarland 2013), it seems that there is fairly strong evidence to support Reiner's 'cop culture characteristics'. Almost all of them are illustrated above in just the examples from a few instances from the study. Ticking off a list of characteristics, however, does not necessarily support the existence of cultural beliefs. One of the benefits of ethnography is to 'see it how it is', but this does not mean that what is on the surface is the whole picture. It would be possible to write an ethnographic story confirming everything that Reiner and others have said about police culture (see Cockcroft 2013; Loftus 2009; Young 1991 for good examples). What lies beneath though and is it 'just talk' as Waddington suggests (1999b)?

Ethnographers often write about becoming part of the group they are studying as a means to achieving the feeling that they are part of the 'insider' culture. In studies of policing there are often 'markers' of confidence where the researcher feels they are now seeing everything 'warts and all'. Sometimes it is achieved by being similar to the group, as Simon Winlow argues (in Westmarland 2011), or having a 'way in', sometimes by being very different, perhaps from another country, and therefore not a threat. In essence, it is about trust, and tests of trust, but also about personality fit, empathy and resilience. Careful attention needs to be paid to information gleaned once these tests have been endured and reflected upon.

Given that this study was about murder investigations, en route at speed to a scene of a particularly grisly sounding death, initially detectives I did not know would seem a little anxious about me, which I came to realize was about how I would react to the sights we would encounter. As details of severed limbs or massive head injuries would be being related over the car radio on the way to the murder, I would reassure them that: 'I'm not squeamish.' They would sometimes ask questions such as: 'Have you see a bad murder before – actually seen the body?' This sort of realization of 'outsiders' being present has been reported by other ethnographers and observers of police behaviour. As P. A. J. Waddington (1999a) reports, a study by Smith and Gray (1983) noted racist and sexist talk in the police canteen, but officers did not enact this on the streets when dealing with suspects and victims. Waddington also notes that talk in the canteen can be an outlet for feelings rather than an example of beliefs (Waddington 1999b). As Michael Rowe argues (2005: 38), police ethnographies have their difficulties and disadvantages, but despite these potential problems, an observational approach was preferable to 'other qualitative methodologies such as interviews or documentary analysis', a point made by Maurice Punch (1979: 4) in his classic study of policing in Amsterdam. Robert Reiner has also argued that participant observations provide an insight that might be missed as accounts by the police would not really get to the detail of police work which is often 'low-visibility' (Reiner 2000: 219) or hidden from the view of the public, supervisors or even colleagues.

There are of course various versions of reality at any given scene or event. In terms of research methods, asking to see as many dead bodies as possible, preferably as a result of homicide, and before they are moved to the mortuary is probably fairly unusual. Negotiating access to this sort of scene is never going to be easy, however, and as Rowe has argued, although some incidents he recounted suggested that the police trusted him, 'ultimately there is no way of establishing the extent to which officers genuinely shared their perspectives on police work and the public at large' (Rowe 2005: 42). Ethnographers often suspect that what they are being shown or told may have been altered or suppressed for the benefit of the researcher, and this is always a possibility. In the case of this study, however, the detectives were working under very high-pressured circumstances, hopefully with little time to hide things, even if they so wished. They were often attending one or two murders a day, having three live inquiries each, and personal clear-up targets that seemed to matter to their professional pride.

Similarly, in some cases ethnographers perhaps have to be careful that they are not simply being given the extreme version of police culture – 'everyone thinks we're racist, let's act it out for them, they think we're cynics – let's show them cynical'. What was also very different from anything I had observed in the UK during my ethnographic research life was the way in which detectives dealt with witnesses, suspects and potential informants. Given that few people came forward to supply evidence, once a suspect was in the frame, some very 'dodgy' means, in UK terms, were used to gain a confession. Similarly, most witnesses were treated as unreliable at best and criminal at worst. Even bereaved families were often talked to with minimal sympathy in public and with disgust in private. So at first it seemed that Reiner's characteristics of cynicism, solidarity and insider/outsider characteristics could be supported without challenge, but there is a danger that the officers were playing a role they thought the research demanded. Police culture is well acknowledged by police officers, especially those who are working in the more cerebral roles such as homicide. Were they, in fact, 'just acting'?

## But is police culture what it seems to me? Reflecting on trust, ethics and ambiguities of ethnography

In his extensive discussion of police subcultures, P. A. J. Waddington has raised the issue of the 'oral tradition' of policing and the way in which what officers say is not always the same as what they do. He questions why police officers spend so much time telling and re-telling 'war stories' and says it is 'especially puzzling in so far as canteen talk is so much at variance with police experience' (Waddington 1999a: 110). His conclusion is that much of police talk is *expressive*. What police officers do in the canteen – and more rarely in private conversations with researchers – is to engage in *rhetoric*, that is, talk that *makes sense* of experience (Waddington 1999: 110, emphasis in original). What he is arguing is that rather than talk influencing behaviour, experience influences talk. Scratch beneath the surface and the cynics become carers, the target followers are clear-up merchants – Asking 'who done this to you?' is about getting the really bad guys locked up for killing the 'average' bad guys, and potentially stopping others in the retaliatory chain being the next homicide victims.

The detectives observed for this study made constant claims to bravado and their desire to catch the bad guys and achieve their clear-up rates. In private moments, however, usually in the dead of night waiting for something to happen, or whilst a suspect was allowed to have a few hours' sleep, confidences would be shared, including their feelings about the work and deeper seated attitudes and approaches. One of the detectives had the following statement on a poster-sized piece of paper attached to his desk directly above his computer:

### The Homicide Investigator

There is no greater responsibility than the investigation of the death of another human being. The duty of a homicide investigator is to seek justice for the dead. The investigator must help the surviving family members through what is often the most difficult ordeal of their lives – the violent death of a son or daughter, husband or wife, parent or sibling. The homicide investigator works hand-in-hand with the evidence technicians in an effort to glean the truth from inanimate objects found at the crime scene – guns and bullets, knives and ligatures, hairs and fibres, fingerprints and body fluids. The homicide investigator must convince witnesses who at best are sceptical, reluctant and fearful, or, at worst are combative, deceitful or fiercely loyal to the murderer. While in harm's way, the homicide investigator must, with the utmost skill and professionalism, apprehend the murderer who has no reservations of taking a person's life. In doing so, the investigator has to develop a rapport so as to overcome the defendant's reluctance to relinquish their constitutional rights and then obtain all admissions and/or denials. Throughout the entire investigation, the homicide investigator must balance objectivity with empathy, compassion with detachment, for the outcome is never as important as the integrity of the process. Most importantly, no matter how convinced of the defendant's guilt, the investigator cannot twist the facts or improve upon the evidence, cannot flout the rules of the court or appeal to anyone's prejudice and cannot hide the missteps of the victim. The homicide investigator is obligated to assist the prosecutor in the preparation of the case during the entire judicial process. In trial, the mission of the homicide investigator is to present truthful and persuasive testimony, in the face of rigorous cross-examination and, in some cases, false or misleading attacks by a defense attorney whose mission is to secure the freedom of the murderer regardless of the truth. And then, as a fruit of your labor, maybe twelve citizens can be convinced to overcome the presumption of innocence and hold the defendant accountable for his/her decision to take the life of another human being. Not until then, can a homicide investigator say that justice, for the dead, has been achieved.

When discussions about the morals and ethics of police work were raised with the detectives, they would say they were only acting like this because of the constraints they face. In a version of 'noble cause corruption' where the playing field is supposedly skewed towards the criminal, the police invoke a number of explanations for the problems they have maintaining what would be viewed from the outside as high moral standards. Another officer offered a poem he had attached to his desk called 'Cop on the Take' by Linney. The theme is the sort of emotional stress officers encounter as part of their daily work, such as taking it 'in his stride when people call him "pig"'.

The poem goes on the explore the other things police officers are said to take, such as;

> He takes . . . time to stop and talk to children.
> He takes . . . your verbal abuse while giving you
> a ticket you really deserved.
> He takes . . . on creeps you would be afraid
> to even look at.
> He takes . . . time away from his family to keep you safe.
> He takes . . . your injured child to the hospital.

In exploring these emotional aspects of police work, the poem goes on to explain the difficulties officers face and how they have to be strong, but this is not without cost to their mental health;

> He takes . . . the job no one else wants–
> telling you a loved one has died.
> He takes . . . criminals to jail.
> He takes . . . in sights that would make you cry.
> Sometimes he cries too, but he takes it anyway
> because someone has to.
> He takes . . . memories to bed each night
> that you couldn't bear for even one day.

Finally, contrasting the ultimate price, his life, with the cost of a cup of coffee, the poem ends;

> Sometimes . . . he takes a bullet.
> And yes, occasionally . . .
> he may take a free cup of coffee.

As 'alternative' moral codes, these two examples provide an insight into deeply held moral beliefs underlying police culture. These are moral messages and standards they feel need to be maintained in the face of the corruption of the people and the world order with which they have to work, such as witnesses, family members and offenders. They illustrate their internal cultural life of 'us against them'. It was within this framework that the project was aimed at understanding their worldview. It could be argued that these statements of ethics, pinned to office desks in their own personal workspace, represent the 'unspoken' ethics or feelings of detectives, unwilling or unable to express such opinions in a macho, competitive, traditionally male value-dominated space. In this version of police culture, 'real cops':

- do not show emotion;
- do not show any sympathy towards 'bad people';
- do not get involved in poor people's lives;
- just care about hitting clear-up targets.

In some ways revealing these confidences seemed more disloyal than the 'outward' cynicism they had displayed. To reveal they really cared about solving the murder for the 'family of the victim' as in the first statement and that they 'sometimes take a bullet' in the second one seemed to reveal a softer, more vulnerable version of police culture. In the second statement there is a line that says 'sometimes he cries too and takes . . . memories to bed each night that you couldn't bear for even one day'. These could be translated as 'sense of mission' from Reiner's list and a type of 'insider/outsider characteristic, but there is something a bit deeper and more subtle here, a different 'take' on police culture perhaps.

## Conclusions

As ethnographies of detectives are fairly rare (exceptions include Hobbs 1989; James 2014; Young 1991) and those focussing on homicide are even more unusual (Innes 2003; Leo 2008), there is little to concur or with which to contradict the finding of this study. The present study could not substantiate or reject Innes' view of the moral careers thesis. Aside from the practical problems of a lack of a comparative spread of victims to pursue the theory, it was clear that the detectives were highly sensitized to issues of race and ethnicity, taking the opportunity to make remarks about it on numerous occasions. It was also difficult to differentiate between the types of victims they saw, as they were largely desensitized to the outcomes of most of the events we witnessed, from a personal, feeling-inducing standpoint. Rather, they were concerned with evidence gathering, deduction and working out who was connected to whom, and whether feuds had been taking pace between certain groups of combatants lately.

From the very first night of the fieldwork, it became apparent that the importance of 'snitches' or informers could not be understated due to the difficulties that the homicide detectives have in deciding what is 'true' intelligence or information. This conclusion had been reached after access negotiations had involved some complicated assurances of confidentiality and numerous informal interviews that ethnographers are often subjected to in the course of gaining trust and cooperation. Direct questions about what the research was about, and comments about their moral and ethics and defence of their practices was common. Their main topic of conversation during these exchanges was about the difficulty of persuading unwilling (or fearful) witnesses to speak to them, despite a complicated and expensive raft of measures to encourage the passing of information to the police.

The lack of evidence the detectives needed to clear up the crimes was seen to be due to the absence of witnesses and the 'snitches get stitches' attitude of potential witnesses, their associates, the victims (if still living) and the victims' families, friends and partners if they were dead. Given this problem and a remark from one of the detectives during the fieldwork enquiring whether it is true that 'detectives in England use a computer to solve homicides?', the study incorporated morals and ethics of investigations with the practicalities of solving homicides without the 'appliance of science' using 'old-fashioned' gut instinct detective methods. This meant that less supervision of their actions was in evidence and little was recorded of their thought processes or motives. More similar to 'Columbo' than 'Morse', these detectives were instinct-driven, working with 'hunches' and dogged, time-consuming follow-ups.

To what extent then can ethnographies turn up some 'truths' about police cultural attitudes? A straightforward study of police culture takes a list of characteristics and looks for confirming events and statements. A more insightful study takes a 'what they say – what they do' approach to the data, looking for evidence that contradicts what other studies might have argued. In this chapter there is considerable evidence that police officers are cynical, want to meet their targets and describe most of the local population as 'knuckleheads'. Scratch the surface, however, and a deeper set of values are evident, as an alternative moral code emerges. This code is based on similar values to those espoused by 'cop culture' and has elements of the same characteristics, but where cynics say 'clear-ups are important for my career', the alternative code says it's for the family. Where macho police culture makes a display of laughing at the unfortunate victims of homicide and 'getting a bone', the underlying emotion is solving murders and locking up perpetrators to prevent others becoming victims and to help the families of the bereaved get over the death. Where there is concordance, however, is in the belief in a 'good and evil' dichotomy which is well documented in police culture literature. Whilst there was a clear feeling of wanting to solve crimes and help families, there were some that were beyond redemption, in the detectives' eyes, such as the family who would not help solve the murder of their brother, even though they knew who did it, and the people who rang up to ask about possessions and compensation the day after their son was killed, and the 'friends' who took the social security card from their dead friend's jacket. It seems that some moral codes, or the lack of them, even US homicide detectives cannot find acceptable.

## Acknowledgements

The author gratefully acknowledges the financial support of the Open University's Research and Development Fund and the support and help of the DC Homicide Unit Detectives and the hospitality of the University of Maryland's Criminology and Criminal Justice Department. Some of this data was originally published in *Policing and Society: An International Journal of Research and Policy.*

## References

Brown, Jennifer M. (1996) 'Police Research: Some Critical Issues', in Frank Leishman, Barry Loveday and Stephen P. Savage (eds), *Core Issues in Policing.* London: Longman, pp. 177–90.

Cockcroft, Tom (2013) *Police Culture: Themes and Concepts.* London: Routledge.

Crawford, Adam (2008) 'Plural Policing in the UK: Policing Beyond the Police', in Tim Newburn (ed.), *Handbook of Policing*, 2nd edn. Cullompton: Willan Publishing, pp. 147–81.

Hobbs, Dick (1989) *Doing the Business: Entrepreneurship, the Working Class and Detectives in the East End of London.* Oxford: Oxford University Press.

Holdaway, Simon (1996) *The Racialisation of British Policing.* London: Macmillan.

Huey, Laura and Ryan Broll (2015) '"I Don't Find it Sexy at All": Criminal Investigators' Views of Media Glamorization of Police "Dirty Work"'. *Policing and Society: An International Journal of Research and Policy*, 25(2): 236–47.

Innes, Martin (2003) *Investigating Murder: Detective Work and the Police Response to Criminal Homicide.* Oxford: Oxford University Press.

James, Adrian (2014) *Examining Intelligence-Led Policing: Developments in Research, Policy and Practice.* London: Palgrave Macmillan.

Klockars, Carl B. (1983) 'The Dirty Harry Problem', in Carl B. Klockars (ed.), *Thinking about Police.* New York: McGraw-Hill, pp. 329–45.

Klockars, Carl B., Sanja I. Kutnjak and Maria R. Haberfeld (eds) (2004) *The Contours of Police Integrity.* London: Sage Publications.

Linney, Wayne, A. (n.d.) 'A Cop on the Take', available at: www.policepoems.com/CopOnTake.htm.

Leo, Richard A. (2008) *Police Interrogation and American Justice.* Cambridge, MA: Harvard University Press.

Loftus, Bethan (2009) *Police Culture in a Changing World.* Oxford: Oxford University Press.

Punch, Maurice (1979) *Policing the Inner City.* London: Macmillan.

Reiner, Robert (2000) *The Politics of the Police*, 3rd edn. Oxford: Oxford University Press.

Rowe, Michael (2005) 'Tripping over Molehills: Ethics and the Ethnography of Police Work'. *International Journal of Social Research Methodology*, 10(1): 37–48.

Skolnick, Jerome H. (1966) *Justice without Trial: Law Enforcement in Democratic Society.* New York: Wiley.

——. (2005) 'A Sketch of the Policeman's "Working Personality"', in Tim Newburn (ed.), *Policing: Key Readings.* Cullompton: Willan Publishing, pp. 264–79.

Smith, David J. and Jeremy Gray (1983) *Police and People in London, Volume 4: The Police in Action.* London: Policy Studies Institute.

Uildriks, Niels A. and Hans van Mastrigt (1991) *Policing Police Violence.* Boston: Kluwer Law.

Waddington, P. A. J. (1999a) *Policing Citizens: Authority and Rights.* London: UCL Press.

——. (1999b) 'Police (Canteen) Sub-culture: An Appreciation'. *British Journal of Criminology*, 39(2): 286–309.

Westmarland, Louise (2001) *Gender and Policing: Sex, Power and Police Culture.* Cullompton: Willan Publishing.

——. (2008) 'Police Cultures', in Tim Newburn (ed.), *Handbook of Policing*, 2nd edn. Cullompton: Willan Publishing, pp. 253–80.

——. (2011) *Researching Crime and Justice: Tales from the Field*. London: Routledge.

——. (2013) '"Snitches Get Stitches": US Homicide Detectives' Ethics and Morals in Action'. *Policing and Society: An International Journal of Research and Policy*, 23(3): 311–27.

Young, Malcolm (1991) *An Inside Job: Policing and Police Culture in Britain*. Oxford: Oxford University Press.

# 4 Forensic criminology as a research problem

## Using traditional processes in a forensic context

*Wayne Petherick and Claire Ferguson*

## Introduction

We begin the chapter with this question: how does the work of practising criminologists relate to that of forensic criminologists? To answer this, we must understand first what forensic criminology is and how it – as a practical sub-branch of criminology – diverges from the more theoretical community. To understand why those studying crime and criminals need to be aware of what their forensic counterparts are doing, we also need to highlight the areas where forensic criminology is applied. This will introduce our argument for how forensic criminology uses well-known criminological research concepts and methods in a forensic capacity in order to educate and answer questions for stakeholders working in the criminal justice system. We will explain, using examples, the methods used by forensic criminologists to apply theoretical knowledge to the study of individuals, including differentiating between inductive and deductive logic. We will describe how forensic criminologists use structured professional judgement as a research method to make conclusions, which are of practical use to investigators, advocates and the court. Finally, we will compare and contrast how research in forensic criminology relates to more traditional endeavours, highlighting the different role that theory plays in the development of research questions across the two branches of the discipline.

## What is 'forensic criminology'?

While gathered under one umbrella term, there are actually a number of different approaches, both theoretical and practical, that encompass criminology. In its most broad definition, criminology is the study of crime and criminals, but like the complexity of crime itself, this base definition does little to help us understand its complex and multi-varied nature. As stated by Stephen E. Brown, Finn-Aage Esbensen and Gilbert Geis (2010: 8), 'criminology is not a field readily reducible to a concise definition'. Larry J. Siegel (2010: 4) suggests that 'criminology . . . uses the scientific method to study the nature, extent, cause and control of criminal behaviour'. Siegel further notes that criminologists come from a diverse array of backgrounds, including sociology, psychology, criminal justice and others. Criminologists can also come from legal backgrounds.

Because of this, the focus of analysis in criminology work can differ greatly. For example, those with a legal background may be interested in formulating legal policy and procedure to better address criminal behaviour; sociologists may be interested in broad societal contributions to crime; those who have training in psychology may concern themselves with the contribution of emotions and cognitions to crime and criminal behaviour. This is to say nothing of the difference between criminology and criminal justice. While the two terms are often used interchangeably, they represent different approaches to understanding the crime problem: the former directs attention to crime and criminal behaviour, while the latter focuses on the role, structure and function of the police, courts and prisons (for an excellent investigation into the 'big bang' that created both disciplines, the reader should consult the history of our discipline, *Academic Politics and the History of Criminal Justice,* by Frank Morn, published in 1995).

Because of this diversity, there will be vast differences in the methods used to problem solve in each sub-branch of criminology. The legally trained will perhaps be less versed in the nuances of science or the scientific method, while those with a social science background may be obsessive in the application of the principle of falsification, the cornerstone of the scientific method. For others still, there may be more of a focus on the abstract: what may be, might contribute to or possibly be the central cause of crime by examining large groups (nomothetic study) rather than individual cases (idiographic study).

These broad definitions and academic backgrounds create multiple intersections between practitioners, crime, criminals, victims and analysis. Some are administrative in their approach, while others focus more on behavioural issues involved in crime and justice. Some examine large groups, while others are more interested in the intricacies of specific cases. These latter individuals adopt the tenets of social science in order to conduct detailed investigations to answer specific questions about a case to a legal standard. These practitioners are known as 'forensic criminologists'.

The gap between traditional criminology and forensic criminology amounts to the difference between theory and practice, or abstract and concrete. Unlike more traditional criminology, forensic criminology seeks to apply criminological research and thought in a tangible way to assist criminal justice practitioners and front-line workers. The term *forensic criminology* is relatively new; however, the concept has a long history involving many different types of practitioners, including lawyers (such as Hans Gross), medical professionals (such as Arthur Conan Doyle) and law enforcement officers (such as August Vollmer). Indeed, history provides many examples of those concerned with using scientific methods, including empirical research, to answer investigative and legal questions. The work of these individuals, whether called criminalistics, crime science, applied criminology or a variety of other terms, has since been rebranded into what is now commonly referred to as 'forensic criminology'.

Despite the recency of its development and more common usage, there is already some debate as to the best definition for the term *forensic criminology.* In the first major text in the field, Wayne A. Petherick, Brent E. Turvey and

Claire E. Ferguson (2010: 3) defined it as 'the scientific study of crime and criminals for the purpose of addressing investigative and legal questions'. In 2015, Andy Williams criticized this definition for being, amongst other things, too vague and inclusive. Williams prefers the definition of 'the applied use of scientific and criminological research and analytical techniques for the purposes of addressing proactive and reactive investigative work, and for aiding in legal cases and issues' (2015: 9). Most notably, this definition stresses the important supporting role that criminological research and theory plays in the practical focus of forensic criminology. He notes (2015: 10) that this definition includes four components: (1) the use of scientific research and techniques, including natural and life science knowledge, analytical tools, physical evidence and interpretation of evidence; (2) the role of criminological research, including sociological, psychological, and crime and criminality research; (3) an application to proactive and reactive investigative work, including investigating and reconstructing crime, crime scene examination and intelligence gathering; and (4) providing assistance for legal issues, such as those surrounding evidential rules, expert evidence, probabilistic inferential reasoning, miscarriages of justice, reconstructing crime narratives and labelling criminals. He adds that, overall, forensic criminology is about involving criminologists in case work 'trying to provide justice based upon robust empirical evidence; and finally, it should be about using strong data and methodological triangulation in developing knowledge about crime and criminality' (Williams 2015: 11).

Although we agree with most of Williams' expansion of our previous definition, a major component of forensic criminological thought is absent from it. That is, forensic criminology is not just about applying traditional criminology concepts and research to specific issues facing investigators or courts. There are many criminologists doing this who would not be considered forensic, as Williams himself notes. The forensic element of our work comes in the application, and involves a shift from examining crime and criminality in abstract or nomothetic terms to examining specific people at specific points in time.

While traditional criminological endeavours are sometimes used for forensic purposes after they are complete, most forensic criminologists actively concern themselves with the forensic applicability of their work from start to finish. They are academics, consultants and researchers who have shifted their research or analytic processes to projects that have a forensic focus to address questions related to case analysis. They recognize that while the process of theory development, evidence gathering and falsification through testing may be similar across criminology communities, the materials used during any phase and the goal behind doing them in the first place are often dramatically different.

Forensic criminologists, then, have changed gears from traditional criminologists, thinking more about individual crimes and individual criminals than about crime and criminality more broadly. Their theory building is about testing whether broader theories hold in the case they are examining at the time they are examining it. In that regard, they are comfortable working with a different set of research materials and with coming to conclusions that potentially have much higher stakes for individuals than those to which we are historically accustomed. This also means that their work will involve more specific types of materials, that is, case material rather than abstract attempts that remain within the realm of theory. Because of this, they must also be adept at working with physical and testimonial evidence.

## Evolution, revolution or history repeating itself?

Criminology is like many other disciplines in that, over time, different theories and practices evolve, invade and dominate discourse. These may be accepted or rejected and, if able to resist falsification over time, may become principles or laws.

In the early days of criminology as an evolving discipline, Italian physician Cesara Lombroso observed physical features of criminals and proposed that they had biological differences, which likely impelled them to commit crimes. Specifically, Lombroso was to propose that criminals had smaller brains than their law-abiding counterparts and also that they possessed many of the same characteristics as our primate ancestors. Criminals were therefore atavists or 'throwbacks' to an earlier stage of evolution. Lombroso founded the biological positivist school of thought – that we are largely slaves to our biology where some of us are wired to commit crimes and some are not. This theory held centre stage for some time until Charles Goring's own examination of Lombroso's findings showed that while there was a difference, it was not statistically significant. This theory died off in Europe, but was still to be a part of criminological thinking in the US for some time following.

With the failing of positivism to explain all aspects of criminal behaviour, future focus turned to the psychological aspects of criminality or the influence of sociology on crime. Further development saw the waxing and waning of interest in these areas, with theorists eventually agreeing that it was a complex interplay of all factors – biology, psychology and sociology – that would make or break the criminal. Eventually interest in biological factors rose again with the advent of new technologies that allowed us to 'look inside' cellular functioning in order to better appreciate the role of biology in our behaviour.

New theorists such as Adrian Raine in works like *The Anatomy of Violence: The Biological Causes of Crime* (2014) have swung the pendulum back, with their research showing that while complex factors play a role, a good deal of our behaviour can be traced back to the way we are wired, with predispositions being tempered by our experience. While quiet for a time, biological theories could be said to have come full circle.

Like neuro-criminology, forensic criminology is not a new discipline at all and has in fact been with us since criminology began. In the late 1800s and early 1900s, Austrian jurist Hans Gross was promoting a scientific approach to the study of crime, later publishing *System der Kriminalistik and Criminal Psychology* before becoming a professor of law and criminology, albeit at different institutions (Turvey and Petherick 2010). At around the same time, Gross was promoting his approach in Austria, Arthur Conan Doyle was making a name for himself in the UK through his fictional detective Sherlock Holmes. While he is most famous for these short stories, few understand that he organized the first system of post-conviction review in Scotland, having been instrumental in having a number of convictions overturned. In essence, Doyle established the first innocence project. In 1910, in Lyon, France, Edmond Locard established the first formal crime laboratory in the world and later published a three-part monograph *The Analysis of Dust*, in which he spoke on the importance of the work of both Gross and Doyle.

The groundbreaking work of these two theorists and practitioners has been stated over and again in the literature and in classrooms around the world. They were the first forensic criminologists. They advocated for good science and practice, and both made their own efforts to improve the community. So why did forensic criminology as a distinct discipline seem to "die off" for a number of decades and when did it come alive again?

August Vollmer was the first Chief of Police in Berkeley, California. He promoted education as an important component of police work and was to suggest that those police seeking advancement would need to undertake tertiary education. He was particularly concerned about the bad reputation that the police had gotten over time, likely as a result of officers being selected based on size rather than reasoning ability. Formal programmes in criminology began with those established by Vollmer and his colleagues in an effort to educate police, with liberal arts being a specific focus.

Eventually, non-police became interested in this relatively new academic discipline and eventually took over many programmes. They criticized the police for not being especially good at thinking, and the police criticized them for not having experience on the streets. The rift this created, along with the in-fighting among academics and practitioners, was to create two separate disciplines – criminology and criminal justice. The criminologists, not typically having experience to rely on, became largely theoretical and ultimately formed the American Society of Criminology. The 'doers' (former and current police) formed the Academy of Criminal Justice Science (ACJS). In time, it appears that criminology lost some of its forensic focus and instead looked at crime as an abstract problem, examining groups, not individuals, and thinking in theoretical terms, not practical ones. In hindsight, this is another trend that led to the demise, or at least dormancy, of forensic criminology for a number of decades.

From early in 2000, one of the authors of this chapter (Petherick) had been working on cases and using criminology to address investigative or legal questions. He had also been teaching forensic criminology to students and approximately halfway through this decade had an idea for a text. One thing that was notable in this endeavour is that there was no competition, and in 2010 we published the book *Forensic Criminology*. While there were practitioners like Daniel Kennedy in the US already doing this work, some responsibility for bringing forensic criminology back from the grave can be attributed to this textbook. It brought together a community of working forensic criminologists doing this work in isolation, and fostered greater interest from students and universities to begin thinking forensically. Perhaps more importantly, it provided a foundation for others to continue and improve upon our work.

Like its parent discipline, forensic criminology has evolved and come full circle over time. Specifically, in line with the title of this book, it is a liquid criminology. It is liquid in that it has changed and developed over time, despite a period of dormancy. It is liquid in that, with the help of theorists and practitioners, it has been re-invented. It is liquid in that it is in a state of flux, with both theory and practice evolving over time as informed by best practice and understanding of the state of criminality.

## The forensic criminologist: generalist or specialist?

The above discussion and definition of forensic criminology raises a further interesting question: what is the breadth and depth of the forensic criminologist's knowledge? To answer this question, we will briefly discuss generalists and specialists in traditional criminology, and then forensic criminology.

A generalist is one who has a broad base of knowledge, usually acquired through a broadly based education. The generalist knows about a lot, but may not have in-depth knowledge of one specific area. Put another way, they do not have a speciality as such. However, the generalist knows a great deal about their area at a macroscopic level and can answer questions related to it using theory and research. For example, they may be able to answer questions related to motive as it applies to groups, but they may not have enough experience with criminal behaviours as seen in case work to identify specific motives in order to tell you what existed in a given case.

A specialist, on the other hand, knows a great deal about a specific or limited area tempered by their education in a general area. Specialists can be found in many different disciplines, such as forensic science, where one may know a great deal about DNA analysis, but little to nothing about fingerprinting. They can also be found in criminology, where they may, for example, possess a great deal of knowledge about security or crime prevention, but very little about what motivates specific criminal behaviours.

The specialist would usually be a generalist first before deciding on a particular area in which to focus their endeavours. That is, they will start out their education with a broad understanding in many areas of theory and research. After developing general skills, the practitioner undertakes further training and education in specific areas that relate to the speciality they wish to acquire. This continued education may be in the form of university qualifications, short courses or other training regimens. It usually requires more than simple self-directed learning. It could be said, then, that the forensic criminologist is a generalist-specialist. They will know much of crime and criminal behaviour, but they are also intimately aware of and versed in how any of this knowledge applies to investigations, the law or legal questions.

## Areas of application

Forensic criminology can be applied to virtually any problem of investigative or legal relevance. Some will be presented later in this section. Any discipline or community with a shared body of knowledge could have a forensic application given the right circumstances of a case or inquiry. Recently we have seen many examples of otherwise non-forensic disciplines being 'forensified' for various reasons, usually associated with a specific inquiry. Many professionals now have careers by adding the word forensic to their job title and tailoring their work to assist those in the justice system. Examples include forensic accounting, forensic linguistics and forensic veterinary science (Kershaw 2009). In reality, though, these individuals are usually accountants, linguists or veterinarians by trade who have simply changed the application of their work or have changed who their clients are (from the general public to criminal and civil justice stakeholders) to become forensically focused. There is no better example of this than Paul Kirk, considered one of the fathers of forensic science. Kirk, a chemist by trade, was asked by a student if there was any way to know whether a dog had died as a result of poisoning versus natural means. Kirk applied his knowledge of the science of chemistry and his training as a scientist to provide an answer. From here, he became one of the most recognizable figures in modern forensics.

The case is slightly different for forensic criminology. As mentioned above, there are many criminologists who have applied their work in a forensic context, but few of these individuals would label themselves as forensic criminologists. True forensic criminologists set about their work with a forensic mind-set, carrying out social science inquiries and research designed to inform on specific investigative or legal issues. They apply their knowledge with the understanding that they are required to draw conclusions of a sufficient quality and certainty to be used in court (that is, they are probative). The subject matter they concern themselves with is vast, but they all work with a set of specific questions to answer which are relevant to an inquiry. They expect that their findings will be used in court, as opposed (or in addition) to being published in a scholarly journal. Because of this expectation and the high stakes which are involved in forensic criminological endeavours, the threshold for drawing conclusions in this research area is necessarily higher regardless of the specific subject matter.

Specifically, forensic criminologists can be, and are, involved in many areas of investigation and adjudication of criminal and civil cases. This includes several sub-areas under the banner of criminal investigation, including, according to Brent E. Turvey and Wayne A. Petherick (2010: 15): crime analysis; crime scene analysis and case linkage; crime scene investigation; criminal profiling; fire scene investigation; interview/interrogation; investigative practice and procedure; medicolegal investigation; pre-sentencing/mitigation investigation; polygraphy; and threat and risk assessment. In addition, Andy Williams (2015: 16) argues that forensic criminologists usually have one of a few roles. These include: aiding investigations; assessment of evidence; aiding legal teams; understanding levels of seriousness and dangerousness; understanding patterns and dynamics of criminality and victimology; proactive crime prevention; and undertaking research. Though Williams notes that this is not an exhaustive list, we think it is important to add that, especially with the final roles listed, there also needs to be a specific forensic focus to include a criminologist's work under this banner. While most criminologists conduct research and understand patterns and dynamics of criminality and victimology, forensic criminologists use this research and understanding for tangible applications, which assist investigations or legal matters pertaining to case work. This distinction is an important one.

In sum, any criminologist who uses their research and understanding of criminality/victimology to conduct a particular type of examination for a specific investigative or legal purpose could consider themselves a forensic criminologist. Some are traditional criminologists by trade, while others have solely concerned themselves with forensic applications of their work, to the exclusion of most others from the outset. There are many different areas where criminological research and theory contributes to the investigation and adjudication of criminal and civil matters, meaning that forensic criminologists have a wide range of expertise and experience. As the discipline gains momentum, no doubt these areas of application will similarly expand.

## Methodology

There are many ways to go about acquiring knowledge, and the suitability of each will depend largely upon what you want to know. Should the inquiry be concerned only with a broad level of understanding of factors that contribute to murder, then the extant research on this topic would be all that needs to be examined. However, should the inquiry revolve around understanding what happened in a single case, crime research will be of less use in the first instance than an in-depth analysis of the features and characteristics of the offence you are trying to understand. It should be noted here that we use the term 'methodology', somewhat non-traditionally, to convey an approach and not as a broader research ethos.

Once a research question is established in a given inquiry (or inflicted upon the practitioner as the case may be), the forensic criminologist approaches their research in much the same fashion as a more traditional criminologist. They compile and examine the necessary background research, develop hypotheses, then search for an appropriate methodology to test them. However, in a strictly case-work scenario, the materials used are often different. Rather than compiling literature exclusively, the forensic criminologist is also compiling as much information on the case or involved parties as they can. This would include, among others, assessing the veracity of witness statements, conducting a victimological examination, determining what is indicated by the physical evidence, making determinations about the crime scene (why/if it was chosen for a particular reason, whether there are other crime scenes, etc.) and establishing the suspect pool. Gathering all the relevant case information is paramount to idiographic study used in the forensic context, as it becomes not only the material used for theory building and hypothesis generating, but also the data on which the assessment is based.

After the literature and/or case evidence is gathered and reviewed, the forensic criminologist uses these materials to develop hypotheses and determine a methodology, which will allow them to be tested. In so doing, the criminologist may apply different levels of analysis and logical styles. These include both nomothetic and idiographic level assessments, as well as inductive and deductive logic. Generally speaking, the criminologist works along a continuum from a nomothetic-inductive level to an idiographic-deductive level of analysis. These are described below.

## Nomothetic-inductive study

While we have included the discussion of nomothetic-inductive and idiographic-deductive as discrete sections, a caveat is warranted. While these approaches are given their own treatment, it should be noted that the distinction between nomothetic and idiographic and inductive and deductive in a practical sense is more a matter of theory and how it is applied in problem solving. In reality, much analysis that occurs within forensic criminology (and more specifically Applied Crime Analysis – see Petherick (2015) for more details) employs both nomothetic and idiographic analysis and inductive and deductive logic to varying degrees, depending on the nature of the case and the material representing it. For example, in developing theories about a case, one relies on nomothetic (group) and inductive (probabilistic) knowledge before determining the idiographic (single case) features by applying the scientific method to inductive theories (that, in a perfect world, result in deductions). Despite the overlap or inter-reliance of one theory on the others, each will be discussed separately for the sake of clarity.

The term 'nomothetic' refers to the study of groups and has perhaps been the most common approach to understanding in criminology. This is true not only in criminology today, but also historically and in many other disciplines. Samuel J. Beck (1953), for example, notes that this approach was the most common for studying human personality in the 1950s and is similarly used in most of the quantitative works published in the contemporary social sciences.

The distinction between 'nomothetic' and 'idiographic' was made first by German historian Wilhelm Windelband (Blackburn 2008), with nomothetic data being useful for formulating general laws. Because nomothetic data are an aggregate, they produce a picture of the average for any given group. This allows us to understand what may be common to a group, or what features, characteristics or traits may be found in or amongst that group. However, nomothetic data may lack complexity because individual information becomes part of a whole. Arthur Conan Doyle said this best through the fictional character Sherlock Holmes in *The Sign of Four* (1896: 60):

> 'Winwood Reade is good upon the subject', said Holmes. 'He remarks that, while the individual man is an insoluble puzzle, in the aggregate he becomes a mathematical certainty. You can, for example, never foretell what any one man will do, but you can say with precision what an average number will be up to. Individuals vary, but percentages remain constant. So says the statistician.'

This means that the nomothetically derived 'group norm' may apply in a given case or it may not, and that it may be rare to find any given individual with all of the features shared by the group. This may lead to errors in prediction based on group data, and is discussed extensively in the literature on risk assessment.

Inductive logic, or induction as it is more commonly known, refers to statistical or analytical reasoning that offers possibilities or probabilities through comparisons with known information (Petherick 2014). Induction is the most common type of reasoning used and can be drawn from a variety of sources. These include direct experience, vicarious experience, research and literature, and generalizations and stereotypes. A good inductive inference will include the nature of the opinion, the strength of certainty that the opinion will be true and exceptions that may undermine the veracity of the claim. When our focus is macroscopic and/or not forensic, inductive reasoning may suffice because the big picture will likely be enough. An example may assist the reader in understanding how nomothetic data and inductive logic can be used to assess a case.

Consider that the authors are asked to work on a homicide in their home state of Queensland, Australia. Should we wish to know what the possibilities are in the case or what may be common or uncommon features, we can consult crime data such as that compiled by a government clearing house or that kept by state or local police agencies. For this example, we will draw from the most recent Annual Statistical Review (2011–12) of the Queensland Police Service.

Considering this data, we discover that homicide in our specific region is a relatively infrequent crime, with 1.6 reported offences per 100,000 of the population. We also know that for the reporting period, males were more likely to be victimized than females. Moreover, victims were known in some capacity to their attacker in 60 per cent of the cases (34 per cent were unknown and the relationship was not stated in 6 per cent of the cases) and homicide was more likely to occur in the home, followed by the street or footpath.

With these probabilities in hand, without considering the unique features of our cases at all, we can know that we are dealing with a statistically infrequent crime, that males were more likely to be victims during this period, that it is more likely than not our victim knew their attacker and that the offence probably occurred in a dwelling. However, there is no guarantee that any of this will be true in *this* case, only that some things may be more or less likely.

While this provides a general guide as to what may have occurred or is likely, there are a number of problems with relying too greatly on nomothetic data and inductive reasoning. In brief, these include, but are not limited to: the ecological fallacy (the degree to which generalizations can be made about individuals from group data); poor or limited statistical probabilities; natural fluctuations in data that occur over time; limitations relating to direct or vicarious experience that result in inductive generalizations; and whether the inductive reasoning is instructive in acquiring knowledge about the case (we would likely know where the offence occurred once briefed on the case and we do not need the local crime data to tell us this).

## Idiographic-deductive study

The word 'idiographic' comes from the Greek and means separate or distinct. It refers to a specific case (Roeckelein 2006). Idiographic study is similar to that referred to in the research as 'N = 1', where the focus is on understanding a specific case rather than trying to understand a large number of cases in the abstract (note that 'abstract' here refers to the fact that the aggregate is an idea that may not exist in any one given physical form).

Inductive logic is more suited to the study of groups owing to the fact that both nomothetic study and inductive logic deal with possibilities or probabilities. When the focus of understanding is the microscopic and we need to know more about a specific case, idiographic study is called for. This by extension makes deductive logic inherently more useful in these cases, as it deals with absolutes. A deductive inference is what is arrived at when the scientific method is applied to a set of inductive possibilities. That is, while some would consider induction and deduction to be polar opposites of the logical spectra, induction is really the starting point for deductive reasoning. When all of the available theories are considered and a careful examination of the evidence has been undertaken, a systematic attempt is made to falsify each theory against the available evidence. When every theory has been falsified, with only one theory remaining that has consistently failed to be falsified, then it can be said we have a deductive conclusion. While this is the goal, it should be noted that not everything can be deductive.

## Structured professional judgement

Structured professional judgement (SPJ) is considered current best practice in many professions. This involves weighting personal opinion against published research and theory in order to avoid the over- or under-prediction of certain values (Petherick 2015). This practice is best known in the area of risk and threat assessment, but has become *de rigueur* in many others. SPJ evolved to account for errors in unstructured clinical judgements where examiners relied on their own education, training and experience rather than the myriad useful and relevant studies to make conclusions.

SPJ does not replace inductive or deductive logic, but it can be seen to augment purely inductive approaches. What SPJ does in practice is to force the examiner to justify their reasoning (i.e. anchor their judgement using the literature) about a specific case (idiographic analysis), which results in more informed judgement about which evidence to use in supporting their opinion. While this provides a solid foundation to case analysis, the authors do not believe that it is as robust as deductive reasoning, nor should it replace deductive logic. Ideally, the case should be analysed with the appropriate inductive theories developed; these theories are then tested against the physical evidence using the scientific method; deductive inferences are then provided. SPJ may be best employed by using research and evidence where deductive conclusions cannot be reached. This will also inform the reader/client of the quality and quantity of the conclusion.

Generally speaking, when compiling a report or assessing a case, forensic criminologists gather information and evidence in much the same vein as other social scientists. They use these materials to develop hypotheses and test them with both nomothetic-inductive and idiographic-deductive analyses. Their conclusions fall along a continuum of certainty based on what they have available to them and how their analysis proceeded. Forensic criminologists then use SPJ to anchor their reasoning and conclusions, and to avoid personal biases.

## Forensic criminology as a research problem

Most criminological research, whether forensic or not, progresses along a predictable series of steps from start to finish. In general, theory leads to research questions which are then refined based on the literature and the goals of the study/ researcher. Necessary background research is compiled, hypotheses are drawn and an appropriate methodology for testing them is established (see above). After this, data are compiled and analysed, and results or implications are determined based on the original theory. To understand forensic criminology as a research problem, it is simplest to compare and contrast how research progresses in a traditional way versus forensic criminological endeavours. Though there are many similarities which make forensic inquiries understandable as a research project, there are also some major differences which need to be highlighted. This is in addition to the more common use of idiographic deductive analysis when practicable. Therefore, before we conclude, it is necessary to explain some of the other differences that exist between traditional and forensic criminologists. Two of the most important differences happen early in the research process, involving how research questions are developed and the role of theory.

## Using theory to develop research questions or vice versa?

Most practising criminologists rely on criminology theory to guide their research. Like the other sciences, criminology theory is the basis for formulating research questions, and eventually understanding the implications of results. For traditional criminologists, theory can provide an explanation as to how or why crime occurs. It can be used to explain different patterns in different places and what the most beneficial reaction might be. Theory, then, often provides a source of many potential research ideas and questions when criminologists work using a top-down approach, that is, from theory to a research question. For forensic criminologists, theory and the questions that need to be answered are linked in a slightly different way.

From the outset of their involvement in a case, the forensic criminologist is usually confronted with a research question which they have been asked to address, such as 'whether the physical and behavioural evidence in this case indicates that this scene has been staged?' or 'can the risk this person poses be mitigated through crime prevention strategies, and if so, how?'. The forensic criminologist then works in a bottom-up fashion to use or develop a specific theory which will allow them to answer the question posed. In this way, forensic criminologists are often less organic in their development of research agendas. Some questions may be posed which are far ahead of the state of the literature/ science in the area, while others may be unanswerable in certain terms based on the information available at the time.

## Narrowing the research questions

Related to the use of theory to develop research questions (or vice versa), forensic criminology often varies slightly in its approach to narrowing down research questions as well. In order to determine which question to study, many traditional criminologists consider three major factors: feasibility; social importance; and scientific relevance (Bachman and Schutt 2012). These refer to: (1) the timeframes for the project and resources available; (2) focusing on areas which are important to the discipline or in the public interest; and (3) the extent to which the current question is grounded in the literature. For the forensic criminologist, feasibility is paramount. This is because very limited timeframes often exist due to rights to a speedy trial, investigations needing to be finalized to protect the public and mounting caseloads. A lack of resources is also often an issue, with the available evidence being finite, and access to important persons limited or absent.

The forensic criminologist, not surprisingly, is less concerned with the social importance of their research, or is perhaps concerned but in a different way. That is, they worry more about whether their work will be of assistance to the specific court or investigating agency involved, and less about whether the answer to their research question will make a difference to society or policy more broadly. Put another way, the forensic criminologist acknowledges that their work usually has implications for one party or one small segment of society (such as law enforcement agents working one case) rather than general effects on the public. This is different from general research endeavours, which are usually focused on informing disciplines or larger communities as to how something works or how common something is.

Finally, as discussed above, forensic criminological research projects often do not develop organically out of the literature as in a more traditional academic environment. They may not have any grounding in the literature and may not seem to be scientifically relevant to the discipline of criminology. Because they deal with discrete and sometime bizarre cases and behaviours, forensic criminologists often find themselves faced with a research question, which is not related to the state of the literature at all. In these instances, they test their theories on the extant evidence available, while extrapolating support from whatever related literature does exist. Research questions are not put on hold until the literature progresses, but are dealt with as comprehensively as possible with what is available. This contrasts to more traditional academic endeavours, which often progress more fluidly. It should now be clear that the forensic criminologists' projects often do not develop organically out of the literature as in a more traditional academic environment. They may not have any grounding in the literature and may not seem to be developing a project, and the threshold for making conclusions is slightly different in the forensic context.

## Conclusion

'Forensic criminology' is a specialist sub-discipline of the general area of criminology, which seeks to answer investigative and legal questions. The forensic criminologist is a specialist, working from a broad base of criminological knowledge and having undertaken further education and training in their chosen specialty. There are virtually no limits to the areas in which forensic criminological knowledge can be applied, requiring only that it is an area where this knowledge could be used to answer a question of law. This can include risk and threat assessment, victimology, deterability, foreseeability, crime analysis and others. While there are multiple pathways to acquiring knowledge, nomothetic and idiographic knowledge were discussed, along with induction and deduction. These styles of analysis and reasoning fall along a continuum, with the forensic criminologist working with the available evidence and literature to move from probability to evidentiary certainties wherever possible. The role and strength of SPJ was also discussed, as it specifically assists with limiting biases, an issue inherently relevant in a high-stakes forensic context. Overall, forensic criminology shares many parallels with the research process used in other social sciences, despite some differences in focus and fluidity, which have been highlighted here where necessary.

## References

Bachman, Ronet D. and Russell K. Schutt (2012) *Fundamentals of Research in Criminology and Criminal Justice*. Thousand Oaks, CA: Sage Publications.

Beck, Samuel J. (1953) 'The Science of Personality: Nomothetic or Idiographic?'. *Psychological Review*, 60: 353–9.

Blackburn, Simon (2008) *Oxford Dictionary of Philosophy*. Oxford: Oxford University Press.

Brown, Stephen E., Finn-Aage Esbensen and Gilbert Geis (2010) *Criminology: Explaining Crime and its Context*, 7th edn. New Providence: Matthew Bender and Company Inc.

Doyle, Sir Arthur Conan (1896) *The Sign of Four*. London: Spencer Blackett.

Kershaw, Alan (2009) 'Professional Standards, Public Protection and the Administration of Justice', in Jim Fraser and Robin Williams (eds), *Handbook of Forensic Science*. Cullompton: Willan Publishing, pp. 546–71.

Morn, Frank (1995) *Academic Politics and the History of Criminal Justice: Contributions in Criminology and Penology No. 46*. Westport: Greenwood Press.

Petherick, Wayne A. (2014) 'Induction and Deduction in Criminal Profiling', in Wayne A. Petherick (ed.), *Profiling and Serial Crime: Theoretical and Practical Issues*, 3rd edn. Boston, MA: Anderson Publishing.

——. (2015) *Applied Crime Analysis*. Boston, MA: Elsevier Science.

Petherick, Wayne, A., Brent E. Turvey and Claire E. Ferguson (2010) *Forensic Criminology*. Boston, MA: Elsevier.

Raine, Adrian (2014) *The Anatomy of Violence: The Biological Causes of Crime*. New York: Vintage Books.

Roeckelein, Jon E. (2006) *Elsevier's Dictionary of Psychological Theories*. San Diego: Elsevier.

Siegel, Larry J. (2010) *Criminology: The Core*, 4th edn. Belmont: Wadsworth Cengage.

Turvey, Brent E. and Wayne A. Petherick (2010) 'An Introduction to Forensic Criminology', in Wayne A. Petherick, Brent E. Turvey and Claire E. Ferguson, *Forensic Criminology*. Boston, MA: Elsevier, pp. 3–50.

Williams, Andy (2015) *Forensic Criminology*. Abingdon: Routledge.

# Part II
# Developing imaginative methods

# 5 Studying the marginalized with mixed methods

*Maggie O'Neill*

## Introduction

This chapter develops a critical recovery of the histories and lives of certain marginalized people using inter-textual research to represent the complexity of lived lives in conditions of liquid modern society. Inter-textual and imaginative methodologies are a response to the fragmentation, plurality and utter complexity of liquid times and seek to counter valorizing discourses and the reduction of the Other to a cipher of the oppressed/marginalized/exploited. Mixing participatory, performative, visual and arts-based research methods, defined as 'ethno-mimesis',[1] and undertaken in participation with the usual 'subjects' of research, can highlight the contradictions of oppression and the complexity of what Paul Piccone (1993) calls 'the permanent crisis of the totally administered society'. Such imaginative mixing of methods may also help criminologists to produce critical reflexive texts that address social harm, foster social justice and approach a radical democratic imaginary.

In what follows, this chapter argues that critical and cultural criminology can make sense of the deep social harms that accompany liquid times into the twenty-first century and articulate, create a space for and practise social justice. Critical and cultural criminology is in many ways indicative of what Bauman sees as characteristic of postmodern sociology: 'a clarifier of interpretive rules and facilitator of communication: this will amount to the replacement of the dream of the legislator with the practice of the interpreter' (1992: 204). This interpretive sociological work, for me, is rooted in Karl Marx's dictum that as philosophers we should not only aim to understand and explain the social world, but should also seek to change it, to transform it. In order to understand the world, we need to engage with lived experience as well as explore structures and practices which serve to enable and/or constrain our actions and meanings and practices.

As a researcher, interpretive ethnography grounded in the standpoints of the co-creators of the research (participatory research with the stereotypical subjects of research) rooted in critical theory, critical and cultural criminology is my chosen methodological approach. This often entails working with artists and communities to create visual representations of lived experience.

## Mixing methods: ethno-mimesis and constellational thinking

As Zygmunt Bauman (1992, 2004, 2007), Anthony Giddens (1984), Maureen Cain (1990), Pat Carlen (1988, 2010), Barbara Hudson (2003), Sandra Walklate (2012), Sandra Walklate and Gabe Mythen (2014), Majid Yar (2003) and other social and criminological theorists have documented, the processes of modernity and globalization are underpinned by deep sexual and social inequalities. Committed to fostering an interpretive role that includes creating spaces for the marginalized/subaltern to speak for themselves, the combination of art and ethnography, as ethno-mimesis, has for me enabled the production of a more sensuous understanding of social relations and lived experience via the inclusion of visual, poetic performance texts in the research process. Collaborating with artists since the mid-1990s to conduct research at the borders of art and ethnography,[2] I have argued that by representing ethnographic data in artistic form, we can access a richer understanding of the complexities of lived experience that may also throw light on broader structures and processes.

The outcomes of this work might reach a wider population beyond academic communities and facilitate understanding, interpretation and action as praxis (or purposeful knowledge). Moreover, this work supports processes of cultural citizenship and social justice (Hudson 2003, 2006, 2012), and connects with principles of a recognitive theory of community as part of a radical democratic process and imaginary (O'Neill 2001, 2008, 2010, 2011, 2014).

The participatory, biographical and visual work shared below provides examples of ethno-mimesis as performative praxis in that it seeks to challenge exclusionary discourses that include negative images and stereotypes and offer representational challenges that are transgressive and transformative, that challenge identity thinking and also represent the multiple subject positions and multi-tiered nature of belonging for women seeking asylum.

This kind of mixed methods research, underpinned by the principles of participatory research, can support and create spaces for the marginalized to speak for themselves as subjects and objects of their own narratives (without intermediaries speaking on their behalf) involving concepts of recognition/mutual recognition (Fraser and Honneth 2004), a relational understanding of social justice (Hudson 2003, 2006) fostering and imagining cultural citizenship (Pakulski 1997), publicness and egalization (Lindner 2006).

Norman K. Denzin argues that qualitative research is inherently multi-method in focus and outlines a case for the interpretive bricoloeur and (following C. Wright Mills) connecting individual experience 'private troubles' with societal relationships and structures:

> In *The Sociological Imagination*, C. Wright Mills challenged us to work from biography to history. He asked us to begin with lived experience but to anchor experience in its historical moment. He invited us to see ourselves as universal singulars, as persons who universalize in our particular lives this concrete historical moment. (Denzin 2012: 86)

Denzin states that it is regrettable that 'this biographically present person disappeared from too much of the MMR dis-course' (2012: 87), but that there is space for hope in that in the next decade there may be 'renewed efforts to embed all our interpretive methodologies in expanded social justice dis-courses. These discourses will interrogate the ways in which power, ethics, and social justice intersect'. This chapter – and indeed the main impulse of my own work over many years – aims to do just this, through a feminist, critical and cultural lens. Denzin describes his thesis, as deceptively simple: 'Those of us in the mixed methods qualitative inquiry community need a new story line, one that does not confuse pragmatism for triangulation, and triangulation for mixed methods research' (2012: 80). He offers instead a 'third way . . . based on interpretive methodologies that show citizens how to confront the obstacles to justice that shape their daily lives' (2012: 81). Moreover, he argues that meaning and understanding in the current age might be 'refracted off of the edges of crystals, not triangles' (2012: 85).

In a recently edited collection, *Advances in Biographical Methods: Creative Applications*, I argued, with co-editors Brian Roberts and Andrew Sparkes (O'Neill, Roberts and Sparkes 2014), for reconnecting the biographical with the sociological imagination – connecting individual experience 'private troubles' with societal relationships and structures, using creative biographical methods. There is a long history of using mixed methods in biographical research and I want to suggest that the 'relational' metaphor of the 'constellation' (rather than the crystal) might offer a more adequate account of a mixed methods 'triangulation' process that offers an interpretive methodology and epistemology towards a recognitive theory and practice of social justice. As Kip Jones (2006) argues, the art/performance process is creative and relational, but so too is the research process.

### Constellational analysis: not triangulation?

For Norman K. Denzin (2012: 82), 'triangulation' is a 'combination of multiple methodological practices, empirical materials, perspectives, and observers in a single study [that] is best understood as a strategy that adds rigor, breadth complexity, richness, and depth to any inquiry'. In a much earlier article, Denzin (1978) identifies four basic types of triangulation: (1) data triangulation (which involves time, space and people); (2) investigator triangulation (which involves multiple researchers in an investigation); (3) theory triangulation (which involves using more than one theoretical scheme in the interpretation of the phenomenon); and (4) methodological triangulation (which involves using more than one method to gather data, such as interviews, observations, questionnaires and documents). Given the backdrop of the paradigm wars of the 1980s described by Teddlie and Tashakkori (2003),[3] Denzin's impassioned article on 'Triangulation 2.0' in the *Journal of Mixed Methods Research* urges scholars to take the discourse 'surrounding this word and retrofit it to a postmodern world where meanings and politics are refracted off of the edges of crystals, not triangles' (Denzin 2012: 85). Moreover, he asks:

> Can we train methodological bricoleurs who seek new third ways through and around obstacles to social justice in a neoliberal world? Can we create a discourse that does not play word games with itself, in methods-centric ways? Can we chart a way out of the present? Can we have a moratorium on mixed methods talk about designs and typologies and *get back to the task at hand, which is changing the world?* (Denzin 2012: 85)

The challenge Denzin puts forward – that existing research methods deal poorly with the fleeting, transitory, multiple, sensory and mobile aspects of people's lives – is correct in part, but at the same time, a wealth of research in ethnography, anthropology, visual and cultural studies, and performance art has absolutely 'interpreted slices, glimpses and specimens of interaction that display how cultural practices . . . are experienced at a particular time and place by interacting individuals' (Denzin 1997: 247).

These creative, sensory, multi-modal, mobile methods and critical interpretive analyses highlighted by Denzin are a central part of my work in criminology, visual studies and biographical sociology. This inter-disciplinary research (which builds upon participatory, biographical, ethno-mimetic work)[4] has examined the creative application of walking (influenced by the artists who use walking as part of their practice) for some time now, as part of a biographical research method for undertaking critical criminological research, as a deeply engaged relational way of attuning to the life of another, that evokes knowing and understanding through 'empathic' and 'embodied learning' (Pink 2007: 245). Through walking with another, we can engage in an embodied/corporeal way and attune ourselves to the narratives and lived experiences of research participants. The methodological process uses 'creativity' and 'imagination' to gain 'understanding' in Pierre Bourdieu's sense, but also I suggest that using the concept of the 'constellation' best explains the process (for me) rather than the 'crystal' or 'triangle'.

### The importance of 'understanding'

Pierre Bourdieu (1999: 608) writes about the craft of social research, the importance of reflexivity, of a sociological 'feel' or 'eye' that allows the researcher to 'perceive and monitor on the spot as the interview is actually taking place, the effects of the social structure within which it is occurring', as well as setting up a relationship that involves active listening that combines a 'total availability' to the participant as well as 'submission to the singularity' of the (life) story being told.

Such reflexivity can become a 'double socioanalysis' (Bourdieu 1999: 608) where both the researcher and the participant are involved in creative thinking, reflecting and learning, and where, without cancelling the social distance between them, the participants can 'be themselves' and the researcher can 'mentally put themselves' in the place of the participant, not to project themselves onto the other. Rather, through 'forgetfulness of self' *understanding* involves the researcher giving 'oneself a generic and genetic comprehension' of who the participants are based upon a 'grasp' of their life circumstances as well as the social mechanisms:

that affect the entire category to which the individual belongs and grasp the conditions, inseparably psychological and social, associated with a given position and trajectory in social space. Against the old distinction made by Wilhelm Dilthey, we must posit that understanding and explaining are one. (Bourdieu 1999: 613)

In this way, thinking about Bourdieu's words, the biographical researcher, engaged in active listening, can connect biography to structure and history (see also Schütze 1992; Wengraf 2006; Roberts 2014) and, taken together, this reinforces the usefulness of the concept of the constellation in making meaning and understanding in the 'relational' research process. The messy business of doing and conducting sociological and criminological research, especially in liquid times, calls for constellational thinking rather than triangulation.

### Constellational thinking

Theodor W. Adorno borrowed the concept from Walter Benjamin, and the metaphor of the 'constellation' suggests a relational relationship to 'illuminate that which eludes individual concepts', indeed, 'relationships of overlapping and tensionality' (Coles 1997: 81) that can inspire creative, imaginative thinking that criss-crosses binary oppositions.[5] Renée J. Heberle (2006: 7) defines the 'constellation', quoting Adorno, as follows: 'a theoretical thought circles the concept it would like to unseal, hoping that it may fly open like the lock of a well-guarded safe-deposit box: in response, not to a single key or a single number, but to a combination of numbers'. Constellations, for Heberle, suggest a move away from what have been the defining terms of feminist method towards using experience 'understood through constellational thinking' and she proffers 'an alternative to thinking about experience as either an authoritative source of truth or as a construction we can only understand through the conditions of its emergence and articulation, but not as an object in itself' (Heberle 2006: 7).

For Adorno, there were no philosophical first principles, and instead of constituting an argument in the usual way, he assembled the whole through a series of parts using the form of the constellation referencing the influence of Walter Benjamin as well as Franz Kafka. Shierry W. Nicholsen, using the term 'exact phantasie' or 'exact imagination', defines constellational thinking as 'an exact imagination is confined by scholarship and science yet goes beyond the material by reconfiguring the material at hand' (Nicholsen 1997: 38). This relational/constellational thinking is, for me, evidenced in Janice Haaken's feminist research. Haaken (2014: 53) states that for herself, as a social action researcher, and the hip-hop artists/participants she worked with, the question of how to 'keep it real' carries both ethical and methodological challenges: 'Yet "the real" inevitably remains contingent on perspectives and points of view, sites of inquiry that require both methods of critical analysis and a theory of subjectivity.' For her:

> in *Moving to the Beat*,[6] our aim was to work against stereotypical and voyeuristic conventions and to create a complex biography of collective trauma,

reparation, and resistance. We sought to create a stage for hip-hop as a shared language for global dialogue on issues affecting marginalized youth.

Haaken writes that working to portray worlds ruptured by collective forms of trauma inevitably gives rise to forms of misrecognition. In creating a picture of the vast scope of humanitarian crises in places such as Sierra Leone, field researchers may enlist visual media in ways that inadvertently reproduce Westernized ways of seeing – ways that perpetuate the narcissism of the Imperial gaze:

> This gaze is often organized around the idea that however bad things are in privileged regions of the world, lives on the margins of the Empire offer no meaningful insights on modernity or alternative ways of thinking about global crises. At the same time, the use of visual media in participatory field projects carries the potential for disrupting Western modes of looking without really seeing, and for creating alternative visions of globalism – visions that attempt to realize its real democratic possibilities. (Haaken 2014: 53)

Haaken's work is an excellent example of relational, constellational thinking in feminist and psychoanalytic research. In 2010–11, we worked together on a participatory project with women who were seeking asylum in Teesside, UK. The project, as an example of the constellational process, mixing methods and disciplines, is described in the following section.

## The asylum–migration nexus: women's lives, well-being and community in criminological research

This section shares research undertaken with women situated in the asylum–migration nexus (refugees, asylum seekers and undocumented people) in Teesside through participatory and biographical research, including arts-based research using film, photography and walking as a method of conducting such phenomenological work. This is an example of constellational thinking in mixed methods research. Key themes addressed include the tension between human rights, human dignity and humiliation in the lived experiences of women, many of whom exist at the margins of the margins, and the possibilities for social justice and a radical democratic imaginary in our criminological work in this area.

### Context to the asylum–migration nexus

Refugees and asylum seekers have become the folk devils of the twenty-first century. The identification of a person as an asylum seeker has become an 'instrument for the refusal of recognition' (Butler 2004: 113). Media representation and the mediatization of the asylum issue provides another source of conflict; the scapegoating of asylum seekers and the tabloid headlines that help to create fear and anxiety about the unwelcome 'others' also serve to set agendas that fuel racist discourses and practices.

What is very clear is the conflict at the centre of Western nations' responses to the plights of asylum seekers and refugees. On the one hand, a commitment to human rights and the 1951 Refugee Convention exists and yet, on the other hand, powerful rhetoric aimed at protecting the borders of nation states is underpinned by the ideology of sovereignty. Yet, in an era of globalization, the sovereignty of states is waning given the rise of supra- national bodies like the United Nations, the International Monetary Fund and the World Bank alongside powerful multi-nationals. As a number of migration scholars (Marfleet 2006; Pickering 2005) have shown, sovereignty is 'vigorously asserted at the borders of nations' (Benhabib 2004: 6). What is very clear from the literature on forced migration is the humiliation of those who bear the label. Something of this humiliation is captured by Zygmunt Bauman in the concept of 'negative globalization'. The 'selective globalisation of trade and capital, surveillance and information, violence and weapons, crime and terrorism' means that 'security cannot be obtained, let alone assured' (Bauman 2007: 7) and neither can justice. 'The perverted openness of societies enforced by negative globalisation is itself the prime cause of injustice' (2007: 7).

As Bauman (2004, 2007) and other theorists have documented (Marfleet 2006; Smith 2006; O'Neill 2010), the processes of modernity and globalization are underpinned by deep social inequalities that lead people to leave home in search of a better life through choice and/or compulsion, or literally to flee for their lives. Forced migration is not 'the result of a string of unconnected emergencies, but an integral part of North–South relations' (Castles 2003: 9). Indeed, 'the numbers of homeless and stateless victims of globalisation grow too fast for the planning, location and construction of camps to keep up with them' (Bauman 2007: 37).

Hannah Arendt (1958) identified the twin phenomena of 'political evil' and 'statelessness' as the most daunting problems of the twentieth and twenty-first centuries. Statelessness for Arendt meant loss of citizenship and loss of rights – indeed, the loss of citizenship meant the loss of rights altogether. Asylum seekers are often represented as nameless and by others; they rarely represent themselves. This void creates space for the withdrawal of humanizing practices and the 'othering' of asylum seekers, refugees and migrants, and what emerges to fill this space is racism, mis-recognition and unbelonging – what Giorgio Agamben (1995) calls 'bare life'. Tyler (2006: 186) argues that 'the figure of the asylum-seeker increasingly secures the imaginary borders of Britain today'.

We know from the available research that forced migration takes place either within or between developing countries, that the cost of enforcing borders is very high in resource terms and that an enormous amount of money is spent securing the borders of Western nations (Castles 2003; Pickering 2005; Marfleet 2006; Sales 2007). Moreover, we know that migration will continue to be a reality of the twenty-first century (Bauman 2007; O'Neill 2010), as the current 'refugee crisis' in Europe makes clear.[7] The social and cultural context that asylum seekers experience is marked by a culture of disbelief, underpinned by law-and-order politics. This is combined with a focus upon strengthening and protecting borders which places responsibility on the asylum seeker for their situation. This impacts upon the experience of seeking safety for people fleeing persecution, human rights violations, violence and war. Their experiences are marked by humiliation, shame, racism and mis-recognition (O'Neill 2010).

## Justice at the borders of community

Barbara Hudson's work on social justice is important here. In *Beyond White Man's Justice* (2006), a justice that has the potential to escape being sexist and racist, she notes that 'we can see the length of time it has taken for racialised as well as sexualised harms to be taken seriously by the law' (2006: 30) and she proposes the three principles that justice should incorporate: discursiveness, relationalism and reflectiveness:

1   *Discursiveness*: Hudson asks that those most excluded are given privileged access to discourse; that the 'outsider' must be able to put their claims in their own terms rather than having to accommodate to the dominant modes of legal/ political discourse. Being able to tell her story in her own words is vital and the goal is to reach inter-subjective understanding. Discursiveness means 'more than allowing a space in proceedings to speak', but also 'opens to challenges to the identity of law and opens to identity claims that are not based on similarity' (Hudson 2006: 35).
2   *Relational*: here Hudson talks about the relational nature of identities as being situationally and relationally contingent (2006: 26). We are all embedded in networks of relationships that help to give meaning and structure to our lives and identities; some of these may be relationships marked by oppression and injustice. Rights are also relational for Hudson: 'Rights are not just posses- sions or rules that limit behaviour, they are also rules of conduct that protect freedom and dignity' (2006: 37).
3   *Reflective*: justice means that each case should be considered in terms of all its subjectivities, harms, wrongs and contexts, and then measured against con- cepts such as oppression, freedom, dignity and equality. Without reflective consideration of the unique circumstances of individual cases against these wider horizons, justice processes collapse into one-dimensionality. The lack of opportunity to decide what is relevant or irrelevant, admissible or inadmis- sible goes against the discursive principle – to be able to tell her story in her own words. It also means that rules and categories formulated by the pow- erful are impregnable against the claims of the powerless (Kerruish 1991, quoted in Hudson 2006: 32). The closure or censure of the law as derived from 'white male idealized characteristics and modes of life' (Hudson 2006: 38) is problematic, as this closure illustrates the abstract generality of law – that acts have to be fitted into categories and liberal justice expels difference with regard to (a) subjectivity and (b) in relation to individual and biographi- cal and situational circumstances (Hudson 2006: 38).

Hudson argues that these principles and concepts are fundamental to moving beyond white man's justice. Thinking in terms of oppression, inequality and domination can guide the practical implementation of justice policies and processes through championing discursiveness, relationalism and reflection towards citizenship and social justice for marginalized groups, such as women seeking asylum. These principles also connect with a holistic concept of social justice defined by myself, Philip A. Woods and Mark Webster (2005), who write about holistic justice as: *distributive justice* – the absence of economic marginalization and destitution; *associational justice* – networks of support to enable people to participate in decision making and governance; *cultural justice* – the right to presence and visibility, the right to dignity and maintenance of lifestyle and the right to dignifying representation. These are also the principles underpinning participatory research and are central to the ethnomimetic research outlined below.

## Women, well-being and social justice: mixing methods in criminological research

Research methodologies, including visual, biographical and participatory, can create spaces for the voices of the marginalized that can serve not only to raise awareness, challenge stereotypes and hegemonic practices, but can also produce critical texts and images that may mobilize and create real change. Hence connecting the discursive, relational and reflective principles of Barbara Hudson's (2006) work with the participatory nature of our research. This is important for social justice as constituted by: distributive justice – the absence of economic marginalization and destitution; associational justice – networks of support to enable people to participate in decision making and governance; and cultural justice as defined above. In 'Who Needs Justice? Who Needs Security?', Hudson asks how do we do justice to those who are outside or at the borders of community? She answers this as follows: for our capacity for empathy for embracing difference and for an ethics of hospitality.

It is more than five years since *Asylum, Migration and Community* was published, the outcome of a decade of Arts and Humanities Research Council-funded research on asylum, migration and belonging. Here I explored the impact of the asylum–migration–community nexus on women. In 2016, there is still a dearth of research on women seeking asylum, the asylum system is still gender-biased and women are still, overall, assumed to be dependants/followers of men. Research and reports by Refugee Action such as *Standing up for Women: Is it Safe Here?* and Refugee Council research such as *Making Women Visible* and *Dignity in Maternity* document women's poverty, exploitation and destitution, their poverty and vulnerability as well as detainment and the impact of dispersal documenting dire housing and maternity issues and inequalities, support for their children and racism. Women also seek asylum for the same reasons as men.

The research project discussed here was developed in collaboration with women situated in the asylum–migration nexus (refugees, asylum seekers and undocumented people) in Teesside through participatory and biographical research including arts-based research using film and photography, as well as walking as a method of conducting phenomenological work. This was 'follow on' research to the regional Race, Crime and Justice research undertaken by Gary Craig et al. (2012) in the North

East.[8] Women's issues and asylum-seeking women's issues in particular emerged as an important focus of further research and so we set about to explore the lives of asylum-seeking women in Teesside – with women. Together we set out to document and share the stories of women seeking asylum in visual form and also how their stories could be woven together to tell a collective tale of the search for sanctuary.

The partners or collaborators were: the regional refugee forum North East, a women's group called Purple Rose, Janice Haaken, a Fulbright scholar/film maker and psychologist/psychoanalyst, ten women who were seeking asylum or were undocumented, one of the women had refugee status, a volunteer from the regional refugee forum who was an artist, and myself. A core group met to discuss how the project might develop and to share ideas for the participatory process and using biographical and arts-based research, including mapping, photography and walking.

Rooted in a long genealogy, biographical approaches have developed from a focus upon a single story, a 'life story', to encompass autobiographical and multi-sensory methods. We lead 'storied lives' and, as part of human understanding, stories and storytelling help people make sense of their lives, cultures, communities and wider society too (O'Neill, Roberts and Sparkes 2014). Brian Roberts (2002) suggests that the growth of interest in biographical methods, also documented in Norman K. Denzin (2012), can be attributed to a variety of factors: disillusionment with static approaches to data collection; a growing interest in the life course; and an increased concern with 'lived experience' and how best to express it.

Walking as an arts-based method (rather than a core part of ethnographic and anthropological research) is participatory, sensory and phenomenological, a deeply relational and per formative method for doing research *with* (not on) marginalized groups, for understanding lived experience (Pink 2007; O'Neill and Hubbard 2010).

*Figure 5.1* Women, well-being and community – a collective walk

Walking and biographical methods together with visual methods helped to explore the experience of 'being-in-place' among this transnational group of women from Africa, Asia and the Middle East, eliciting dialogue, biographical remembering and relational, embodied engagement. In the participatory process, a collective story emerged, a collaborative knowledge production that included empathic witnessing.

We explored ways of seeing women's lived experiences, well-being and sense of community in the context of their lives in the North East by walking with them along a route they had agreed that took in the important places and spaces for them; they shared their sense of belonging or community in Middlesborough.

> Asylum Accommodation: when you are an asylum seeker, life is everywhere with the least facilities. We just want to be alive.

The aims of the research were to: (a) conduct a critical recovery of women's lives, journeys and histories; (b) using storytelling and visual/photographic and walking methods to help make visible women's lives, experiences, issues and what community means; (c) exhibit the work, producing an exhibition, a short film and a collaborative research report.[9] The research was made up of three phases. The first phase was a workshop where we agreed the qualitative methods and specifically the participatory approach, biographical interviews/conversations recorded whilst walking and in the workshop setting; as well as the use of photography and film. In this day-long workshop, women drew a map from a place they called home to a special place in Teesside. The maps were then shared and we discussed the places

*Figure 5.2* Women, well-being and community – empathic witnessing

*Figure 5.3* Women, well-being and community – friendship

and spaces women had placed on their maps. In the second phase, the group agreed that they would like to do a collective walk and they agreed the route together. We discussed the use of film and filming was agreed so long as no faces were shown. The flip video camera was held predominantly by Lucy, the volunteer. The women were given a disposable camera to take photographs along the way of their choosing and we stopped and listened and recorded conversation around these places (eventually we would choose a number of the images for the exhibition of the project that launched in a community venue in Stockton, and Durham and Teesside Universities). This second phase was made up of collective/shared walks, recording conversations at each of the places on the route, women taking photographs and talking about why the places in particular were important. The third phase involved further workshops where we talked about the photographs the women had taken. We also explored some of the video footage with Janice Haaken and talked about the themes emerging from the work to date. A fourth phase took place after Janice had returned to Portland University. Images were collectively chosen for exhibition; Margareta Kern, a Leverhulme-funded artist in residence with me at Durham, supported the research as part of her residency and made broadcast-quality recordings of one of the women's poetry. The woman was an asylum seeker (who now has refugee status) who was a former academic from Sri Lanka. Meanwhile, Janice worked on a short nine-minute film of the project from Portland, sending versions to and fro for us to discuss and give feedback on. Finally a celebration, an exhibition, an exhibition booklet and a film were created as well as two publications that documented the process, journey and methods, that were sensory and phenomenological, deeply relational and performative (Haaken and O'Neill 2014; O'Neill, Mansaray and Haaken 2016).

The research developed a critical recovery of the histories and lives of marginalized women using inter-textual, mixed methods to research and represent the complexity of lived lives in conditions of liquid modernity. A collective story emerged through a constellational process and journey about the women's connection with places and spaces in Teesside and a picture emerged of the safe zones and dangerous zones that the women navigate in their daily lives. The struggle for recognition emerged as a strong theme amidst migrant trajectories of suffering, resistance and resilience. Their stories tell a collective tale of the search for sanctuary, belonging and being in place. Using visual, participatory and arts-based research, a picture emerges of the liveable lives made out in the margins.

> There is a wall here so she cannot pass from here she has to pass from this fence this dangerous fence. This is a symbol of many people who cannot stay in their country and they have to go to another country and they are damaged they were damaged from moving. All of we [sic] understand what is damaged because we all experience. Some of the people they have too many.

> Every asylum seeker relates to the police station. Most of us here have never been to police station in our home country, so for me to go to police station I could not believe it on top of everything else you are going through you have to go to police station to sign. For me because of my journalistic background I was probing saying why, why the police station just to put my signature

*Figure 5.4* Barrier to moving forward

*Figure 5.5* Police HQ

down. I go there and they say are you living at the same address. And we sign for our support. It does not make sense I do not like to go there I really dislike it. But we comply it does not make any sense, I hate and dislike it but then I have no choice.

I hate this place it is the worst place in this town. It is the police station. Any asylum seeker will not like this any time you go every two weeks I don't sleep if I go to sign, this stress I have it is too much for me, it is 50/50 they may detain you.

I signed today and all night I did not sleep all night, I feel sick, I did not know what would happen to me.[10]

Very close to my house, I feel that I am living when I see the University. When I was 22 I studied for four years, then I became an assistant lecturer and then a lecturer and senior lecturer, I feel like my life is the University. This picture of the main gate the concept of the University is very important and no-one can kill that.

The film *Searching for Asylum* (available on YouTube) created by Janice Haaken from research video files, sounds files, photographs and narrative opens with a narrator's voice:

Offering protection to imperiled strangers is an ancient cultural practice, deeply bound to traditions of hospitality. But during periods of social and

*Figure 5.6* Teesside University

economic crisis, this spirit of openness may readily yield to moral panic, and rampant fear of foreigners.

Imaginary threats can mask real ones. As capital flows with accelerating speed across national boundaries, migrants are confronted with mounting xenophobia and militarized borders with heavily armed border guards.

Although asylum seekers represent a small percentage of migrants seeking residence in Britain each year, the asylum seeker occupies centre stage in media portraits of the causes of social crises, from unemployment, cutbacks in housing, to crime. The asylum seeker's presence in the UK also reaffirms the public fantasy of the state as compassionate and generous, yet firm in separating the genuine from the so-called bogus cases. But is the state so generous? And what social borders do these newcomers navigate when they do enter the United Kingdom?

*This story* maps the world of asylum seekers in a town in North East England – one of many sites where the British government began dispersing asylum seekers in the early years of 2000. Ten women asylum seekers and two women academics set out to create a picture of safe zones and danger zones that asylum seekers navigate as they find their way in the communities where they have been placed, often waiting years for a final decision on their cases.

What emerges through the women's narratives both reinforces and challenges some of the dominant tropes we find in the mass-media representation of asylum seekers and what is clear is that the stories that emerged in the course of the research and captured in the film offer oppositional discourses and representations to the rather simplistic message of 'deviant' outsiders. As an example of mixed methods research in criminology, the concept of the constellational is appropriate and useful. The commitment to social justice and praxis is, we hope, made clear. The project created a space for women to speak and be listened to, one which counters valorizing discourses and, as stated in the introduction, the reduction of the Other to a cipher of the oppressed/marginalized/exploited. And, in doing so, it addresses social harm, fosters social justice and approaches a radical democratic imaginary.

## Conclusion

The importance and methodological impact of the mixed methods research documented here is in connecting the small scale, the micrology of a life to history, culture and social structure. In mixing participatory, performative, visual and arts-based research methods, defined as 'ethno-mimesis' (O'Neill 2001), a collective story of the search for freedom and sanctuary emerged through the research with women. The sociological imagination, thinking otherwise, is absolutely the driver for this work, as is the important relationship with social justice, the potentially transformative, change-causing nature of our research as criminologists for understanding, for practice and for policy.

This example of generating understanding and meaning through constellational thinking rather than triangulation supports Norman K. Denzin's (2012: 85) statement that the 'combination of multiple methodological practices, empirical materials, perspectives, and observers in a single study is best understood as a strategy that adds rigor, breadth complexity, richness, and depth to any inquiry'. A clinical psychologist, a criminologist, ten women seeking asylum/undocumented and an artist volunteer member of the regional refugee forum worked together through participatory, constellational processes to conduct participatory, visual and biographical research that led to images, an exhibition, an exhibition booklet, a film and academic papers/outputs. The relational metaphor of the constellation is central to the methodological impact of using creative, multi-modal and performative, biographical (mixed) research methods in this project. It is also central to understanding and practising social justice too, as evidenced in my use of Barbara Hudson's important work (Hudson 2006, 2012).

Using the concept of the 'constellation' in criminological mixed methods research is, for me, the methodological promise and challenge of doing critical and cultural criminology. It enables and invites a methodological approach that asks how our criminological research might challenge sexual and social inequalities, and how might it support processes and practices and theories of social justice, in this case doing research with the usual 'subjects' of research to recover, document, analyse and share in inter-textual and multi-sensory ways the utter complexity of women's lives as asylum seekers, refugees or undocumented people in current times, in conditions of liquid modernity.

## Notes

1 Ethno-mimesis combines ethnographic research and the re-presentation of ethnographic data in visual/artistic form. I have defined it as a process and a practice for doing research – often this has been conducted with artist and community groups/community artists as part of the participatory collaborative process of doing participatory action research.
2 The most recent example being artist Jimini Higgnett's text *Mulier Sacer* (2013) in his 'The How to Go on Series' that brings together stories and photographs of women who have escaped forced prostitution in the Netherlands with a section of *Prostitution and Feminism*, alongside a blog by an ex-sex worker and an interview with a sociologist working in support of access to sex for disabled clients.
3 Teddlie and Tashakkori (2003), summarized by Denzin (2012: 84): (a) the post-positivist-constructivist war against positivism (1970–90); (b) the conflict between competing post-positivist, constructivist and critical theory paradigms (1990–2005); and (c) the current conflict between evidence-based methodologists and the mixed methods, interpretive and critical theory schools (2005–present).
4 Usually working in collaboration with artists as well as marginalized groups/individuals-sex workers, homeless, asylum seekers, refugees and undocumented people.
5 In my work on Theodor W. Adorno (1999, 2001), I suggest that it is only by trying to say the 'unsayable', the 'outside of language', 'the mimetic', the sensual, the non-conceptual that we can we approach a 'politics' that undercuts identity thinking, refuses to engage in identity thinking, but rather criss-crosses binary thinking and remains unappropriated. Works of art, as ciphers of the social world, help us to access the sedimented stuff of society, what may be unsayable, and help to reveal the unintentional truths of society.
6 See http://moving2thebeat.com.
7 See https://policypress.wordpress.com/2015/09/22/how-have-attitudes-changed-in-the-last-five-years-towards-asylum-and-migration.
8 See https://www.dur.ac.uk/research/directory/view/?mode=project&id=503.
9 The exhibition booklet can be found at: https://www.dur.ac.uk/resources/sass/research/RaceCrimeandJusticeintheNorthEast-WomensLivesWell-beingExhibitionBooklet.pdf.
10 One of the women was detained and sent to a detention centre following 'signing' at the police station during the project; she was eventually deported despite a campaign and petitions delivered to the centre.

## References

Adorno, Theodor W. (1978) *Minima Moralia: Reflections from a Damaged Life*. London: Verso.
——. (2005) *Critical Models: Interventions and Catchwords*. New York: Columbia University Press.
Agamben, G. (1995) *Homo Sacer: Sovereign Power and Bare Life*. Stanford: Stanford University Press.
Arendt, Hannah (1958) *The Human Condition*. Chicago: University of Chicago Press.
Bauman, Zygmunt (1992) *Intimations of Postmodernity*. London: Routledge.
——. (2004) *Wasted Lives: Modernity and its Outcasts*. Cambridge: Polity Press.
——. (2007) *Liquid Times: Living in an Age of Uncertainty*. Cambridge: Polity Press.
Becker-Schmidt, Regina (1999) 'Critical Theory as a Critique of Society: Theodor W. Adorno's Significance for a Feminist Sociology', in Maggie O'Neill (ed.), *Adorno, Culture and Feminism*. London: Sage Publications, pp. 104–18.

Benhabib, Seyla (2004) *The Rights of Others: Aliens, Residents and Citizens*. Cambridge: Cambridge University Press.

Bourdieu, Pierre (1999) *The Weight of the World: Social Suffering in Contemporary Society*. Cambridge: Polity Press.

Butler, Judith (2004) *Undoing Gender*. London: Routledge.

Cain, Maureen (1990) 'Towards Transgression: New Directions in Feminist Criminology'. *International Journal of Sociology of Law*, 18(1): 1–18.

Carlen, Pat (1988) *Women, Crime and Poverty*. Milton Keynes: Open University Press.

——. (2010) *A Criminological Imagination: Essays on Justice, Punishment, Discourse*. Farnham: Ashgate.

Castles, Stephen (2003) 'Towards a Sociology of Forced Migration and Social Transformation'. *Sociology*, 37(1): 13–34.

Coles, Romand (1997) *Rethinking Generosity: Critical Theory and the Politics of Caritas*. New York: Cornell University Press.

Craig, Gary, Maggie O'Neill, Bankole Cole, Georgios A. Antonopoulos, Carol Devanney and Sue Adamson (2012) *'Race', Crime and Justice in the North East Region*. Durham: Durham University.

Denzin, Norman K. (1997) *Interpretive Ethnography*. London: Sage Publications.

——. (2012) 'Triangulation 2.0'. *Journal of Mixed Methods Research*, 6(2): 80–8.

Fraser, Nancy and Axel Honneth (2004) *Redistribution or Recognition? A Political-Philosophical Exchange*. London: Verso.

Giddens, Anthony (1984) *The Constitution of Society: Outline of the Theory of Structuration*. Cambridge: Polity Press.

Haaken, Janice (2014) 'Keepin' it Real: Social Action Research, Psychoanalytic Theory and the Moving to the Beat Project', in Barbara O'Neill, Brian Roberts and Andrew Sparkes (eds), *Advances in Biographical Methods: Creative Applications*. London: Routledge, pp. 43–54.

Haaken, Janice and Maggie O'Neill (2014) 'Moving Images: Psychoanalytically-Informed Visual Methods in Documenting the Lives of Women Migrants and Asylum-Seekers'. *Journal of Health Psychology*, 19(1): 79–89.

Heberle, Renée J. (2006) *Feminist Interpretations of Theodor Adorno*. Philadelphia: Pennsylvania State University Press.

Hudson, Barbara (2003) *Justice in the Risk Society: Challenging and Re-affirming 'Justice' in Late Modernity*. London: Sage Publications.

——. (2006) 'Beyond White Man's Justice: Race, Gender and Justice in Late Modernity'. *Theoretical Criminology*, 10(1): 29–47.

——. (2012) 'Who Needs Justice? Who Needs Security?', in Barbara Hudson and Synnove Ugelvik (eds), *Justice and Security in the 21st Century*. London: Routledge, pp. 6–23.

Jones, Kip (2006) 'A Biographic Researcher in Pursuit of an Aesthetic: The Use of Arts-Based (Re)presentations in "Performative" Dissemination of Life Stories'. *Qualitative Sociology Review*, 2(1): 66–85.

Lindner, Evelin (2006) *Making Enemies: Humiliation and International Conflict*. Westport, CT: Praeger Security.

Marfleet, Phillip (2006) *Refugees in a Global Era*. Basingstoke: Palgrave Macmillan.

Nicholsen Shierry W. (1997) *Exact Imagination, Late Work: On Adorno's Aesthetics*. Cambridge MA: MIT Press.

O'Neill, Maggie (2001) *Prostitution and Feminism: Towards a Politics of Feeling*. Cambridge: Polity Press.

——. (2008) 'Transnational Refugees: The Transformative Role of Art?'. *Forum Qualitative Sozialforschung/Forum: Qualitative Social Research*, 9(2).

——. (2010) *Asylum, Migration and Community*. Bristol: Policy Press.

——. (2011) 'Ethno-Mimesis and Participatory Art', in Sarah Pink (ed.), *Advances in Visual Methodology*. London: Sage Publications, pp. 153–72.

——. (2014) 'Participatory Biographies: Walking, Sensing, Belonging', in Maggie O'Neill, Brian Roberts and Andrew Sparkes (eds), *Advances in Biographical Methods: Creative Applications*. London: Routledge, pp. 73–89.

O'Neill, Maggie and Phil Hubbard (2010) 'Walking, Sensing, Belonging: Ethno-mimesis as Performative Praxis'. *Visual Studies*, 25(1): 46–58.

O'Neill, Maggie, Susan Mansaray and Janice Haaken (2016) 'Women's Lives, Well-Being and Community: Arts Based Biographical Methods', in Norman K. Denzin, Mike Ball and Greg Smith (eds), *The International Review of Qualitative Research* (Special Edition on *Working with Images: Practices of Visualisation, Representation & Pattern Recognition*). London: Sage Publications, forthcoming.

O'Neill, Maggie, Brian Roberts and Andrew Sparkes (eds) (2014) *Advances in Biographical Methods: Creative Applications*. London: Routledge.

O'Neill, Maggie, Philip A. Woods and Mark Webster (2005) 'New Arrivals: Participatory Action Research, Imagined Communities and Social Justice'. *Social Justice*, 31(1): 75–88.

Pakulski, Jan (1997) 'Cultural Citizenship'. *Citizenship Studies*, 1(1): 73–86.

Piccone, Paul (1993) 'Beyond Pseudo-culture? Reconstituting Fundamental Political Concepts'. *Telos*, 95: 3–14.

Pickering, Sharon (2005) *Refugees & State Crime*. Annandale, NSW: Federation Press.

Pink, Sarah (2007) 'Walking with Video'. *Visual Studies*, 22(3): 240–52.

Roberts, Brian (2002) *Biographical Research*. Buckingham: Open University Press.

——. (2014) 'Biographical Research: Past, Present and Future' in Maggie O'Neill, Brian Roberts. B. and Andrew Sparkes (eds). *Advances in Biographical Methods: Creative Applications*. London: Routledge, pp. 11–29.

Sales, Rosemary (2007) *Understanding Immigration and Refugee Policy: Contradictions and Continuities*. Bristol: Policy Press.

Scheff, Thomas J. (2006) 'Silence and Mobilization: Emotional/Relational Dynamics'. Available at: www.humiliationstudies.org/documents/ScheffSilenceandMobilization. pdf.

Schütze, Fritz (1992) 'Pressure and Guilt: War Experiences of a Young German Soldier and Their Biographical Implications'. *International Sociology*, 7(2): 187–208; 7(3): 347–67.

Smith, Anna Marie (1998) *Laclau and Mouffe: The Radical Democratic Imaginary*. London: Routledge.

Smith, Dennis (2006) *Globalization: The Hidden Agenda*. Cambridge: Polity Press.

Tashakkori, Abbas and Charles Teddlie (eds) (2003) *Handbook of Mixed Methods in Social & Behavioral Research*. Thousand Oaks, CA: Sage Publications.

Tyler, Imogen (2006) ''Welcome to Britain': The Cultural Politics of Asylum'. *Cultural Studies*, 9(2): 185–202.

Wengraf, Tom (2006) 'Interviewing for Life Histories, Lived Situations and Personal Experience: The Biographic-Narrative-Interpretive Method (BNIM)'. Available at: www.uel.ac.uk/wwwmedia/microsites/cnr/documents/Wengraf06.rtf.

Walklate, Sandra (2012) *Gender and Crime*, 4 vols. London: Routledge.

Walklate, Sandra and Gabe Mythen (2014) *Contradictions of Terrorism: Security, Risk and Resilience*. London: Routledge.

Yar, Majid (2003) 'Honneth and the Communitarians: Towards a Recognitive Critical Theory of Community'. *Res Publica*, 9: 101–25.

# 6 The 'typical victim'

## No story to tell and no one to tell it to

*Ross McGarry*

The history of biographical methods in the social sciences seems to have been one of fits and starts, moments of creativity having usually been followed by a normal marginal position. (Gelsthorpe 2007: 536)

## Introduction

A central concern within C. Wright Mills' *The Sociological Imagination* (1959) was a preoccupation within occidental sociological knowledge that seeks to quantify and rationalize human experience, abstracting it from the constructed realities of everyday interactions. Mills (1959: 129) went on to state that the intellectual undergirding of such rational 'bureaucratic social science' cannot be separated from its close affinity with political state ordering; indeed, 'the whole social science endeavour has been pinned down to the services of prevailing authorities'. For Mills this way of thinking epitomized understanding the social world as informed by 'abstracted empiricism' (Mills 1959); accepting social life to be measured 'scientifically', preferring to observe human experiences rationally from a distance rather than in more intimate and personal ways. In a challenge to such sociological and methodological conservativism Mills (1959) advocated that the method of biography was fundamental to developing a 'sociological imagination'. The ability to reflect upon one's own personal experiences facilitated a recognition of what he termed 'personal troubles' (Mills 1959): life as experienced within your own 'social milieu' engaged with social issues that are particular to you and prescient for those around you. Once cognizant of your surroundings in this way thinking about them more deeply as being social, historical and cultural issues would give way to connecting more immediate social relationships with the world at large. This is what Mills (1959) called 'public issues', to be considered from a variety of perspectives rather than one's own disciplinary viewpoint. Indeed, for Mills (1959: 7), 'the sociological imagination is the most fruitful of the self-conscious'. Stating this is nothing new of course and unpicking the dominance of positivism within social science and the paradigmatic nuances which set qualitative and quantitative research apart methodologically is beyond the remit of this chapter. So why mention this at all?

There is a clear message in Mills' (1959) work that in order to fully understand the complexities of social experience and be able to coherently situate oneself within social and political structures, it is imperative for social science to embrace pluralism in its methodological approaches and permit reflection and introspection into who we are, where we came from and how we got here. While these types of issues are well-trodden ground within some areas of social science, for others – where recounting personal experiences are perhaps most germane - this is not necessarily the case. As Mills (1959: 6) continues: 'No social study that does not come back to the problems of biography, of history and of their intersections within a society has completed its intellectual journey.'

Taking his lead from Mills (1959), Jock Young (2011) levelled this accusation against criminology having a widespread obsession with generating and using generalizable quantitative information to measure the extent of crime and devise its control. Focusing on a mystifying enumerated explanation of policing drug deals as a 'full-blown example of abstracted empiricism', Young (2011: 11–12) depicts the positivistic uses of criminological data as a means to 'detach themselves from their subject matter and lose all context in an abstraction of reality'. For Young (2011), abstracting the experience of crime from the contexts within which it occurs – including the thoughts, decisions and emotions of those involved – is how the criminological imagination is 'closed down', stripped of its creativity and jettisoned of personal biographical reflection. Whilst Young's (2011: 15) lampooning of criminology as an unreflexive 'Datasaur' hits at the heart of this sense of 'self-consciousness' with disciplinary interests, there is another conversation of a similar nature waiting to be had here. At what point has victimology engaged with 'imagination' in the ways advocated by Mills (1959) and Young (2011), and has this imagination ever been developed far enough within victimological theorizing to have the opportunity to be 'closed down' at all?

These questions are yet to be unpacked within academic victimology. However, the perceived value of biography as a methodological device for the study of victimization appears to exist on two opposing sides of an under-developed debate. Tim Hope (2007) has previously described the victimological use of biography a 'teleological fallacy', inasmuch as studying victimization through an engagement with personal experiences has no purpose for victimology. Basia Spalek (2006) once advocated for the wider use of biography within victimological research to assist in understanding victims' identities and the experience of victimization as being something felt emotionally and existentially. Unfortunately Spalek offered no elaboration on what this pursuit might look like. In one sense this indicates something of a methodological stalemate: neither position has particularly committed to strongly refuting or advocating the uses of biography for victimology, meaning that old ways of 'doing' victimological research (as we shall see) remain the norm, leaving innovations with few creative footholds. Looked at another way, this duality perhaps creates a false positive. For example, research on the 'voice' of the victim within criminal proceedings by Kim M. E. Lens et al. (2013) recently indicated that a traumatic experience of victimization was more likely to compel a person to claim their 'right' to 'victim allocution' (i.e. a Victim Personal Statement) (see Walklate 2007a). This might suggest that we would hear directly from the victim and their personal experiences of crime. Instead we are led to this not insignificant finding through a web of abstracted empiricism detached from the *lived experience* of victimization (Young 2011).

As advocated throughout this edited collection, this chapter intends to create some space to disrupt an inherent 'solidity' within victimological methodology through the uses of biographical methods. In order to do so, this chapter makes its case across several interconnected parts. First, it will outline some of the historical features of biographical work within the discipline of criminology, reflecting critically upon the work of the Chicago School of Sociology as not only a gendered school of thought on these issues, but with little attention paid to the victim of crime. Next the absence of biographical methods in victimological research will be aligned with the long-standing influences of positivist victimology and the closed imagination of victimological methodology. Once outlined, Jo Goodey's (2000) hegemonic masculine biography will be used to illustrate the *teleological efficacy* of biographical methods for victimology through an exploration of a case study depicting a hegemonic masculine experience of violence, injury and recovery. The final section will lead this chapter into a closing discussion reflecting upon the uses of critical victimology to bring an alternative analysis to the victimological imagination that is not fixated with abstracting and generalizing the lived experience of harm.

## Biography, deviance and marginality

Following Mills' (1959) instruction on the value of biography for the study of sociology, the methodological importance of biographical research for the social sciences continued to be noted elsewhere (see, for example, Berger and Berger 1976; Bertaux 1981; Denzin 1989). In Ken Plummer's *Documents of Life* (1983: 8–10), we are introduced to a variety of materials that constitute what he considered the 'rise of the personal tale' in sociology. Included within these sources are diary entries, written letters, fictional illustrations of factual events, photographs and film. Other sources assume a verbal depiction of the experiences of individual lives that are captured in ways peculiar to the method adopted and presented as idiographic portrayals of social life. These methods often include, but are not limited to, the uses of narrative, life course (Hatch and Wisniewski 1995) and life story research (Goodley et al. 2004). For Plummer, included alongside these accounts of social life are less detailed journalistic reports, oral history and life history:

> The cornerstone of social science life document research is akin to the literary biography and autobiography: it is a full length book account of one person's life in his or her own words . . . What matters, therefore, in life history research is the facilitation of as full a subjective view as possible, not the naive delusion that one has trapped the bedrock of truth. (Plummer 1983: 14)

Although life history research is not the purview of sociology and has been used in cultural studies, social work, psychology and indeed historical research (see Dollard (1935) for further instruction on the interdisciplinarity of life history research, particularly on interpreting works from the Chicago School), the popularity of this 'personal tale' within sociology is most notably associated with the symbolic interactionist and ethnographic work of the Chicago School of Sociology (see Rock 2001). Despite the view of a distinct sociological 'tradition' emanating from the Chicago School in this way being contested ground (see Becker 1999), for Plummer (1983) it was the 'Chicago vision' that paved the way for the use of life documents in sociology. In particular, William I. Thomas and Florian Znaniecki's *The Polish Peasant in America and Europe* (1918) illustrated the 'important distinction (which now runs right through sociology) between *objective* factors of the situation and the *subjective* interpretation of that situation' (Plummer 1983: 41). Such methods of understanding lived experiences by placing a pre-eminence on subjective interpretation are understood as fundamental approaches to studying society from a humanistic perspective (see Berger 1963), a position that had been 'persistently minimised, maligned and rendered marginal by social scientists' (Plummer 1983: 11). Ten years after this statement was made, a special issue of the journal *Sociology* was dedicated to the continued and growing intellectual relevance of biography and autobiography as sources of sociological scrutiny, in particular for gender studies and feminist research (see, for example, Cotterill and Letherby 1993; Stanley 1993; Wilkins 1993). We will return to some of these points in the closing observations of this chapter, but for now taking note of these methodological origins of biography for sociology is sufficient enough to turn our attention to their relevance for criminology.

### The Chicago School and the 'deviant'

It is beyond the confines of this chapter to outline the completeness of the ethnographic work that was produced from the Chicago School and the totality of their influences on sociological and criminological work; others have outlined this successfully elsewhere (see, for example, Deegan 2001; Reed-Danahay 2001). It is necessary, however, to briefly connect some of the popularly held influences of the Chicago School to the discipline of criminology.

Some attempts to adopt biographical approaches to social problems from the Chicago School during the early twentieth century came as a reaction against biological and psychological tendencies to explain criminal behaviour in terms of degeneracy and fatuity. For a number of Chicagoan scholars, the lived experiences of individual criminals became a prolific source of empirical data to be analysed and theorized to research deviant subcultures (i.e. gangs, petty criminals and delinquency) in order to understand how criminals and their environment interacted and were influenced by one another. Several books are illustrative of this ethnographic research, including Frederic Thrasher's *The Gang* (1927) and William Foote Whyte's *Street Corner Society* (1943). Other work more explicitly employing biographical methods included Nels Anderson's (1923) *The Hobo*, adopting a vast number of life histories to depict a 'cultural universe' of homeless men in Chicago. Edwin Sutherland (1937/1956) followed this tradition sometime later by researching the biographical accounts of one petty criminal (Chic Cornwell) in

*The Professional Thief*, illustrating the inherent corruption of the criminal justice process through his biography. However, the most lauded example of biography used in this way – for criminology at least – is Clifford Shaw's *The Jack-Roller* (1930/1966), the culmination of six years of research into the early biography of one adolescent boy (Stanley) from an unstable background, who subsequently experienced deprivation and homelessness before ending up in prison and being rehabilitated under the guidance of Shaw. Upon introducing biography as a method, we are informed by Shaw (1930/1966: 1) that although this may be a new approach for research concerned with the study of crime and deviance – as outlined above – it was not so for other disciplines (see Plummer (2001) for a comprehensive overview of life story research in ethnography).

Each of these works is a noteworthy contribution to the criminological canon. However, the significance of *The Jack-Roller* was singled out in a special issue of *Theoretical Criminology*, presenting numerous appreciative interpretations of Shaw's (1930/1966) work. Although this special issue was published to celebrate the 100th anniversary of Stanley's birth and to illustrate the importance of Shaw's work for criminological theory, Lorraine Gelsthorpe (2007), as the opening quotation of this chapter suggests, also sagely observed that despite biographical research in criminology being intermittent, it was also progressive enough to be populated by a 'new generation' of criminological work. Robert J. Sampson and John H. Laub's (1993) life course research and Shadd Maruna's (2001) phenomenological work on desistance from crime are perhaps the most prominent of these literatures. Other more recent 'newcomers' have adopted ethnographic (see Cromwell 2010), life course (see Benson 2013) and autoethnographic (see Wakeman 2014) approaches to the (auto)biographical scene in criminology.

We are told by Shaw (1930/1966) that the life history approach being adopted by his research (and, by implication, others in the Chicago School) was concerned with *individual* first-person accounts, not generalizations, and the means of recording experiences of social life comes in various forms including autobiographies, diaries and interviews (as noted above by Plumber (1983)). Taking *The Jack-Roller* as our point of orientation within biographical criminological research, we can begin to note a number of implicit themes within this body of work from Dick Hobbs (2001). First, the subject matter with which the above work from the Chicago School had concerned itself was *criminal and deviant behaviour*. Second, those who were the focus of the ethnographic and biographical work of the Chicago School were disproportionately *male deviants and criminals*. Third, the work of the Chicago School was disproportionately conducted by *male social scientists*. As such, the influential starting point of biographical work within criminology was conducted by men researching male criminal activity. This is not to suggest that women were inactive in conducting sociological research within the Chicago School (see Deegan 1996) or have not been the focus of criminological studies (see Millman 1976; Carlen et al. 1985; Miller 2010). Taking stock of some of these observations does, however, lead us to ask a broader set of questions that appear to sit within the 'interstitial spaces' (*qua* Thrasher 1927) of criminological literature on ethnography, biography and the Chicago School: where in all of this activity was the victim?

## Biographical research and the 'marginalized'

To help address the above question we briefly return to the comments of Plummer (1983: 81), who states that 'the central thrust of personal document research is to enable the voices to be heard that are usually silenced: the victims of what Becker calls a "hierarchy of credibility" . . . for such research has a democratising thrust to it: each person has a life and a story to tell'. There are two particular problems herein that need to be reflected onto the concept of victimhood. First, although almost exclusively depicting the lives of (mostly young, male) criminals and deviants, those being researched by the Chicago School were people who occupied the interstitial spaces of social life (Thrasher 1927): those who did not have a 'voice' or whose voices were marginalized. Inasmuch as they were 'silenced', they were invisible save for the research that brought their stories to light. Reflecting upon *The Jack-Roller*, it has been noted that the depiction of Stanley's life experiences illustrated his marginalized and vulnerable status – a 'victim' status that Mechthild Bereswill (2007) unpicks (and rejects) as a self-justification for deviance. For Bruce Hoffman (2009), however, Stanley was subjugated by his life experiences, the imposition of an academic authority upon his biography, and his eventual reform coming under the supervision of an academic (Shaw). As such, one might suggest that *some* criminals and deviants under research within the Chicago School have the capacity to be depicted as individuals with past exposures to vulnerability and *victimization*.

Second, the overlapping of these issues does perhaps create a 'hierarchy of credibility' (Becker 1967), but not in the way that has been understood previously as 'underdog sociology'. Although now changed considerably, it has long been established that the 'credibility' of the victim with criminology and criminal justice had frequently caused them to be forgotten in terms of both academic and policy interest. Although the intentions of the ethnographic work of the Chicago School were to get closer to the lives of certain groups in order to understand them in depth rather than to offer a complete analyses of all aspects of the social worlds being studied, it is still possible to raise important questions about the presence and absence of the victim within this work. It is often assumed that biographical and autobiographical research is only concerned with individual lives, but 'it is a very rare autobiography that is not replete with the potted biographies of significant others in the subject's life' (Editorial 1993: 2). Taken in this way, if the main concerns of much biographical research of the Chicago School were the lives and experiences of criminals and deviants, then the types of activities that such people would have been engaged with would surely have illustrated – at one time or another – the 'significant others' who they had *victimized*. As Richard Quinney (1972) observes, without a victim to speak of, there is no crime. What has therefore been assumed by Ken Plummer (1983) (and no doubt countless others), when noting the 'democratic thrust' of biographical work that recognizes that all people have a story to tell, is that when addressing the criminologically focused work of the Chicago School, offenders and victims share an equal relationship. The absence of the victim within this type of research illustrates that this is not the case.

The language of silence and invisibility has hitherto been used to describe the status of the victim of crime within the discipline of criminology and criminal justice policy, particularly in the US and UK (see the edited collection by Bottoms and Roberts 2010). Yet, despite reclaiming prominence within these arenas, it appears that the victim remains within the margins of this area of influential criminological literature. The next task of this chapter will be to begin addressing why, despite Becker (1992: 45–7) suggesting that empirical phenomenological research is an appropriate means of studying the lived experience of criminal victimization by seeing the world through the eyes of the victim, it remains the case that studies such as these are said to be rarely found within victimology (Hope 2007).

## A view of mainstream/empirical victimology

Popularly understood as being formed by several 'Founding Fathers', the academic study of victimology was shaped at the outset by the concept of *victim precipitation* from the work of Hans von Hentig (1940) and Martin F. Wolfgang (1958), and later *victim culpability* by Benjamin Mendelsohn (1963). Within this body of work, victimization was understood as the product of interaction between the 'penal couple' (Mendelsohn 1963) and was aimed at demonstrating that the victim had a role to play in their own victimization. From the outset, this was perhaps a precarious way to set the scene for victimology. Victims were to be understood as complicit in their own victimization, causing themselves to become the targets of crime; a line of thought that would come back to haunt victimology some years later in what came to be known as *victim blaming* following the contemptible work of Menachem Amir (1971).

A further development from the work of these 'Founding Fathers' of victimology included von Hentig's (1948) *The Criminal and His Victim*. Continuing the notion of victim precipitation, this book developed what came to be known as *victim proneness*. For von Hentig (1948), some people were more prone to criminal victimization than others based upon social variables (i.e. class and nationality) or biological characteristics (i.e. sex and intelligence) which he devised into discrete categories of victims, including women, children, the elderly and mentally 'subnormal'. The categorization of likely victims in this way illustrated a 'principle of differentiation' (Walklate 2006: 276), identifying the (abnormal) victim from the (normal) non-victim. Sandra Walklate (2006) has suggested that in von Hentig's terms the latter constituted the white heterosexual male against which the (abnormal) victim should be measured.

Von Hentig's (1948) work on proneness has had lasting influences on victimological research and can be most notably traced in the concepts of 'Lifestyle' or 'Routine Activities' theory (see, for example, Hindelang et al. 1978; Cohen and Felson 1979; Gottfredson and Hindelang 1981). This particular type of work within victimology emphasizes the value placed on 'scientific' knowledge across much of the discipline in being able to accurately measure and predict criminal victimization by taking account of people's daily activities, the places they frequent, the times of day that they do so and their exposure to high-risk situations where victimization might occur. These early concepts of victimology shaped what David Miers (1989) later termed positivist victimology, broadly understood to consider the occurrence of victimization being influenced by rational choice and predictability (i.e. repeat victimization), and for victimization to be of a very specific type (i.e. interpersonal crime).

The influential work of the early victimologists has thereby shaped the discipline with a concern for the scientific measurement of victimizing factors which reliably perpetuate and reproduce *criminal* victimization. Considered more broadly, this has been variously referred to as mainstream or 'conventional victimology' (Walklate 1989). This seeks to deal with crime that occurs in public (street crime, acquisitive crime, etc.) and pays little attention to crimes that go on in private (i.e. in the home) or in corporate domains. Highlighting this begins to shed some light on why biographical methods have been side-lined within victimological research. The preferred methodological approaches to studying victims, in what has been described as 'empirical victimology' – the study of people and their experiences of *crime* victimization (Hope 2007) – have been co-opted by intra-state and state-led criminal justice organizations (particularly in the West) for several decades. Emblematic of Mills' (1959) 'bureaucratic social science', examples include the British Crime Survey of England and Wales (now the Crime Survey of England and Wales) (see Hough and Mayhew 1983), national criminal victimization surveys from the Bureau of Justice Statistics (2013) in the US, the European victimization survey (see Van Dijk et al. 2005) and the International Criminal Victimization Survey (see van Dijk and Mayhew 1993). For Tim Hope (2007), despite the associated issues of selectivity, bias and methodological ambiguity, victimological research has been tied to these particular (statistical) methods. Reflecting upon the opening comments of this chapter, it is fair to suggest that victimological research has undergone a similar dominance of abstracted empiricism (Mills 1959) and has had much of its imagination 'closed down' by abstracting the lived experience of victimization into preferred methods advocating comparability and generalizability (Young 2011). These theoretical and methodological starting points place us far from where we need to be in understanding biography in victimology.

There is, however, a paucity of victimological work that has similarly distinct influences to it as the incomplete 'intellectual journey' (Mills 1959) of biography in criminological research. Let us now turn our attention to some of the deeper issues within conventional victimology that inhibit biography from being a vital part of a victimological imagination.

### Introducing Polly, the 'typical victim'

In Leah E. Daigle's (2012) textbook/reader on *Victimology*, an early chapter covering the theories of victimization – as described above – opens with the story of 'Polly'. In an image Polly is depicted as a young white female, described in the narrative as a student deviating away from her usual studies in the college library, instead meeting up with friends for a drink before walking home alone in the dark. During her walk home, Polly is accosted by two unknown young men whilst passing an alley; they overpower her and take her purse, despite her best physical efforts. We are told that following her victimization, Polly begins to question why she had been targeted for victimization as she continues her walk home: was it misfortune, bad timing or placing *herself* in harm's way? The example of Polly is meant to depict Nils Christie's (1986) notion of the 'ideal victim'.

Christie (1986) typifies the ideal victim as an old lady who is assaulted and robbed of her belongings by an unknown (stronger) male aggressor. Like Polly, her victimization takes place on the way home from doing a 'good deed' (caring for her sister). Both victims are 'ideal' as they have the following characteristics which are key components to gaining requisite public sympathy and being legitimately ascribed a victim status:

1    The victim is weak. Sick, old or very young people are particularly well suited as ideal victims.
2    The victim was carrying out a respectable project – caring for her sister.
3    She was where she could not possibly be blamed for being – in the street during the daytime.
4    The offender was big and bad.
5    The offender was unknown and in no personal relationship to her.

A sixth condition of the ideal victim is being powerful enough to make your case known and successfully claim an 'ideal' victim status (Christie 1986: 18–19, 21).

For Christie (1986), the ideal victim is intended to pose a conceptual problem to help illustrate the differentiation between the victim and the non-victim (Walklate 2006); it becomes the standard against which other forms of victimization can be measured for the purposes of critique and to illustrate normative assumptions about victimization. However, the depiction of Polly is a literal interpretation used to illustrate what Daigle (2012: 14) calls 'the 'typical' crime victim', which we are told to be 'fortunate' enough to be able to develop an understanding of through conventional (positivist) victimology. Despite there being no other acknowledgements of alternative victimological perspectives on offer (i.e. radical, feminist or critical, as discussed later), there are further conceptual problems at work here that further render the uses of biography a non-starter for victimological research.

We are told that despite the difficulties of ever really knowing why Polly was victimized, the solution to understanding her experience is to 'compare her to other victims to see how similar she is' (Daigle 2012: 14). It is at this juncture that the literal use of the ideal (or typical) victim becomes analytically problematic. First, we are encouraged to understand the personal experience of her victimization in the context of the 'penal couple' (Mendelsohn 1963). As Daigle (2012) repeatedly reminds us, given the 'close relationship' between the victim and the offender, if we have a deficit of knowledge within victimological literature to understand the experience of victimization, then we can do so through similar approaches taken by criminologists to understand criminal behaviour. This assumes once again that the relationship between offenders and victims are on an equal footing. Second, it suggested that the best way to understand the experience of victimization is to abstract it from the personal experience itself and hold it comparatively against others with the hope of understanding its similarities to other experiences of victimization. As an ideal victim, Polly is not just without agency and choices, she is also without a personal experience to speak for herself and there is no one to listen to it.

This not only leaves the experience of victimization with no biographical relevance, it also shores up a normative and polarized view of the 'victim'. Von Hentig's (normal) non-victim is a white heterosexual male, whereas Christie's 'ideal' victim and Daigle's depiction of the 'typical' crime victim assumes the characteristics of a white vulnerable female (Polly). This represents some long-standing conceptual problems for the victimological imagination regarding gender, vulnerability and agency. To help unpack some of these issues, we now turn to a biographical case study of violence and harm experienced far beyond the confines of the polarized view of the penal couple within the criminal justice system.

## Hegemonic masculinity, violence and victimization

The above discussion reflects the sentiments of the opening quotation from Gelsthorpe (2007) on how biography can frequently be reduced to marginal positions within social science. Encouraging the importance of a biographical tradition of research within criminology, criminologists and victimologists, Jo Goodey (2000) proposed that a particular way of understanding the experience of victimization is through 'hegemonic masculine biography'. By centring on the life stories of male offenders, Goodey suggests that mapping their biographical experiences onto a 'biographical continuum' would allow the individual to become central to criminological analysis and facilitate a re-assessment of their social and structural situations. In doing so we do not lose the personal from view in lieu of the social, and as Mills (1959) encouraged, the historical and structural features of everyday experiences are able to be acknowledged (i.e. who they are, where they emerge from and how their experiences influence the trajectory of their lives) (Goodey 2000).

As Goodey (2000) avers, it is the points at which people deviate from social norms and engage in criminal activity or experience victimization that become the focus of our analysis. In centring on biography, we are reconstructing the lives of others for our analysis not simply leading with our research interests, allowing for a more attentive view of how individuals adapt to their circumstances and the powerful structural processes (i.e. masculinity) that impact upon their lives (Goodey 2000). This approach provides a frame of analysis to help map personal biography and connect the past experiences of individuals with the present; seeking to identify any convergences and divergences in the lives of others that led them into crime and/or victimization. One indication of this is via 'epiphany moments', 'interactional moments and experiences which leave marks on people's lives' (Denzin 1989: 70), either influencing a person's entire life course, being experienced cumulatively or symbolically, or afforded meaning once recounted (Goodey 2000).

Having coined the term 'victimology' to have relevance only when associated with criminology (Mendelsohn 1963), Mendelsohn (1974) later advocated that victimological research explore all types of victimization, including those involving the 'danger complex' relating to war, atrocity and genocide. To help understand the biography of Stanley in *The Jack-Roller*, we are provided with a pen-picture of his life as covered within the scope of Shaw's (1930/1966) work. Taking some direct methodological influences from these two approaches, the following case study illustrates the biography of 'Carl',[1] a British soldier from the 2003 war in Iraq. Carl was interviewed near the end of his service career following recovery from a serious injury that left him with a lifelong disability. Before we reflect upon the victimological nuances of his experiences, it will be worth reviewing his biography using Goodey's (2000) approach to hegemonic masculine biography.

Figure 6.1 presents the casualties and field hospital admissions of all British service personnel during the war in Iraq. The following case study includes the lived experiences of one individual tallied within this table. Presenting data in this tabulated way illustrates the political uses of 'bureaucratic social science' (Mills 1959) that sanitizes highly emotive personal experiences of institutionalized violence and victimization. To help disrupt the 'solidity' of this data, the following biography includes the story of Carl, whose experience is abstracted somewhere within Figure 6.1 as one of those accounted for as an evacuated casualty of war.

### *Illustrating victimization with biography*

For the purposes of clarity, Carl is a white British, heterosexual, working-class male in his late twenties. He was interviewed during 2009 using Tom Wengraf's

**OP TELIC CASUALTY AND FATALITY TABLES**

Number of Op Telic UK Military and Civilian casualties [1][2][3][4][5]
1 January 2003 to 31 July 2009

| Year | Casualties (excluding Natural Causes) | | | Field Hospital Admissions | | | Aeromed Evacuations |
|---|---|---|---|---|---|---|---|
| | Total | Very Seriously Injured or Wounded | Seriously Injured or Wounded | Total | Wounded in Action | Disease or Non Battle Injury | |
| Total | 222 | 73 | 149 | 3,598 | 315 | 3,283 | 1,971 |
| 2003 | 46 | 14 | 32 | | | | |
| 2004 | 45 | 14 | 31 | | | | |
| 2005 | 20 | 5 | 15 | | | | |
| 2006 | 32 | 11 | 21 | 1,302 | 93 | 1,209 | 701 |
| 2007 | 69 | 24 | 45 | 1,300 | 202 | 1,098 | 603 |
| 2008 | 9 | 5 | 4 | 778 | 20 | 758 | 433 |
| 2009 | 1 | - | 1 | 218 | - | 218 | 234 |
| Aug-08 | 0 | - | - | 63 | - | 63 | 34 |
| Sep-08 | 0 | - | - | 67 | - | 67 | 29 |
| Oct-08 | 0 | - | - | 57 | - | 57 | 36 |
| Nov-08 | 0 | - | - | 51 | - | 51 | 41 |
| Dec-08 | 0 | - | - | 60 | - | 60 | 46 |
| Jan-09 | 0 | - | - | 38 | - | 38 | 48 |
| Feb-09 | 0 | - | - | 45 | - | 45 | 32 |
| Mar-09 | 0 | - | - | 69 | - | 69 | 42 |
| Apr-09 | 1 | - | 1 | 39 | - | 39 | 40 |
| May-09 | 0 | - | - | 10 | - | 10 | 35 |
| Jun-09 | 0 | - | - | 10 | - | 10 | 28 |
| Jul-09 | 0 | - | - | 7 | - | 7 | 9 |

Source: NOTICAS          Source: UK and Coalition Medical Facilities          Source: AECC

1. These data are provisional and subject to change.
2. The personnel listed as VSI and SI may also appear in the UK field hospital admissions and Aeromed Evacuations data.
3. The admissions data contain UK personnel admitted to any Field Hospital, whether operated by UK or Coalition Medical Facilities.
4. Civilians are not included in the figures previous to 01/01/2006.
5. The VSI and SI injury data includes records classified as 'Other Causes'. This classification is used when there is insufficient information to attribute a casualty to injury or natural cause.

*Figure 6.1* Bureaucratic accounting of violence
(Source: Ministry of Defence 2009)

(2001) Biographical Narrative Interpretive Method (BNIM) and his experiences are illustrated below in a diagrammatic depiction employing Jo Goodey's (2000) biographical continuum.

In the interests of getting closer to Carl's experiences and engaging with them as situated accounts of his life, what follows is a brief pen-picture illustrating his biography, depicting his intersection with the social structures of civic life and a total institution (Goffman 1961), and illuminating where he came from and how he ended up nestled within the data in Figure 6.1.

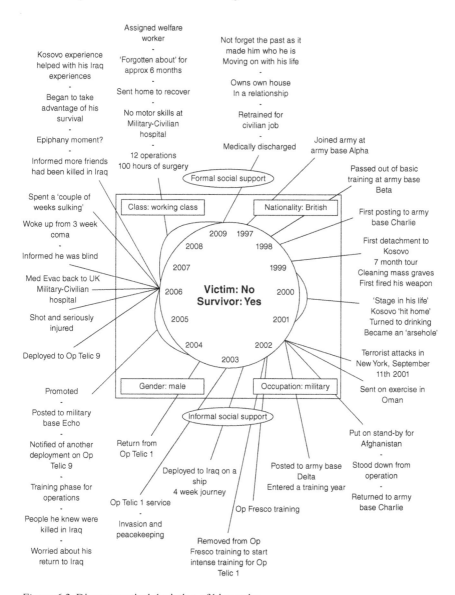

*Figure 6.2* Diagrammatical depiction of biography

### *Introducing Carl: a hegemonic masculine biography*

Carl joined the army in 1997, completing his basic training at army base Alpha before progressing on to his trade training at army base Beta. During 1998, Carl successfully passed out of trade training and was posted to army base Charlie, where he served until 2001. Whilst at army base Charlie he was deployed on his first operational detachment to Kosovo in 1999. During this seven-month tour, he was not only involved in clearing mass graves resulting from the genocide committed against ethnic Albanians, but was also required to discharge his weapon for the first time against an enemy; he recalls no 'confirmed kills' as these were not his interest. Upon returning from Kosovo, Carl states that his involvement in this conflict at a young age had an impact on his life which 'hit home' on returning to his family and being away from the other soldiers in his unit. Between 2000 and 2001, he states that he went through a 'stage in his life' where he turned to drinking more than usual and – in his words – became more of an 'arsehole' than he needed to be. In 2001, he went on an exercise to Oman, knowing little of the terrorist attacks that had occurred in North America (9/11); during this time, he was put on standby to deploy to Afghanistan, but was subsequently stood down and returned to army base Charlie. Upon his return during 2001, he was posted to army base Delta, where he entered a training year, eventually being redeployed to take part in training for Op Fresco in 2002. He was subsequently removed from training for Op Fresco to start intensive training for Op Telic, the invasion of Iraq, following which in 2003 he was deployed to Iraq by ship, taking four weeks to arrive. Having participated in Op Telic 1 in both invasion and peace-keeping capacities, Carl returned from operations having now participated in two major conflicts with the British army. On returning to the UK following his participation in the Iraq invasion, he was promoted on posting in 2003 to army base Echo, whereby he was also notified that he would be returning to Iraq on Op Telic 9 in 2006. During his time at army base Echo, he underwent further training for operations in Iraq and began to hear of people he knew being killed in Iraq, causing him to worry about his return on Op Telic 9 in the capacity of a commander. Then, as expected, in 2006 he was deployed once again for his second tour of Iraq, during which he recalls witnessing a young member of his unit being shot and killed – having to take a commander's responsibility for informing the rest of his unit – in addition to once again having to discharge his weapon system to suppress enemy forces, again claiming no 'confirmed kills'. However, it was also during this tour in Iraq that he was shot and seriously injured while conducting his primary duty in 2006. Having kept himself alive following being shot, he was medically evacuated back to a civilian-military hospital in the UK and was placed in a medically induced coma for three weeks – an experience he recounts as being horrific. He awoke to discover that he was blind and had sustained other extensive facial injuries and scarring as a result of being shot, news which he states caused him to 'sulk' for a couple of weeks. However, in 2007, he was informed that more people he knew had been killed in Iraq, encouraging him to take advantage of his survival from his injuries – he was alive. From 2006 until his interview in 2009, Carl was in recovery from his injuries, undergoing 12 operations and 100 hours of surgery. At the start of his recovery, he states the army could not send him for treatment at a civilian-military hospital due to there being no motor skills rehabilitation available; rather, he praises the army for sending him home to recover and adjust to his injuries. However, he states that he was 'forgotten about' by the army for approximately six months following his return home to his family, following which he was eventually assigned a welfare worker who put him into contact with a UK charity for the blind, who he credits with his recovery. Now Carl is due to be medically discharged from the army in 2009; he is a home owner, in a relationship and intends to put his retraining to good use in his civilian life, leaving his army career behind and moving on. Despite his experiences in the army and sustaining life-changing injuries in Iraq, he remains proud of his service in the army and to his country.

## Discussion

As Goodey (2000) continues, biographies are important touchstones for evaluating our theoretical ideas about crime and victimization, and we must avoid purely descriptive accounts of people's lives; looking to how the individual intersects with social structures assists in overcoming this. In order to study victims, Rob Mawby and Sandra Walklate (1994) acknowledged the need for objective scientific measurement (as did Fattah (1992)) in addition to the pursuit of a depth of meaning. Part of this meaning making comes from an understanding of the relationship between structure and agency (Giddens 1984) and includes researching the victims we 'see' (Polly) as well as those we do not (Carl). For Mawby and Walklate (1994), the victim is considered a human agent who can be active (resisting ascribed labels and making choices of their own) as well as being passive (like Polly), but all the time situated within political processes that can mobilize victimhood for the furthering of state interests. With these things in mind, let us now consider some elements of Carl's biography to move it beyond the descriptive and into a victimological frame of reference that is more aligned with critical victimology (Mawby and Walklate 1994).

### *Direct and secondary victimization: experiencing violence as injury*

The most obvious harm that Carl experienced during his service in the British army was the physical injury that he suffered whilst serving in Iraq; this can be readily identified as direct victimization, the personal experience of harm. His injury was almost fatal and set him on a path that included medical evacuation, hours of surgery and a significant change to his life through a permanent disability. Having been informed that he was blind and in need of rehabilitation, whilst not critical of the military, he admits to being unsupported by the Ministry of Defence and returned home to his family, newly disabled and 'forgotten about'. Although eventually assigned the support he required for his recovery from a UK charity, this lack of assistance from the support structures that supposedly existed to provide for him is translatable as a secondary victimization.

### *Primary victimization: perpetrating and witnessing violence*

During his service in Kosovo, Carl was exposed as a young man to the consequences of genocide and had first discharged his weapon against an opposing force. These experiences had 'hit home' when he found himself removed from the closeness of his military unit and returned to his family; changing one supportive structure for another less equipped to deal with what he had experienced had consequences for him and entered him into a temporary period in his life where he was drinking alcohol more than usual and had a change of character for the worse. Ironically, it is these experiences of war as a young man that had prepared him for Iraq, although perhaps nothing could have prepared him for the life-changing injuries he sustained at war.

### Epiphany and the road to recovery

The impacts of service in Kosovo and witnessing atrocity were not the only times that service life had an impact upon Carl's emotional stability. He had been acutely aware that people he knew were being hurt in Iraq – a sobering thought that made him cognizant of the dangers ahead. The challenges that Carl faced following his injury were not only physical but also emotional, which he modestly referred to as 'sulking'. However, his recovery was not only due to his rehabilitation but also to his recognition that other people were continuing to be harmed in Iraq. The deaths of other British soldiers he knew served as an epiphany moment (Denzin 1989) that had helped him transgress his initial emotional trauma following his injury and encouraged him to take advantage of having not been killed.

### Dealing with dualities

The account of Carl's biography as depicted here illustrate a complex range of experiences that highlight instances of vulnerability which could easily be translated as a challenge to his hegemonic masculine biography. When asked to consider if he thought of himself as a victim of his experiences, Carl had this to say:

> I think I'm less a victim than most because at least I got hurt fighting . . . we we're in a battle, we were fighting, we were doing what soldiers do . . . so I feel even less of a victim because at least I know that I was hurt being a soldier . . . at least this person had the balls to fight . . . within a range of bullets so . . . I feel . . . slightly less a victim . . . than anyone else might feel.

> Victim makes you seem weak.

> We're not victims are we, we're soldiers, or Airmen, Marine, Navy . . . we're not victims as such coz you know we're out there doing a job, we know what we're doing . . . we trained for that.

Asked to consider if his experiences made him think of himself as a survivor, he responded:

> I survived a horrific thing, you know, and . . . I think meself very lucky.

> I think that everyone who comes home whether you're hurt or not is a survivor . . . you survived a [sic] six months of intensive conflict and . . . there'll be

no one who comes back and doesn't tell you at least three or four stories of where they could have actually died.

It is the case then that Carl's perception of hegemonic masculinity is intertwined with a sense of vulnerability that he rejects, and an awareness that he has over-come his physical injury and is getting on with his life in different ways.

### Returning to the ideal and 'typical' victim

There is very little to recognize about Carl's experience that sits comfortably with the ideal victim (Christie 1986): he is male, was an aggressor in his role as a sol-dier, and the geopolitics of the Iraq war make it difficult to illustrate his service as a 'good deed'. However, whist the perception of soldiering is symbolized by mascu-linity, toughness and the means to be resilient in the face of adversity, one would be mistaken – despite Carl's protests – that the hegemonic masculinity of soldiering is unlikely to be understood as victimizing. In the post-war era of Iraq and Afghanistan, the rise in what has been referred to as elsewhere as 'military victimhood' (McGarry 2015) has witnessed British service personnel – injured or not – being warmly received into the embrace of the public, state and charitable sectors. The injured body and mind of the soldier has become ground to be competed over and these pursuits tell us much about the interests and manipulations of the state and its moves to revive civil–military relations in over a decade of war (Walklate and McGarry 2015).

However, the use of biography as a victimological device in the ways demon-strated here is also illuminative of other issues. Given the gendered assumptions relating to victimization being the purview of women, the biography of Carl illus-trates that conventional victimological archetypes of young, white, heterosexual males being 'normal' non-victims of crime is a wholly limiting way of conceptual-izing harm and victimization. Men (particularly young men) are frequently absent from the victimological imagination for precisely these reasons, despite being the most likely to experience violent crime: men can be and are victims in a variety of different contexts (see Walklate 2007b). However, the blurring of these distinc-tions does not stop here; in rejecting his victim status and embracing the notion of 'survival', Carl's biography reaches out to feminist discourses and literature which highlight that victims (such as those suffering from domestic violence) have choices, they can indeed reject labels ascribed to them by the state (or through the processes of research as we have here) and – as the uses of autobiography does for feminist research (see Stanley 1992, 1993; Cotterill and Letherby 1993) – assist in negotiating their identities in dynamic and empowering ways.

Finally, the depiction of the 'typical' victim by Daigle (2012) also directs us towards the use of a particular method which appears to indicate using the personal experiences of victims, but in ways that keep the victimological imagi-nation 'closed down' (Young 2011) and the uses of biographical methods abated. Daigle (2012) encourages us to use the 'life course' perspective as a vehicle for understanding victimization stemming from (1) a lack of self-control or – as an alternative – (2) routine activities theory. The main fault of this advocacy is that it provides a gendered view of victimization, that is 'unsurprisingly' – as Daigle (2012: 26) explains – experienced more outside of the home (i.e. on the way to work; see Cohen and Felson 1979) and is reduced by cohabitation and marriage (see Sampson and Laub 1997). Being urged to view life course research in this way dramatically overlooks the realities of victimization for women for whom the marital home is the most dangerous place of all. This conventional view of victimology also says nothing for acts of violence that are random and indiscriminate, such as terrorism and war (as experienced by Carl), it overlooks structural inequalities that are routine facets of the 'terrorism of everyday life' (Furedi 1995) and provides an ethnocentric view of victimization. Following Young (2011), this chapter therefore proposes that if criminology has yet to fully complete its 'intellectual journey' as a social science engaged with biography (Mills 1959), victimology has barely taken its first steps.

## Conclusion

This chapter has made clear that the uses of biographical work have been conspicuously absent from victimological research, despite their prominence within the symbolic interactionist and ethnographic methods employed by the Chicago School of Sociology. The early scholars of victimology have inadvertently played some part in the 'closing down' (Young 2011) of biographical methods within victimological research due to the influences of positivism within the study of crime victims. However, as this chapter has demonstrated, the uses of biography have a distinct value for the victimological imagination that allow us to tap into the lived experiences of harm and victimization in order to understand how people negotiate their lives and to understand the complexities of victimhood. As a concluding note, it is worth stating what the uses of biography as a method allow for the occurrence of victimization to *not* be abstracted as a comparable event, but indulged as an *experience*, meaning that victims are trusted to speak for themselves and on behalf of others with similar experiences. As methodological victimologists, our task is to think through the conventional uses of the ideal and 'typical' victim to illustrate that victims' experiences are stories to be told and to demonstrate that biographical work within victimology has creative scholars prepared to listen.

## Note

1 This biography is taken from the PhD research of the author of this chapter. Carl is not the participant's real name; it is a pseudonym, for this soldier's given identifier as Participant D within the original research he took part in. The author has afforded this name as a reflection upon the author's PhD fieldwork has illustrated that the use of names rather than identifiers – particularly in biographical research – assists in making the telling of life stories more relatable and personal.

## References

Amir, Menachem (1971) *Patterns of Forcible Rape*. Chicago: University of Chicago Press.
Anderson, Nels (1923) *The Hobo: The Sociology of the Homeless Man*. Chicago: University of Chicago Press.

Becker, Carol S. (1992) *Living and Relating: An Introduction to Phenomenology*. London: Sage Publications.

Becker, Howard S. (1967) 'Whose Side are We on?' *Social Problems*, 14(3): 239–47.

——. (1999) 'The Chicago School, So-Called'. *Qualitative Sociology*, 22(1): 3–12.

Benson, Michael L. (2013) *Crime and the Life Course: An Introduction*, 2nd edn. Abingdon: Routledge.

Bereswill, Mechthild (2007) 'A Deep Hermeneutic Interpretation of *The Jack-Roller*'. *Theoretical Criminology*, 11(4): 469–84.

Berger, Peter L. (1963) *Invitation to Sociology: A Humanistic Perspective*. London: Penguin.

Berger, Peter, L. and Brigitte Berger (1976) *Sociology: A Biographical Approach*. Harmondsworth: Penguin.

Bertaux, Daniel (ed.) (1981) *Biography and Society*. Beverley Hills, CA: Sage Publications.

Bottoms, Anthony and Julian V. Roberts (eds) (2010) *Hearing the Victim: Adversarial Justice, Crime Victims and the State*. Cullompton: Willan Publishing.

Bureau of Justice Statistics (2013) *National Crime Victimization Survey* (NCVS) API. Available at: www.bjs.gov/developer/ncvs/index.cfm.

Carlen, Pat, Jenny Hicks, Josie O'Dwyer, Diana Christina and Chris Tchaikovsky (1985) *Criminal Women: Autobiographical Accounts*. Cambridge: Polity Press.

Christie, Nils (1986) 'The Ideal Victim', in Ezzat A. Fattah (ed.), *Crime Policy to Victim Policy*. London: Macmillan, pp. 17–30.

Cohen, Lawrence E. and Marcus Felson (1979) 'Social Change and Crime Pattern Trends: A Routine Activity Approach'. *American Sociological Review*, 44: 588–608.

Cotterill, Pamela and Gayle Letherby (1993) 'Weaving Stories: Personal Auto/Biographies in Feminist Research'. *Sociology*, 27(1): 67–79.

Cromwell, Paul (ed.) (2010) *In Their Own Words: Criminals on Crime*, 5th edn. Oxford: Oxford University Press.

Daigle, Leah E. (2012) *Victimology: A Text/Reader*. London: Sage Publications.

Deegan, Mary J. (1996) '"Dear Love, Dear Love": Feminist Pragmatism and the Chicago Female World of Love and Ritual'. *Gender & Society*, 10(5): 590–607.

——. (2001) 'The Chicago School of Ethnography', in Paul Atkinson, Amanda Coffey, Sara Delamont, John Lofland and Lyn Lofland (eds), *Handbook of Ethnography*. London: Sage Publications, pp. 11–25.

Denzin, Norman K. (1989) *Interpretive Biography*. London: Sage Publications.

Dollard, John (1935) *Criteria for the Life History: With Analysis of Six Notable Documents*. New Haven: Yale University Press.

Editorial (1993) 'Editorial Introduction'. *Sociology* (Special Issue on Biography and Autobiography in Sociology), 27(1): 1–4.

Fattah, Ezzat A. (ed.) (1992) *Critical Victimology*. London: Macmillan.

Furedi, Frank (2005) *Politics of Fear: Beyond Left and Right*. London: Continuum.

Gelsthorpe, Lorraine (2007) '*The Jack-Roller*: Telling a Story?' *Theoretical Criminology*, 11(4): 515–42.

Giddens, Anthony (1984) *The Constitution of Society*. Cambridge: Polity Press.

Goffman, Erving (1961) *Asylums: Essays on the Social Situation of Mental Patients and Other Inmates*. London: Penguin.

Goodey, Jo (2000) 'Biographical Lessons for Criminology'. *Theoretical Criminology*, 4(4): 473–98.

Goodley, Dan, Rebecca Lawthom, Peter Clough and Michelle Moore (2004) *Researching Life Stories: Method, Theory and Analyses in a Biographical Age*. London: Routledge/Falmer.

Gottfredson, Michael R. and Michael J. Hindelang (1981) 'Sociological Aspects of Criminal Victimization'. *Annual Review of Sociology*, 7: 107–28.

Hatch, J. Amos and Richard Wisniewski (eds) (1995) *Life History and Narrative*. London: Taylor & Francis.

Hindelang, Michael J., Michael R. Gottfredson and James Garofalo (1978) *Victims of Personal Crime: An Empirical Foundation for a Theory of Personal Victimization*. Pensacola, FL: Ballinger Publishing.

Hobbs, Dick (2001) 'Ethnography and the Study of Deviance', in Paul Atkinson, Amanda Coffey, Sara Delamont, John Lofland and Lyn Lofland (eds), *Handbook of Ethnography*. London: Sage Publications, pp. 204–19.

Hoffman, Bruce (2009) 'Conquest Traditions, Conflict Transformation and the Cultural Boundaries of Criminology: Rigoberta Menchú and Criminological Science'. *Contemporary Justice Review*, 12(2): 171–89.

Hope, Tim (2007) 'Theory and Method: The Social Epidemiology of Crime Victims', in Sandra Walklate (ed.), *Handbook of Victims and Victimology*. Cullompton: Willan Publishing, pp. 62–90.

Hough, Michael and Patricia Mayhew (1983) *The British Crime Survey: First Report*. Home Office Research Studies No. 76. London: HMSO.

Lens, Kim M. E., Antony Pemberton and Stefan Bogearts (2013) 'Heterogeneity in Victim Participation: A New Perspective on Delivering a Victim Impact Statements'. *European Journal of Criminology*, 10(4): 479–95.

Maruna, Shadd (2001) *Making Good*. Washington DC: APA Press.

Mawby, Rob I. and Sandra Walklate (1994) *Critical Victimology: International Perspectives*. London: Sage Publications.

McGarry, Ross (2015) 'War, Crime and Military Victimhood'. *Critical Criminology: An International Journal*, 23(3): 255–75.

Mendelsohn, Benjamin (1963) 'The Origins of the Doctrine of Victimology'. *Excerpta Criminologica*, 3: 239–45.

——. (1974) 'Victimology and the Technical and Social Sciences: A Call for the Establishment of Victimology Clinics', in Israel Drapkin and Emily Viano (eds), *Victimology: A New Focus*. Lexington: D. C. Heath, pp. 25–35.

Miers, David (1989) 'Positivist Victimology: A Critique, Part 1'. *International Review of Victimology*, 1 (1)1–29.

Miller, Jody (2010) 'Gender and Victimization Risk among Young Women in Gangs', in Paul Cromwell (ed.), *In Their Own Words: Criminals on Crime*, 5th edn. Oxford: Oxford University Press, pp. 324–37.

Millman, Marcia (1976) 'She Did it All for Love: A Feminist View of the Sociology of Deviance', in Marcia Millman and Rosabeth M. Kanter (eds), *Another Voice: Feminist Perspectives on Social Life and Social Science*. New York: Octagon Books, pp. 251–79.

Mills, Charles Wright (1959) *The Sociological Imagination*. New York: Oxford University Press.

Ministry of Defence (2009) 'Op Telic Casualty and Fatality Tables'. Available at: webarchive.nationalarchives.gov.uk/20121026065214/http://www.mod.uk/NR/rdonlyres/7E86BD05-D4FF-4677-97AA-CCFBDCFE4E34/0/optelic_31jul09.pdf.

Plummer, Ken (1983) *Documents of Life: An Introduction to the Problems and Literature of a Humanistic Method*. London: George Allen & Unwin.

——. (2001) 'The Call of Life Stories in Ethnographic Research', in Paul Atkinson, Amanda Coffey, Sara Delamont, John Lofland and Lyn Lofland (eds), *Handbook of Ethnography*. London: Sage Publications, pp. 395–406.

Quinney, Richard (1972) 'Who is the Victim?' *Criminology*, 10: 314–23.

Reed-Danahay, Deborah (2001) 'Autobiography, Intimacy and Ethnography', in Paul Atkinson, Amanda Coffey, Sara Delamont, John Lofland and Lyn Lofland (eds), *Handbook of Ethnography*. London: Sage Publications, pp. 407–25.

Rock, Paul (2001) 'Symbolic Interactionism and Ethnography', in Paul Atkinson, Amanda Coffey, Sara Delamont, John Lofland and Lyn Lofland (eds), *Handbook of Ethnography*. London: Sage Publications, pp. 29–38.

Sampson, Robert J. and John H. Laub (1993) *Crime in the Making: Pathways and Turning Points through Life*. Cambridge: Harvard University Press.

——. (1997) 'A Life-Course Theory of Cumulative Disadvantage and the Stability of Delinquency', in Terence P. Thornberry (ed.), *Developmental Theories of Crime and Delinquency: Advances in Criminological Theory, Volume 7*. New Brunswick, NJ: Transaction, pp. 133–61.

Shaw, Clifford R. (1930/1966) *The Jack-Roller: A Delinquent Boy's Own Story*. Chicago: University of Chicago Press.

Spalek, Basia (2006) *Crime Victims: Theory, Policy and Practice*. Basingstoke: Palgrave Macmillan.

Stanley, Liz (1992) *The Auto/biographical I*. Manchester: Manchester University Press.

——. (1993) 'On Auto/Biography in Sociology'. *Sociology*, 27(1): 41–52.

Sutherland, Edwin H. (1937/1956) *The Professional Thief, by a Professional Thief*. Chicago: University of Chicago Press.

Thomas, William I. and Florian Znaniecki (1918) *The Polish Peasant in America and Europe: Monograph of an Immigrant Group, Volume I: Primary Group Organization*. Boston: Gorham Press.

Thrasher, Frederic (1927) *The Gang: A Study of 1,313 Gangs in Chicago*. Chicago: University of Chicago Press.

Van Dijk, Jan J. M. and Patricia Mayhew (1993) *Criminal Victimisation in the Industrialised World: Key Findings of the 1989 and 1992 International Crime Survey*. Amsterdam: Directorate for Crime Prevention/Ministry of Justice. Available at: www.unicri.it/services/library_documentation/publications/icvs/publications/04_industr_countries.pdf.

Van Dijk, Jan J. M., Robert Manchin, John van Kesteren, Gegerly Hideg and Sami Nevala (2005) *The Burden of Crime in the EU: Research Report: A Comparative Analysis of the European Survey of Crime and Safety in Europe (EU ICS)*. Brussels: European Commission. Available at: www.unicri.it/services/library_documentation/publications/icvs/publications/EUICS_-_The_Burden_of_Crime_in_the_EU.pdf.

Von Hentig, Hans (1940) 'Remarks on the Interaction of Perpetrator and Victim'. *Journal of Criminal Law and Criminology*, 31(3): 303–9.

——. (1948) *The Criminal and His Victim*. Hamden: Archon Books.

Wakeman, Stephen (2014) 'Fieldwork, Biography and Emotion: Doing Criminological Autoethnography'. *British Journal of Criminology*, 54(5): 705–21.

Walklate, Sandra (1989) *Victimology: The Victim and the Criminal Justice Process*. London: Unwin Hyman.

——. (2006) 'Changing the Boundaries of the "Victim" in Restorative Justice: So Who is the Victim Now?', in Dennis Sullivan and Larry Tifft (eds), *Handbook of Restorative Justice: A Global Perspective*. Abingdon: Routledge, pp. 273–85.

——. (2007a) *Imagining the Victim of Crime*. Maidenhead: Open University Press.

——. (2007b) 'Men, Victims and Crime', in Pamela Davies, Peter Francis, and Chris Greer (eds), *Victims, Crime and Society*. London: Sage Publications, pp. 142–64.

Walklate, Sandra and Ross McGarry (2015) 'Competing for the "Trace": The Legacies of War's Violences', in Sandra Walklate and Ross McGarry (eds), *Criminology and War: Transgressing the Borders.* Abingdon: Routledge, pp. 180–97.

Wengraf, Tom (2001) *Qualitative Research Interviewing.* London: Sage Publications.

Whyte, William Foote (1943) *Street Corner Society: The Social Structure of the Italian Slum.* Chicago: University of Chicago Press.

Wilkins, Ruth (1993) 'Taking it Personally: A Note on Emotion and Autobiography'. *Sociology*, 27(1): 93–100.

Wolfgang, Martin F. (1958) 'Victim Precipitated Criminal Homicide'. *Journal of Criminal Law, Criminology and Police Science*, 48(1): 1–11.

Young, Jock (2011) *The Criminological Imagination.* Cambridge: Polity Press.

# 7 Doing visual criminology

## Learning from documentary, journalism and sociology

*Eamonn Carrabine*

## Introduction

Across the social sciences, there has been a resurgence of interest in visual methods, which has been accompanied by a rise in scholarship on visual culture that has now established itself as an exciting and expanding intellectual field. In criminology, while there is a rich tradition of research on 'crime and the media', specific attention to the *visual*, or indeed on the role and place of the *image* in crime, in crime control and in criminal justice has long been lacking. This omission is particularly surprising given just how deep-seated the cultural fascination with the iconography of crime and punishment is in the popular imagination. Of course, there have been some significant interventions in recent years, including Katherine Biber's (2007) *Captive Images*, Judith Resnick and Dennis Curtis' (2011) *Representing Justice*, Jonathan Finn's (2009) *Capturing the Criminal Image* and Alison Young's (2005) *Judging the Image*, which have each made ambitious attempts to understand the power of representation and bring new ways of thinking to bear in the discipline. Today images are everywhere, and they have a profound impact on our sense of ourselves as 'modern' (Jervis 1998). Indeed, the term 'ocularcentralism' was coined to describe a world saturated by visual experiences and the privileging of vision in Western philosophy and social theory (Jay 1993).

In criminology, Keith Hayward (2010: 1) too has made the point that the West is 'suffused with images and increasingly images of crime' in his opening essay to an edited collection exploring the multifaceted ways in which crime is constructed visually. Yet he goes on to insist:

> It is not just a case of image proliferation – contemporary society's keen sense of the visual demands that images also be both mutable and malleable. Here the 'logic of speed' . . . meets liquidity of form, as images bleed from one medium to the next. Uploaded and downloaded, copied and cross-posted, Flicker-ed, Facebook-ed and PhotoShop-ped, the image today is as much about porosity and manipulation as it is about fixity and representation. This, of course, poses a question: what does the term 'image' actually mean under contemporary conditions? (Hayward 2010: 1)

This is a vital question, and Hayward highlights how the distinction between representation and seeing has become increasingly blurred and is especially prominent in the 'spectacle' of crime and punishment as it has developed since the birth of modernity, which is indelibly tied to the rise of a mass culture of spectatorship (Carney 2010). In this chapter I explore what it is to do visual criminology under such circumstances, which involves using images for social science purposes under these conditions of liquid modernity and opening up criminology to 'disciplinary outsiders, heretic ideas and imaginative methodologies' (Walklate and Jacobsen, Introduction to this volume).

The challenge then is to construct an approach that can do justice to both the power of images in social life and their place in social research, and it is to such matters that we now turn. There are now several accounts of how to conduct research with visual materials and they each survey the different ways in which images have been used to understand the world (some recent examples include Harper 2012; Rose 2012; Pink 2013). Anthropologists and sociologists, for example, have used photographs from the beginning as both disciplines began to explore societies near and distant, but they gradually fell out of favour as they were deemed too subjective, unsystematic and eccentric. As Howard S. Becker explains:

> Sociologists lost interest in reformist uses of photography as they shifted their attention from reform to scientific generalization . . . and very few photographs accompanied sociological articles and books. Anthropologists complained that their colleagues made photographs that were no different from ones tourists made of exotic places and that served no better purpose than those amateur works. (Becker 2004: 193–4)

To take the example of sociology, the ties with photography were established very early on, and practitioners sought to promote social reform by exposing the injustices associated with the modern age. Crusading journalists like Jacob Riis photographed the crushing slum poverty in New York in the 1880s (an undertaking pioneered several decades earlier in British cities by a number of different urban explorers), while Lewis Hine's involvement with the sustained campaign against child labour is often said to have led to the passage of laws ending child slavery. Between 1907 and 1918, he travelled around the US, taking over 5,000 photographs of children at work, often tricking the managers, to create what he termed a 'photo story', where words and pictures combine to produce a powerful, non-linear narrative (Marien 2010: 207). At around the same time, early editions of the *American Journal of Sociology* routinely included photographs to accompany the 'muckraking' reformist articles it published during the first 15 years of its existence. This tradition was much later reclaimed and reworked by Howard S. Becker (1974, 1982/2008, 1995) across a series of influential publications that argued for a more ambitious use of visual material to explore society.

So far I have largely been discussing visual methods as they have developed within specific academic disciplinary contexts. However, it is important to recognize how photography developed in diverse ways from the outset, not least since the emergence of criminology itself has some very close connections with these regimes of representation. Of course, Cesare Lombroso's criminal anthropology will be the most well-known example, to criminologists at least, of how photography was used to classify bodies into distinguishable types in the nineteenth century. Alan Sekula (1989) and John Tagg (1988) have each argued that the photographs taken for police and prison records should be understood in relation to the boom in portraiture, whereby people were encouraged to measure the respectable citizen against the criminal body and visualize social difference. They both present forceful Foucauldian understandings of the institutional power at work in police and prison photography. However, they have been criticized for not considering a broader range of photographic practices, and for ignoring the gendered dynamics at work in the collection, exchange and display of photographs in domestic settings (Smith 1998; di Bello 2007). As Gillian Rose (2012: 234) suggests, these nineteenth-century female photographers were creating images that did not 'replicate the surveillant gaze of the police mug-shot or the family studio portrait' and in doing so they 'thwart the classifying gaze by strategies such as blurred focus, collage and over-exposure'. This more recent historical research presents the possibility of a richer understanding of the uses of photography and the practices that accompany it.

Consequently, it is helpful to identify three distinctive, but overlapping, genres that can help sharpen the discussion. Documentary photography, photojournalism and visual sociology all see it as 'their main business to describe what has not yet been described' and 'to tell the big news' in their respective explorations of society (Becker 1974: 3). Each has different uses and diverse histories, but the boundaries between them are occasionally blurred, so considering them as distinctive genres will help shed light on what they are trying to achieve in particular contexts. There then follows a discussion of what visual criminology can learn from each by concentrating on some contemporary projects that speak to crime, deviance and punishment in powerful ways. However, visual analysis should never be an end in and of itself, but must always have the goal of social and political explanation firmly in sight.

## Documentary photography

One immediate difficulty facing any attempt at defining 'documentary photography' is that practically every photograph is a document of something, and from the beginning the medium itself has largely been understood through its capacity to record an objective and faithful image of events with an unprecedented authority. It has even been claimed that to most nineteenth-century minds, 'the very notion of documentary photography would have seemed tautological' as photography itself was regarded as 'innately and inescapably performing a documentary function' (Solomon-Godeau 1991: 170). The term 'document' means 'evidence', and has been traced to the medieval term *documentum*, which referred to an official paper providing a form of evidence 'not to be questioned' and 'a truthful account backed by the authority of the law' (Clarke 1997: 145). The particular magic of photography lay in its ability to capture a moment in time and faithfully record this reality in a two-dimensional space of representation. Although all photos are documentary in the sense that they have an indexical relationship with whatever was in front of the lens when the image was made, we can make some broad distinctions between photographs intended for 'public' or 'private' viewing, and those which are 'caught' in 'candid' moments as opposed to those which are 'arranged' in some 'covertly contrived' ways (Goffman 1979: 14). A 'documentary' photograph, however, is best defined by the use to which it is put, or asked to perform, rather than by some essential or innate quality of the image itself (Snyder 1984).

A further way out of the definitional difficulties is to situate documentary in relation to a distinctive kind of social investigation and it was this practice that John Grierson had in mind when he coined the term 'documentary' in 1926. Although he was using it to describe a form of film making that would have the power of both poetry and prophecy, replacing the escapist fantasies of Hollywood cinema with a bolder vision of what the medium could offer, the term was quickly applied to certain kinds of photography, popular literature, radio programmes, arts movements and social science writing. Indeed, the documentary movement would flourish in the 1930s and combined both physical activity (constructing a text, object or image) and ethical task (explaining the truth of the world), which are tied together in his formulation of documentary as 'the creative treatment of actuality' (Grierson 1966: 147). The juxtaposition between the creative (artistic licence) and the actual (reality as it is) lies at the heart of the tradition and has been the cause of much controversy.

Despite being a 'genre of actuality', the main purpose of documentary, as it developed in the 1930s, was to 'educate one's feelings', as practitioners concluded that while we 'understand a historical document intellectually', we also 'understand a human document emotionally' (Stott 1973: 8) and so the affective came to be prioritized in the movement. As Roy Stryker, another leading figure, put it:

> Truth is the objective of the documentary attitude . . . A good documentary should tell not only what a place or a thing or a person *looks* like, but it must also tell the audience what it should *feel* like to be an actual witness to the scene. (Cited in Phillips 2009:65, emphasis in original)

The tension between fact and feeling is further underlined by the didactic function of the tradition, where the combination of the claim to transcend subjective bias with a desire to convince spectators of the need for social change became an essential feature of the movement. As one of most influential critics of documentary has put it, it is 'a practice with a past' and how it came to 'represent the social conscience of liberal sensibility presented in visual imagery' (Rosler 1981/2004: 176) suggests a need to situate it in its historical context. In revisiting this past, it is clear that photography became bound up with social advocacy and exposing injustice in ways that had close ties with journalism and sociology almost from the outset.

All the characteristic photographic practices now associated with the documentary form were well established by the 1860s: alongside war images, historical sites, sacred places and exotic natives, each became the subjects of the lens as colonial empire expanded, while other practitioners travelled into 'the abyss' to explore those dark, dangerous and ungovernable places in which the urban poor lived (Carrabine 2012). Thomas Annan in Glasgow, John Thomson in London and Jacob Riis in New York are examples of the latter, where explorations of slum conditions in the modern metropolis were driven by an uneasy mix of public curiosity and social concern. Their approaches differed from the sheer sensationalism of much of the journalistic attention given to immigrant neighbourhoods and street life in the burgeoning 'yellow press' of the time.[1] Instead, a sense of social injustice pervades the early documentary photographs and the images seek to expose wrongs in an effort to prompt social reform. There is a clear moral vision at work, where the poor are divided into distinct categories – the deserving and undeserving – or into typological figures of suffering. They strongly spoke to the deep-seated 'worry that the ravages of poverty – crime, immorality, prostitution, disease, radicalism – would threaten the health and security of polite society, and their appeals were often meant to awaken the self-interest of the privileged' (Rosler 1981/2004: 177). In doing so, they tended to depict their subjects as passive victims of social conditions, yet playing on the danger of (and the desire to know) the Other.

The 1930s saw large-scale documentary projects like the Farm Security Administration's (FSA) Information Division, which eventually produced over 80,000 images of the human suffering endured in the Great Depression in the US. The photographers include Walker Evans, Dorothea Lange, Russell Lee, Arthur Rothstein and Ben Shahn, among many others, who strove for advocacy and reform in an effort to engender support for New Deal relief policies. As commentators subsequently noted, 'it was images of the "worthy" as opposed to the "unworthy" poor that were promoted' (Solomon-Godeau 1991: 179). The dominant tone is that the victims of the Depression are ordinary people, who have fallen on hard times, where poverty and misfortune are personalized and individualized, rather than the structural product of a breakdown in economic, political and social relations – a view put in the following way:

> In the liberal documentary, poverty and oppression are almost invariably equated with misfortunes caused by natural disasters: Causality is vague, blame is not assigned, fate cannot be overcome . . . Like photos of children in pleas for donations to international charity organizations, liberal documentary implores us to look in the face of deprivation and weep (and maybe send money . . . ). (Rosler 1981/2004: 179)

This critique of the politics of representation at work in documentary is an important one and has often been repeated since the 1970s, yet the work of the FSA has endured because it sought not only to inform, but also to move us through a dramatic visual language.

Lewis Hine is arguably the quintessential socially concerned documentary photographer, and his work from the end of the nineteenth century up to the 1930s embodies the achievements, limitations and contradictions of using images in the pursuit of social reform. His work rejected fine art photography and he declared himself a 'sociological' photographer, with considerable care taken to preserve his subjects' dignity, in well-crafted images conveying the complexities of working-class life (Clarke 1997: 147). Much has been made of how his images never exploit, but always speak to the exploitative conditions in which the poor live. Howard S. Becker (1995: 7), for example, notes how in a classic 'image of "Leo, 48 inches high, 8 years old picks up bobbins at fifteen cents a day", in which a young boy stands next to the machines which have, we almost surely conclude, stunted his growth'. It was while working for social welfare organizations that Hines perfected his technique of the 'photo story', which combined word and pictures in arresting non-linear narratives published in journals and magazines read by professional and volunteer social workers.

## Photojournalism

The images Hine produced were similar to those made by journalists, but were less preoccupied with narrating current events or illustrating news stories, and instead the approach anticipates the 'golden age' of photojournalism (1930s–1950s) when 'reportage' became a staple of newspaper and magazine coverage. Indeed, the rapid expansion of the market during this period, when magazines like *Look* and *Life* in the US, *Illustrated* and *Picture Post* in Britain and *Vu* in France gave outlets for influential photographers like W. Eugene Smith, Robert Capa and Henri Cartier-Bresson to have their work commissioned and published. These mass-circulation picture magazines emerged between the wars, initially in Germany, and then quickly spread to other countries. Using innovative juxtapositions of image and text, the term 'photojournalism' came to describe the new practice. Yet it is important to note that photography has a long and troubled history in Western journalism and Karin Becker (1990/2003) has charted some of these dynamics across distinct types of publication. She highlights how it was in the tabloid newspapers of the 1920s that large, eye-catching photographs of crime, violence, disaster and society scandals came to prominence – telling stories quickly, through sensational pictures and short captions. Press historians see this as a nadir for journalism and the 'abundant use of pictorial material' was regarded 'as conclusive proof both of declining literary standards and a nefarious plan to exploit hopelessly naïve and illiterate people' (Carlebach 1997: 145). If the tabloid press undermined the credibility of the photograph as a medium for serious news, then it was the simultaneous rise of picture magazines that established the genre of the photo essay, where images and text could be spread out as running narratives across several pages.

Assignments from these publications were especially coveted and the magazines became a global phenomenon. With their distinctive styles and expert photography, they underlined the importance of the 'camera as witness', where the photojournalist takes pictures to fulfil an editorial requirement and 'answer the essential journalistic questions: who, what, where, when, and why' (Gefter 2009: 123). By the 1970s, their popularity had fallen, with the likes of *Life* and *Look* closing, partly as a result of the rise of television and changes in press ownership, while new kinds of colour newspaper supplement appeared that were mainly led by advertising and lifestyle features. As the business of journalism has changed, so photojournalists have had to adapt to new constraints and find fresh outlets to pursue their practice. Indeed, a case can be made that socially conscious photojournalism has flourished independently of the print media for decades now, where the pictures are more likely to be seen on the walls of galleries, museum exhibitions and elegant books than in newspapers and magazines. Photojournalism retains a somewhat elevated status and there are a number of elements contributing to this:

> the formal structural properties of the ideal photo essay; the determination of the single photograph as an idealized moment – fetishized as 'the decisive moment' either alone or at the centre of the essay; and the reconstruction of the photojournalist as artist. (Becker 1990/2003: 297)

In many respects Margaret Bourke-White is the prime example of the photojournalist, chronicling rural poverty in *You Have Seen Their Faces* (1937) and those excluded from the 'American Dream'. During the Second World War, she photographed the German bombing of Moscow, was the first woman to fly in an air raid, and sent back harrowing pictures of the Nazi concentration camp at Buchenwald. In addition, she insisted on documenting the 'buffalo soldiers', so-called military units composed of all-black soldiers during combat in Italy (Marien 2003: 287).

War is a major subject for photographers and the Second World War effaced the distinction between civilian and combatant to the extent that since then, those caught up in the conflict have received as much attention as the soldiers themselves. Indeed, it is often said that the stream of horrific images from Vietnam provided normative criticism of the war. The 1972 photograph of a naked Vietnamese girl running away from a village just napalmed by US planes is one of the most distressing images of the era and brought home the terror of the indiscriminate killing. Robert Capa's statement that 'if your pictures aren't good enough, you're not close enough' (cited in Marien 2003: 303) has long been the credo of the war photographer rushing off to battle to capture the death and destruction. It was the Spanish Civil War (1936–9) that was the first to be covered by corps of professional photographers from the frontline, and Capa's photograph of a Republican soldier 'shot' by his camera at the same time as bullets rip through his crumpling body is one of the defining images of the war. As Susan Sontag (2003: 20) explains, it 'is a shocking image, and that is the point'. Or as Peter Howe, a former picture editor at *Life*, put it, 'the job of the photojournalist is to witness those things that people don't want to think about. When they're doing the job right, they are taking photographs that people don't want to publish by their very nature' (cited in Lowe 2014: 211). Alongside this socially concerned photography,[2] which is dedicated to bearing witness and political critique, there remained a mass market for sensationalized images of working-class life and the urban condition. Indeed, the picturing of 'news' was absolutely central to the development of a global visual economy and one that shows no sign of diminishing in today's digital age.

Among the most infamous photographers exploiting this appetite was Arthur Fellig, more well known by his nickname Weegee, who in graphic black-and-white photography captured the gruesome detail of gang executions, car crashes and tenement fires that he then sold to the New York City tabloid editors. Such brutal pictures became the staple images of the mass-circulation press in the 1930s and effectively changed journalistic practices overnight (Lee and Meyer, 2008). His bestselling book *Naked City* (1945/2002) was the first collection of his tabloid photography and was published in the same year that the Museum of Modern Art held an exhibition of his work. It has been noted how his images 'may appear as realistic representations of the underside of New York urban life', but they also 'convey complex ideas of guilt and voyeurism' (Blinder 2009: 9).

In a nuanced essay, Phil Carney (2010: 26) situates Weegee in a broader account exploring the relationships between photographic spectacle, predation and paparazzi, suggesting he was 'the first photographer to stalk and ensnare his prey with stealth and speed', establishing practices that would become increasingly popular as a market devoted to publishing candid images of celebrities' unguarded moments came to prominence. These 'stolen images' undermined what a 'good' photograph should look like, with their 'awkward composition, harsh contrasts and uncertain focus' (Becker 1990/2003: 301) and are now an integral feature of tabloid celebrity culture. Weegee provides an important bridge from the conventional topics of documentary photography into the new directions taken in the post-war period, when the 'new' documentarists began exploring more 'subjective' approaches to image making, which re-opened important debates about photography's complex relationship with reality (Carrabine 2012). Yet it is important to note that crime photographers are rarely able to capture the criminal act itself and represent the act by focusing on its 'after-effects and constituent parts' so that 'weapons, suspects, victims, locations, accomplices, and bloody crime sites are usually photographed separately, often at some remove in time and space from the crime itself' (Straw 2015: 139). The resulting visual coverage is then fragmented and overlaps to an extent with official forensic photography, but tends to draw from a fairly stable repertoire of disparate images with varying degrees of documentary credibility and journalistic value.

## Visual sociology

For much of the twentieth century, sociology has shown little interest in the use of images, and remains dominated by words and figures. Yet, visual illustration was a central feature of the investigations of urban life pioneered in the work of nineteenth-century social commentators like Henry Mayhew in his studies of *London Labour and the London Poor* (1851–62), while Cesare Lombroso famously used images to highlight the criminal nature of certain bodies, and social reformers used photographs as both illustration and evidence. It has been noted that the *American Journal of Sociology* routinely published images in articles pressing for 'social amelioration' from the beginning, but once Albion Small took over the editorship of the journal in 1914, photographs disappeared from its pages and were replaced by 'causal analysis,

high-level generalisations and statistical reports' (Stasz 1979: 133). The clear implication is that images are too unscientific and undermine the intellectual credibility of
the discipline, which is bound up with a more general disdain for mixing advocacy
with scholarly objectivity as academic sociology took shape in American universities in the early twentieth century (Turner 2014). It is this attempt to make sociology
a science that would come to define the discipline and was the target of C. Wright
Mills (1959) in his famous indictment of the then-dominant positivist methods and
functionalist theorizing.

Although the use of visual material has remained a marginal activity in the
discipline, there have been some significant interventions that have looked at photographs for their sociological value. One important example is Pierre Bourdieu's
(1965/1990) collaborative work on photography, which he sees as an ordinary,
'middlebrow art form' through which class taste is pictured in family snapshots,
holiday souvenirs and wedding portraits. In Bourdieu it is a practice that is sociologically important because it both *portrays* the social world and it *betrays* the
choices made by the photographer. He explains:

> While everything would lead one to expect that this activity, which has no
> traditions and makes no demands, would be delivered over to the anarchy
> of individual improvisation, it appears that there is nothing more regulated
> and conventional than photographic practice and amateur photographs: in
> the occasions which give rise to photography, such as the objects, places
> and people photographed or the very composition of the pictures, everything
> seems to obey implicit canons which are very generally imposed and which
> informed amateurs or aesthetes notice as such, but only to denounce them
> as examples of poor taste or technical clumsiness. (Bourdieu 1965/1990: 7)

The book demonstrated how a cultural practice like photography, which in principle was open to almost everyone and had not yet acquired an elaborate set of
aesthetic judgment criteria, could still sustain social hierarchies and class divisions.
The work opened up the questions of what can be learned from analysing the photographs people take and what is it that people do with them – revealing how taste
is far from being an inimitable personal faculty, but is instead an essentially social
phenomenon structuring perceptions of the world. Recent research has focused on
how class, gender, place and identity shape amateur photographic practice (Rose
2004), while the conventions informing the 'digital turn' in distinctive communities and their legitimation has become the focus of attention as photography has
become ever more ubiquitous in everyday life (Murray 2008; Hand 2012).

Few sociologists have done more than Howard S. Becker to rework and
reclaim the importance of the visual in the discipline. His essay on 'Photography
and Sociology' (Becker 1974) highlights how both are interested in social problems and exotic subcultures, while many photographers have been drawn towards
capturing the ambience of urban life in ways that parallel the sociological thinking of Simmel and his subsequent followers. These arguments are developed in
his edited collection *Exploring Society Photographically* (Becker 1981), which

originally accompanied an exhibition of 12 distinctive projects exploring social worlds. It begins with Gregory Bateson and Margaret Mead's (1942) study of *Balinese Character: A Photographic Analysis*, which is now regarded as a key intervention in anthropology, as it moved well beyond what were the conventional ethnographic uses of visual material. By presenting the images in large, detailed sequences, the intention was to capture those aspects of a culture that words could not. Other examples include the photographer Euan Duff's exploration of the 'Working World', which examines how the nature of work impacts on other aspects of life, and builds on his earlier collaborative work with the sociologist Dennis Marsden in their study of the unemployed in *Workless* (Marsden and Duff 1975). Also included is a selection of images from Bruce Jackson's (1977) *Killing Time* taken from Cummins Prison Farm in Arkansas. A Professor of English, Jackson has been documenting prison life[3] across various media since the early 1960s, and his other work includes *A Thief's Primer* (1969), *Portraits from a Drawer* (2009) and most recently *In This Timeless Time: Living and Dying on Death Row in America* (with Diane Christian (2012)), which clearly speaks to criminological issues in compelling and provocative ways. Indeed, imprisonment has proved to be a particularly important site for photographers and the website and blog at www.prisonphotography.org lists some 120 professional practitioners who have sought to convey the pains of confinement in visually striking ways. In a subsequent essay, Becker (1995: 9) maintained that there is much to be gained from reading photographs against their generic grain in order to explore how 'context gives images meaning'.

The last foundational text I want to discuss is Erving Goffman's (1979) *Gender Advertisements*, which reproduces a large number of commercial advertisements and uses them as visual data. As the title suggests, the book addresses how gender relations are displayed in them and he explains they work by exploiting a specific set of social conventions:

> The magical ability of the advertiser to use a few models and props to evoke a life-like scene of his [sic] own choosing is not primarily due to the art and technology of commercial photography; it is due primarily to those institutionalized arrangements in social life which allow strangers to glimpse the lives of persons they pass, and to the readiness of all of us to switch at any moment from dealing with the real world to participating in make-believe ones. (Goffman 1979: 23)

His discussion draws on his previous work deploying dramaturgical metaphors to examine social interaction and he suggests that advertisements can be productively compared to stage scenes, where the ritual displays in them tell us much about gendered social relations in society at large. Much of the book is organized to indicate the various ways in which gender inequalities are enacted through the sheer attention to detail. The section on the 'ritualization of subordination', for example, has an account of how 'women frequently, men very infrequently, are posed in a display of the "bashful knee bend"' (Goffman 1979: 45) and the accompanying array of visual evidence featuring this form of deferent gesture gives a social scientific understanding of how gender differences are expressed. The book provides both a nuanced study of the gender politics displayed in print advertisements and an exploration of the interaction rituals governing conduct in everyday life, and is justly regarded as one of the best examples of visual sociology.

Some of these issues have been imaginatively taken up the photographer and documentary film maker Lauren Greenfield (2002), who has explored the various 'body projects' young women pursue in light of the exhibitionist tendencies of contemporary American femininity and the difficulties of living up to the expectations posed by popular culture in their daily grooming rituals. In some respects this is indicative of a post-feminist sensibility based on sexual confidence and autonomy, where 'raunch culture' is understood as a shift 'from an external, male judging gaze to a self-policing narcissistic gaze' in a new sexualized culture that is changing the boundaries between public and private spheres (Gill 2010: 103). Here new forms of 'public intimacy' are developing in a 'striptease culture', which is preoccupied with self-revelation and confessional exposure in ever louder and more mediatized ways (McNair 2002). Indeed, the phrase 'oversharing' has come to describe the phenomenon where 'too' much is revealed about ourselves on social media through the constant documenting and display of private lives to others (Agger 2015). Of course, much of this is taking place in 'acts of visual communication on a scale that is unprecedented' (Hand 2012: 194) and the full implications of this transformation have yet to be addressed. However, I now want to turn to some recent work exploring similar avenues as Greenfield, which uses a photographic project to dissect consumer society, but focuses on explicitly criminological themes and topics.

## Doing visual criminology

There is a long and influential line of critique on photographic representation that is deeply suspicious of how the camera aestheticizes all that it pictures. It features in the writing of Allan Sekula, Martha Rosler and Susan Sontag, and can be traced back to Walter Benjamin's (1934/1982) dire warnings on photography's ability to beautify suffering. What each thinker shares is the conviction that 'aestheticizing suffering is inherently both artistically and politically reactionary, a way of mistreating the subject and inviting passive consumption, narcissistic appropriation, condescension, or even sadism on the part of viewers' (Reinhardt 2007: 14). Elsewhere I have described how some contemporary practitioners have responded to the complaint that much photojournalism and social documentary exploits the other and reinforces the differences between the superior and inferior (Carrabine 2012, 2014, 2015). During the 1970s and 1980s, the very practice of documentary critique came under sustained critique, when the movement was charged with exploiting the other and 'truth claims' were debunked as stage-managed fictions. Under these and other criticisms, documentary fell out of fashion, but more recently there has been a resurgence of interest in the genre. Contemporary practitioners seem to be less troubled by terms like 'truth', 'evidence' and 'reality', which is not to say that they are blind to the way in which photographs are constructed, but are more attuned to them as 'carefully fabricated cultural objects' (Price 2009: 107).

One recent development has been the turn to making documentary-style pictures that appear devoid of 'any significant or identifiable subject matter' (Batchen 2012: 233). An example of such an approach is the work of the French photographer Sophie Ristelhueber, who has paid particular attention to the ruins and traces left by war and the scars it leaves on the landscape. In her series 'WB (West Bank)', she 'refused to photograph the great separation wall that embodies the policy of a state and the media icon of the "Middle Eastern problem"'; rather, she took photographs of the small roadblocks the Israelis had built on 'country roads with whatever means available' and from such an elevated 'viewpoint that transforms the blocks of the barriers into elements of the landscape' (Rancière 2011:104). This more allusive approach is also exemplified in the work of the Chilean artist Alfredo Jaar, who has produced several works on the Rwandan genocide of 1994, none of which depicts a single instant of the carnage. Across a series of pieces he has explored the limits of representation, exposing media culture's inability to see and stop the slaughter. Likewise, the failure of Western governments to intervene in the conflict in the former Yugoslavia is a theme explored in Simon Norfolk's *Bleed* (2005), which revisits the frozen landscapes of eastern Bosnia where thousands were massacred, and the almost abstract images become powerful allegories for the secrets buried beneath the ice. For Norfolk, it was crucial to know the exact location of the gravesites in order to give the work a forensic credibility and visual power. As he explains, 'it's even more important when the picture uses metaphors; if the detective work was poor then the whole project would unravel quickly. The only way you can come at it in such a symbolic way is if you are one hundred percent sure that here are the locations – otherwise it's a weak, feeble approach' (cited in Lowe 2014: 225). The tension between the arresting beauty of the images and the fact that something terrible is contained in them enables him to make a strong moral argument about the nature of guilt.

A rather different exponent of the method is Bruno Serralongue, who in his *Fait Divers* series traced crime and accident scenes as they were described in the regional newspaper *Nice-Matin*. Working between late 1993 and April 1995, he would take pictures of the deserted scene in and around Nice, France, where only very recently something terrible had happened. Although the photos 'look too suspiciously banal' on their own, once they are accompanied by text below the image, the effect is disconcerting and is an ironic comment on the 'role of the photographer-as-detective', albeit 'one who always arrives at the scene too late' (Van Gelder and West 2011: 159). Others too have become preoccupied with conveying traumatic events that for various reasons have left hardly any visual traces. This is especially the case in Antonio Olmos' (2013) efforts to photograph all the sites where murders occurred in London, England, between 1 January 2011 and 31 December 2012, which are collected in his profoundly moving book *Landscape of Murder*. The sites were visited within a few days of the crime, and the images not only capture fleeting moments of grief (huddled friends, wilting flowers, messages of condolence) and remnants of forensic investigation (fluttering police tape, scattered traffic cones), but occasionally nothing at all remains to indicate that a life has ended violently at the site. The book is not so much about violence and death, but is rather a way of seeing place and giving memory to mostly forgotten events, and in doing so presents a very different portrait of the city. In this it shares much with the genre of 'aftermath photography' and the 'forensic turn', where there is an acknowledgement that the camera is a 'secondary witness' that does not depict the trauma itself, but rather the spaces in which it occurred and the traces left behind, so that the 'act of secondary witnessing takes on an overly moral character as the witness is actively choosing to make their statement about the past rather than passively being there at the time of the occurrence' (Lowe 2014: 217).

The question of photography's roles as a credible eyewitness is taken up by Taryn Simon (2003) in her work with the Innocence Project in the US, which was established in 1992 and primarily uses DNA testing to overturn wrongful convictions. As she explains:

> The primary cause of wrongful conviction was mistaken identification. A victim or eyewitness identifies a suspect perpetrator through law enforcement's use of photographs and lineups. These identifications rely on the assumption of precise visual memory. But through exposure to composite sketches, mugshots, Polaroids, and lineups, eyewitness memory can change. Police officers and prosecutors influence memory both unintentionally and intentionally – through the ways in which they conduct the identification process. They can shape, and even generate, what comes to be known as eyewitness testimony. (Simon, Neufeld and Scheck 2003: 7)

Images in these cases were deeply implicated in transforming innocent citizens into violent criminals and securing their convictions. In 2002 Simon photographed a number of these men at locations that had profound significance in their wrongful imprisonment – often the scene of crime. This particular place is both arbitrary and crucial; it is somewhere they had never been, yet changed their lives forever. The haunting narrative portraits she produced highlights photography's ability to blur truth and fiction and the devastating consequences this can have. Each photograph is accompanied by commentary from the two lawyers who co-founded the Innocence Project, Peter Neufeld and Barry Scheck (who both also worked on the O.J. Simpson defence team in 1995), and it quickly becomes apparent that there remain many still falsely imprisoned because of failings in the legal system. Her images directly confront the contradiction between truth and justice, and in them we see a 'mixture of anger, resignation, and fear in the photographed images of the innocents forged by the unimaginable horror of spending a decade or more in prison because they happened to be a person of the wrong color or class, in the wrong place, at the wrong time' (Courtney and Lyng 2007: 189).

A different example of this more reflexive approach can be seen in the collabo-ration between anthropologist Phillipe Bourgois and photographer Jeff Schonberg (2009) in their compelling visual ethnography of homelessness and drug addiction in San Francisco. *Righteous Dopefiends* is the result of a ten-year project chroni-cling the suffering, friendships and betrayal that characterize survival among the destitute, while also analysing the structural forces and institutions (police, wel-fare and hospital) that they negotiate in their daily lives. The role of the photos is described in the following way:

> The composition of the images recognizes the politics within aesthetics; they are closely linked to contextual and theoretical analysis. Some photographs provide detailed documentation of material life and the environment. Others were selected primarily to convey mood or to evoke the pains and pleasures of life on the street. Most refer to specific moments described in the sur-rounding pages, but at times they stand in tension with the text to reveal the messiness of real life and the complexity of analytical generalizations. (Bourgois and Schonberg 2009: 11)

The tension between text and image comes especially to the fore as Bourgois the-orizes how forms of institutional violence further weaken the vulnerable, while the photos suggest different kinds of relationship between homeless addicts and those who appear devoted to their care (in public health work and emergency hospital services) via a detailed critique of the dysfunctional US medical sys-tem. These leave open the question of which interpretive framework to follow. As Douglas Harper (2012: 54) suggests, this might be because the 'theory best describes the reality of the addicts' world and this cannot be visualized', or per-haps the 'theorist and photographer experienced a different social world', or maybe 'the essences of the culture is a partly contradictory combination of the two.' In any case, the work stands as one of the best recent examples of visual ethnography on explicitly criminological themes and is a clear attempt to repre-sent intimate suffering in ways that acknowledge the politics of representation at work in and across their text.

Other contemporary documentary projects that confront criminological issues in striking visual ways include Richard Ross' (2012) *Juvenile in Justice*, which combines powerful imagery with excerpts from life stories that the young people in custody shared with him.[4] The work builds on his earlier *Architecture of Authority* (2007), a book capturing carceral spaces ranging from the innocuous to the notori-ous, but in such a way that the oppressive structures look strangely inviting and even seductive, to unsettling effect. The pictures encountered include a Montessori pre-school environment through diverse civic spaces (including a Swedish court-room, the Iraqi National Assembly hall and the United Nations) to more ominous manifestations of authority: an interrogation room at Guantánamo, segregation cells at Abu Ghraib and, finally, a capital-punishment execution chamber. A less epic examination of confinement is Jürgen Chill's (2007) study of German prison cells, which are largely unexplored as living spaces. His distinctive approach deploys a central overhead view of what initially looks like a budget hotel room or a university hall of residence, but it slowly becomes apparent that we are looking into a different kind of institutional space. Chill has explained that his method was to talk to prisoners to get to know them a little and explain his project. Then, and only with their permission, he took a series of overhead photographs that were then digitally collaged back in his studio to create the final image with a single view.[5] On one level the photographs provide an intimate insight into how dehumanized spaces are individualized by prisoners, but on another the absence of the inhabitants themselves speaks to the largely anonymous lives prisoners lead.

A somewhat different example of a visual study of prison as a cultural site is Bruce Jackson's (2009) *Pictures from a Drawer*, which uses around 200 discarded prison identification photographs, likely dating from 1915 up to 1940, given to him in 1975 to provide a remarkable account of prisons, portraiture and US social history. As Jackson argues, the function of these photos was not portraiture; rather their function was to 'fold a person into the controlled space of a dossier'. Here, freed from their prison 'jackets' and printed at sizes far larger than their originals, these one-time ID photos have now become portraits. Jackson's restoration transforms what were small bureaucratic artifacts into moving images of real men and women. As he suggests, these photographs are second only to 'coroners' photographs of the newly dead, prisoner identification portraits are perhaps the least merciful, the most disinterested, the most democratic, and the most anonymous portraits of all' (Jackson 2009: 11). Neither the sitters nor the photographers who took them have any interest in the photographs they are making, and they strive only for the literal. Unlike arrest identification photographs, or 'mugshots' as they are often known, the people having their picture taken in the police station face an uncertain future. But in prisoner identification photographs, all possibility is foreclosed, the individuals sitting for them have already been through gaol, through trial and have been unambiguously removed from ordinary life.

By moving from the still-life genre to portraiture, we can how contemporary practitioners are attempting to say something visually new about imprisonment using both 'made' and 'found' images. This brief discussion of a handful of recent examples should demonstrate that the documentary tradition is not only flourishing, but has much to offer a visually informed criminology. Although the genre can be condemned and dismissed for its morbid fascination with human suffering, it also offers new ways of seeing social practices. Despite all the contradictions running through the tradition, the desire to bear witness to the suffering and violence of the age remains paramount, and requires of us to learn new ways of seeing, especially in those places where seeing is not simple and is often hidden from view. Indeed, it is also clear that accompanying this resurgence of interest in using images to tell stories about social worlds, there has also been an emergence of a formidable body of theoretical writing focusing on the ethical and political implications of the visual, working within, around and against the traditions described in this chapter.

## Conclusion

Recent years have seen a substantial wave of theoretical writing on photography by Ariella Azoulay, Judith Butler, Georges Didi-Huberman, Susie Linfield, Jacques Rancière and many others (see Stallybrass 2013 for a collection of this work) that see fresh roles and revaluations of the medium in new social and political situations. Each of these thinkers can help us make sense of contemporary media landscapes and the dynamics of ethical responsibility in them. Azoulay (2008), for example, has made much of the citizenship of photography in her discussion of how the camera is an instrument of considerable political power, arguing that we need to transform our relationship to images from one of passivity and complaint to one of creativity and collaboration. Rancière (2007: 22–31) has drawn an important distinction between three different kinds of image – 'naked', 'ostensive' and 'metaphoric' – in an effort to query the radicalism of art and its emancipatory powers. Elsewhere I have described how Didi-Huberman's (2008) controversial analysis of the few pictures taken from inside the Holocaust provide evidence of the 'crime of crimes' (Carrabine 2014) also reminds us that the attempt to destroy all that documented it was an integral part of the extermination.

Despite their differences, it is clear that Azoulay, Rancière and Didi-Huberman are each striving to enlarge the political imagination and are each emphasizing that images, when used critically and inventively, can enable 'us to think through the essential questions of our time' (Lübecker 2013: 405). A rich strain of theoretical writing has emerged that has taken issue with some of the orthodox positions adopted in the debates surrounding the politics of representation, and it is from them that we have much yet to learn. Although visual social science is nearly as old as photography, it is hard to dispute the view that 'we are really still at the beginning, with a lot of work yet to do' (Becker 2004: 197). The material covered in this chapter should be seen then as offering a few starting points from where the journey can commence, but it promises to be one that opens up exciting, new possibilities for the discipline.

## Notes

1 The term 'yellow press' was coined in the 1890s to describe the sensationalist journalism associated with two New York papers, Joseph Pulitzer's *World* and William Randolph Hearst's *Journal*, which were caught up in an intense rivalry and in their efforts to increase circulation included scare headlines, bold layouts, graphic pictures, comic strips and distinctive use of yellow ink to attract readers.
2 Cornell Capa, younger brother of Robert, coined the term 'concerned photographer' in 1968 to describe work that passionately sought to enlarge understanding and was committed to social justice by producing 'images in which genuine human feeling predominates over commercial cynicism or disinterested formalism' (cited in Gefter 2009: 144).
3 A similar project was at work in Danny Lyon's (1971) extraordinary visual portrait of the Texas prison system in his *Conversations with the Dead*, which alongside photographs of the dehumanizing conditions includes text taken from prison records, convict letters and inmate artwork. Lyon had also worked in the civil rights movement, and the book can be seen as contributing to that activism, while also continuing his interest in outlaw biker subcultures from earlier in the decade (Lyon 1968).

4  For further details, see www.juvenile-in-justice.com.
5  See http://issuu.com/mikecarney/docs/confined_singles.

## References

Agger, Ben (2015) *Oversharing*. London: Routledge.
Azoulay, Ariella (2008) *The Civil Contract of Photography*. New York: Zone Books.
Batchen, Geoffrey (2012) 'Looking Askance', in Geoffrey Batchen, Mick Gidley, Nancy Miller and Jay Prosser (eds), *Picturing Atrocity: Photography in Crisis*, London: Reaktion Books, pp. 227–39.
Bateson, Gregory and Margaret Mead (1942) *Balinese Character: A Photographic Analysis*. New York: New York Academy of Sciences.
Becker, Howard S. (1974) 'Photography and Sociology'. *Studies in the Anthropology of Visual Communication*, 1: 3–26.
——. (1982/2008) *Art Worlds*. Berkeley, CA: University of California Press.
——. (1995) 'Visual Sociology, Documentary Photography and Photojournalism: It's (Almost) All a Matter of Context'. *Visual Sociology*, 10(1–2): 5–14.
——. (2004) 'Afterword: Photography as Evidence, Photographs as Exposition', in Caroline Knowles and Paul Sweetman (eds), *Picturing the Social Landscape: Visual Methods and the Sociological Imagination*. London: Routledge, pp. 193–7.
Becker, H. (1981) *Exploring Society Photographically*. Mary and Leigh Block Gallery, Evanston: Northeastern University.
Becker, Karin (1990/2003) 'Photojournalism and the Tabloid Press', in Liz Wells (ed.), *The Photography Reader*. London: Routledge, pp. 291–308.
Benjamin, Walter (1934/1982) 'The Author as Producer', in Victor Burgin (ed.), *Thinking Photography*. London: Macmillan, pp. 15–32.
Biber, Katherine (2007) *Captive Images*. Abingdon: Routledge-Cavendish.
Blinder, C. (2009) 'Not So Innocent: Vision and Culpability in Weegee's Photographs of Children', in M. Kadar, J. Perreault and L. Warley (eds), *Photographs, Histories and Meanings*. New York: Palgrave Macmillan, pp. 9–23.
Bourdieu, Pierre (1965/1990) *Photography: A Middlebrow Art*. Cambridge: Polity Press.
Bourgois, Phillipe and Jeff Schonberg (2009) *Righteous Dopefiend*. Berkeley, CA: University of California Press.
Carlebach, Michael (1997) *American Photojournalism Comes of Age*. Washington DC: The Smithsonian Institution Press.
Carney, Phil (2010) 'Crime, Punishment and the Force of Photographic Spectacle', in Keith Hayward and Mike Presdee (eds), *Framing Crime: Cultural Criminology and the Image*. London: Routledge, pp. 17–35.
Carrabine, Eamonn (2012) 'Just Images: Aesthetics, Ethics and Visual Criminology'. *British Journal of Criminology*, 52(3): 463–89.
——. (2014) 'Seeing Things: Violence, Voyeurism and the Camera'. *Theoretical Criminology*, 18 (2): 134–58.
——. (2015) 'Visual Criminology: History, Theory and Method', in Heith Copes and Mitch Miller (eds), *The Routledge Handbook of Qualitative Criminology*. London: Routledge, pp. 103–21.
Clarke, Graham (1997) *The Photograph*. Oxford: Oxford University Press.
Courtney, David and Stephen Lyng (2007) 'Taryn Simon and *The Innocents* Project'. *Crime, Media, Culture*, 3(2): 175–91.
Di Bello, Patrizia (2007) *Women's Albums and Photography in Victorian England: Ladies, Mothers and Flirts*. Aldershot: Ashgate.

Didi-Huberman, Georges (2008) *Images in Spite of All: Four Photographs from Auschwitz*. Chicago: University of Chicago Press.

Finn, Jonathan (2009) *Capturing the Criminal Image: From Mug Shot to Surveillance Society*. Minneapolis: University of Minnesota Press.

Gefter, Phillip (2009) *Photography after Frank*. London: Aperture.

Gill, Rosalind (2010) 'Supersexualise Me! Advertising and the "Midriffs"', in Feona Attwood (ed.), *Mainstreaming Sex: The Sexualization of Western Culture*. London: I. B. Tauris, pp. 93–109.

Goffman, Erving (1979) *Gender Advertisements,* London: Macmillan.

Greenfield, Lauren (2002) *Girl Culture*. San Francisco, CA: Chronicle Books.

Grierson, John (1966) 'The First Principles of Documentary', in Forsyth Hardy (ed.), *Grierson on Documentary*. London: Faber & Faber, pp. 35–46.

Hand, Martin (2012) *Ubiquitous Photography*. Cambridge: Polity Press.

Harper, Douglas (2012) *Visual Sociology*. London: Routledge.

Hayward, Keith (2010) 'Opening the Lens: Cultural Criminology and the Image', in Keith Hayward and Mike Presdee (eds), *Framing Crime: Cultural Criminology and the Image*. London: Routledge, pp. 1–16.

Jackson, Bruce (1969) *A Thief's Primer*. London: Macmillan.

——. (1977) *Killing Time*. Ithaca, NY: Cornell University Press.

——. (2009) *Pictures from a Drawer: Prison and the Art of Portraiture*. Philadelphia: Temple University Press.

Jackson, Bruce and Diane Christian (2012) *In This Timeless Time: Living and Dying on Death Row in America*. Chapel Hill, NC: University of North Carolina Press.

Jay, Martin (1993) *Downcast Eyes: The Denigration of Vision in Twentieth-Century French Thought*. Berkeley, CA: California University Press.

Jervis, John (1998) *Exploring the Modern*. Oxford: Blackwell.

Lee, Anthony and Richard Meyer (2008) *Weegee and the Naked City*. Berkeley, CA: University of California Press.

Lowe, Paul (2014) 'The Forensic Turn: Bearing Witness and the "Thingness" of the Photograph', in Liam Kennedy and Caitlin Patrick (eds), *The Violence of the Image: Photography and International Conflict*. London: I. B. Tauris, pp. 211–34.

Lübecker, Nikolaj (2013) 'The Politics of Images'. *Paragraph*, 36(3): 392–407.

Lyon, D. (1968) *The Bikeriders*. New York: Macmillan.

Lyon, D. (1971) *Conversations with the Dead*. New York: Henry Holt.

Marien, Mary (2010) *Photography: A Cultural History*. London: Laurence King.

Marsden, Dennis and Euan Duff (1975) *Workless*. London: Penguin.

McNair, Brian (2002) *Striptease Culture: Sex, Media and the Democratisation of Desire*. London: Routledge.

Mills, C. Wright (1959) *The Sociological Imagination*. New York: Oxford University Press.

Murray, Susan (2008) 'Digital Images, Photo-Sharing and Our Shifting Notions of Everyday Aesthetics'. *Journal of Visual Culture*, 7(2): 147–63.

Norfolk, Simon (2005) *Bleed*. Stockport: Dewi Lewis.

Olmos, Antonio (2013) *Landscape of Murder*. Stockport: Dewi Lewis.

Phillips, David (2009) 'Actuality and Affect in Documentary Photography', in Richard Howells and Robert Watson (eds), *Using Visual Evidence*. Maidstone: Open University Press, pp. 55–77.

Pink, Sarah (2013) *Doing Visual Ethnography*, 3rd edn. London: Sage Publications.

Price, Derrick (2009) 'Surveyors and Surveyed: Photography Out and About', in Liz Wells (ed.), *Photography: A Critical Introduction*. London: Routledge, pp. 65–115.

Rancière, Jacques (2007) *The Future of the Image*. London: Verso.

——. (2011) *The Emancipated Spectator*. London: Verso.

Reinhardt, Mark (2007) 'Picturing Violence: Aesthetics and the Anxiety of Critique', in Mark Reinhardt, Holly Edwards and Erinna Duganne (eds), *Beautiful Suffering: Photography and the Traffic in Pain*. Williamstown, MA: Williams College Museum of Art, pp. 13–36.

Resnick, Judith and Dennis Curtis (2011) *Representing Justice*. New Haven: Yale University Press.

Rose, Gillian (2004) '"Everyone's Cuddled Up and it Just Looks Really Nice": An Emotional Geography of Some Mums and Their Photos'. *Social & Cultural Geography*, 5(4): 549–64.

——. (2012) *Visual Methodologies*, 3rd edn. London: Sage Publications.

Rosler, Martha (1981/2004) 'In, Around, and Afterthoughts on Documentary Photography', in Martha Rosler (ed.), *Decoys and Disruptions: Selected Writings, 1975–2001*. New York: October, pp. 151–206.

Ross, Richard (2007) *Architecture of Authority*. New York: Aperture.

——. (2012) *Juvenile in Justice*. Santa Barbara, CA: Richard Ross Publications.

Sekula, Alan (1989) 'The Body and the Archive', in Richard Bolton (ed.), *The Contest of Meaning*. Cambridge, MA: MIT Press, pp. 343–89.

Simon, Taryn, Peter Neufeld and Barry Scheck (2003) *The Innocents*. New York: Umbrage.

Smith, Lindsay (1998) *The Politics of Focus: Women, Children and Nineteenth-Century Photography*. Manchester: Manchester University Press.

Snyder, Joel (1984) 'Documentary without Ontology'. *Studies in Visual Communication*, 10: 78–95.

Solomon-Godeau, Abigail (1991) *Photography at the Dock*. Minneapolis: University of Minnesota Press.

Sontag, Susan (2003) *Regarding the Pain of Others*. London: Penguin.

Stallybrass, Julian (ed.) (2013) *Documentary*. London: Whitechapel Gallery.

Stasz, Clarice (1979) 'The Early History of Visual Sociology', in Jon Wagner (ed.), *Images of Information: Still Photography in the Social Sciences*. London: Sage Publications, pp. 119–36.

Stott, William (1973) *Documentary Expression and Thirties America*. Chicago: University of Chicago Press.

Straw, Will (2015) 'After the Event: The Challenges of Crime Photography', in Jason Hill and Vanessa Schwartz (eds), *Getting the Picture: The Visual Culture of the News*. London: Bloomsbury, pp. 139–44.

Tagg, John (1988) *The Burden of Representation: Essays on Photographies and Histories*. Basingstoke: Macmillan.

Turner, Stephen (2014) *American Sociology: From Pre-disciplinary to Post-normal*. London: Palgrave Macmillan.

Van Gelder, Hilde and Helen Westgeest (2011) *Photography Theory in Historical Perspective*. Oxford: Blackwell.

Young, Alison (2005) *Judging the Image*. London: Routledge.

# 8 Liquid crime history

## Digital entrepreneurs and the industrial production of 'ruined lives'[1]

*Barry Godfrey*

### Introduction

Recent exhibitions at art galleries across Europe have raised some interesting questions about modernity and the celebration of decay caused by the passing of time. The works featured under the title of 'Ruin Lust' depict fallen structures, relics, buildings and monuments (for example, John Constable's *Hadleigh Castle* or William Turner's *Temple of Poseidon at Sunium*). These works have aroused interest amongst visitors, art critics and cultural theorists (as well as members of the viewing public). There is also much to interest social scientists, historians and digital theorists, as this chapter goes on to prove. There is a clear community of interest that joins the viewers of 'ruin lust' with many criminologists who are seeking to understand how and why some people suffer 'ruined' lives, and who want to do something about it. This chapter argues that a significant strand of criminological inquiry shares a similar and long-standing interest in ruins (of lives rather than buildings) and makes three main points. First, it asserts that one strand within criminological research and practice has always contained a latent and unacknowledged romanticism which seeks to investigate, understand and 'repair' ruined lives through a more sophisticated analysis of how and why life-chances are damaged or restricted.[2] In other words, this strand of criminology is fundamentally concerned with lives that appear to be ruined, but which can be rescued. The second assertion is that crime historians are similarly affected; in fact, the chapter argues that they are perhaps even more prone than criminologists to the 'redemption impulse' which seeks to recover ruined lives. Third, the chapter argues that the new forms of crime history which utilize digital resources have changed the character of biographical research to the extent that it has taken on a 'liquid' character, and this chapter suggests that the availability of digital data on the Internet (which is quite staggering) offers a hyper-extension of criminology's reach towards uncovering and recovering the lives of the dispossessed and powerless.

### Ruin lust

Humans revere, cherish and are fascinated by ruins. This is a fascination that Christopher Woodward (2001) believes originated in nostalgic contemplations on the fall of Ancient Rome:

When we contemplate ruins, we contemplate our own future. To statesmen, ruins predict the fall of Empires, and to philosophers the futility of mortal man's aspirations. To a poet, the decay of a monument represents the dissolution of an individual ego in the flow of Time; to a painter or architect, the fragments of a stupendous antiquity call into question the purpose of their art. Why struggle with a brush or chisel to create the beauty of wholeness when far greater works have been destroyed by Time? (Woodward 2001: 2–3)

In eighteenth-century England, Classical virtues were lauded, and the Imperial Roman Empire became an aspirational model for the emerging British Empire. By the late nineteenth century, London had reached the same size, population, stature and visual splendour as the glory that once was Rome. But Rome had fallen, and therefore there was the possibility that London and the rest of the British Empire could suffer the same fate: 'Imperial imaginaries create particular topographies, temporalities, scopic regimes, and modes of representation. Their scopic regimes include . . . imperial ruin gazing – that is, scenes in which the imperial subject contemplates the metropole of a mighty empire in ruins while thinking about the future of his own empire' (Hell 2010: 170). Accordingly, the melancholy contemplation of ancient glories now turned to rubble began to seep into nineteenth-century political dialogue and artistic production. The early nineteenth-century Romantic movement is particularly associated with painted depictions of ruined churches, classical facades and elegiac landscapes. The ruins were emblematic of human virtues, vices, regrets and decline. Percy Bysshe Shelley's poem 'Ozymandias' musing on the fall of the empire created by the Egyptian Pharaoh Ramesses II typifies the poetic response to hubris and loss:

'My name is Ozymandias, king of kings:
Look on my works, ye Mighty, and despair!'
Nothing beside remains. Round the decay
Of that colossal wreck, boundless and bare
The lone and level sands stretch far away. (Shelley 1826: 100)

Engravings and paintings of the late nineteenth and early twentieth centuries persisted with themes of loss, destruction and decay through their depiction of ruined buildings and monuments: Gustave Dore's *The New Zealander*, Picasso's *Guernica* or the war paintings of Nash, for example (Boym 2001: 11–12; Dillon 2011; Nead 2005: 212–15). Whilst it seems conceivable that 'the semantic instability of the ruin owes much to the fact that it bespeaks a potential vacuity of meaning' (Hell and Schonle 2010: 6), it seems equally likely that ruins are actually the *perfect* canvas upon which meanings can be ascribed. The paintings of ruined buildings were understood by nineteenth-century viewers as metaphors of hubris, just as more modern depictions of derelict buildings are 'read' by modern viewers as metaphors for unemployment, recession, poverty, disillusionment and the failures of twenty-first-century capitalism.

As photography came to rival painting in the twentieth century, decaying urban environments, and particularly decommissioned institutions, have featured strongly. Brinkley and Eastman (2008) photographed closed-down diners, drive-ins, shops and other parts of 'Vanishing America'; Hinkley and James (2011) did something similar when travelling the iconic highway Route 66; Romany (2010) provided a more poetic interpretation of former factories, theatres and other institutions in the US; whilst Margaine (2012) continued the theme for similar institutions across Europe. Payne (2009) produced an interesting volume of photographs of decommissioned US 'State Mental Hospitals' and Moore (2010) composed an eloquent photographic essay on the abandoned factories and houses of Detroit (a city which declared itself bankrupt in 2014), continuing a theme started by the celebrated American photographer Danny Lyons. *The Destruction of Lower Manhattan* (originally published in 1969, but reprinted in 2005) was Lyons' attempt to document the large-scale demolition of part of New York in 1967. He photographed buildings which would soon be laid-low and also the people living in that area who would soon be moved out. Both buildings and the residents had seen better days, but all retained dignity in the photographs: 'I liked the buildings. I liked being alone in them. I liked the dirt. I liked the danger. And I liked that I was the last person to see them . . . The buildings, all doomed, spoke to me. I was there to save them, to be witness, to pass on to the future, forever, what they looked like, at their best, alone in the light' (Lyon 2014: 134).

However, the strongest theme within modern ruin lust is that of decaying carceral institutions. There are now numerous photographic collections of prisons across the world. Bolze and Delarue (2013) includes photographs of Lyon's three gaols through their various historical incarnations. The cells of Holmesburg Prison, Philadelphia, with their peeling paint and faded graffiti, are depicted by Roma and Szarkowski (2005). Finger (2010) produced an illustrated history of Queensland's St Helena Colonial Prison, and O'Sullivan (2009) did the same for Dublin's Kilmainham Prison. There are many others. Almost no decommissioned prison that has been turned into a hotel or a museum lacks an official 'biography' (complete with photos).

The photographs of former carceral institutions allow us a glimpse into a hidden world and they allow us to wallow in nostalgia in a similar way that eighteenth-century paintings of ruined churches or Roman temples did. The buildings also seemed to show, if not resilience, then a quality of survivability that raised them to the heroic. Like Lyons, Dillon (2011) saw the buildings as heroic and resilient: 'The ruined building is a remnant of, and portal into, the past; its decay is a concrete reminder of the passage of time. And yet by definition it survives, after a fashion.' The remains of these buildings are poignant not merely because they have lost their place in the social and physical landscape, but also because they have now been stripped of their authority, context and purpose. The factories do not contain workers; the prisons have no prisoners; the asylum has no inmates. The ruined buildings seem to echo the ruined lives of the people who once dwelt or worked in them, and even contain the faint remnants of their thoughts etched in graffiti on the walls, and we have been just as interested in the people who inhabited these carceral institutions, and wonder whether they too survived the harsh conditions they experienced?

## 'Ruined' people

Since the 1970s, photographers have started to focus on prisoners, inmates and other people who lived or who were once kept in those now-crumbling carceral institutions. For example, Danny Lyon, after photographing buildings and structures in the 1960s, then started to photograph prisoners in six American penal institutions, published as *Conversations with the Dead* in 1971. In *The Seventh Dog* (2014), he talked about the people featured in those photographs:

> Charlie Lowe, who I knew from Ellis, had been a child prisoner in Gatesville. That was the prison where Texas used to send the kids before they were old enough to be sent to the TDC [Texas Department of Corrections]. Notorious for its brutality to the child prisoners, Gatesville was closed by the state in 1980. Charlie, who was seventeen years old, hatched an escape plan from Gatesville with four of his abused teenage buddies. After they created a commotion, the over-six-foot-tall guard entered the dorm and Charlie hit him over the head with a baseball bat. In Charlie's version, the guard kept getting back up so Charlie kept hitting him. In one of Charlie's partner's versions, Charlie lost it and kept hitting the guard until his eye popped out. Charlie got life, and his buddies got fifty, forty, thirty, and twenty years each, showing that Texas juries know how to deduct by ten. (Lyon 2014: 133)

Lyon's work between 1971 and 2014 provided a glimpse of prison life (which had rarely been revealed to the public gaze). Modern prison photography continues to pull back the curtain to reveal the realities of incarceration, and appears to seek to fulfil three further aims: to *visualize* those who have been hidden or ignored; to *humanize* those who have been demonized; and to *critique* social structures or social policy. Writing about the photographs of serving prisoners in three European gaols, Bart de Visser said that:

> They were quite ordinary people really, perhaps a bit more introvert than the average. The look in their eyes is mostly melancholy or reserved . . . The question is what to make of the knowledge that these are prisoners, if all we know about them are names and dates. What does this project tell us about the way society looks at 'others'? The photos show vulnerable, lonely men and women, thrown into relief by their chosen backgrounds . . . Is it too far fetched to argue that *Portraits in Prisons* shows Foucault's criticism is still relevant? That the neat, spotlessly clean lines of prison cells and the exercise yards are so many poignant illustrations of a doomed system? (Visser, quoted in Gariglio 2007)

Prison(er) photography therefore fits into a longer visual tradition of portraying the lower sections of society that has existed since at least the eighteenth century

(Shesgreen 2002; Hitchcock 2004). Drawings and paintings of debtors, paupers, vagrants, drunks and lunatics by William Hogarth, Thomas Rowlinson, and Theodore Gericault joined the woodcuts and public broadsides which depicted the hangings at Tyburn (Bates 2014; Crone 2012) in order to reveal (and also parody, to use as illustrations of immorality or to satirize social policy) the lives of the poor. Readers seeking more knowledge about the condemned could also buy the Ordinary (the chaplain) of Newgate's accounts, which recounted tales of the poor unfortunates who were condemned to be executed (see Gatrell 1996). The accounts outlined the twists of fate and moral failings that had brought the prisoner to the shadow of the gallows and could be seen to be the first popular set of accounts of the lives of convicted criminals. These biographies and broadsides provided a visual and literary foundation for nineteenth-century social investigation to build upon.

Although attempting to be more systematic in their approach, devising categories and so on, social investigators such as Henry Mayhew were also keen to visualize the people and lives they were examining. Between 1851 and 1861, Mayhew carried out an investigation into the lives of London's working classes (including a volume on a selected group of individuals who laboured at the margins of society that the Victorians came to call the 'criminal classes'). In *London Labour and the London Poor*, Mayhew drew pen portraits of the 'soiled doves', fallen angels, street-sellers, beggars, vagrants, flower-girls and tramps that he met in London. However, what made Mayhew interesting is that he interviewed over 100 Londoners and gave his readers an idea of the lives of working people – and what circumstances in their lives had brought them to their particular social situation. He even showed a remarkable degree of sympathy for those who found themselves in dire straits because of their infirmity or some kind of malevolent misfortune (Quennell 1951). His work, of course, also helped to create the preconditions for the emergence of the criminal classes (Chesney 1970; Godfrey, Lawrence and Williams 2007). One could see Mayhew's work as useful in explaining the lives of poor labouring Londoners or assisting in the creation of a set of myths about a core of criminals preying on respectable society. Either way, it was his in-depth approach to the personal histories of the people he interviewed that began to create an interest in the reasons why some people had ended up in trouble with the police and the courts, a theme which was taken up by criminologists in the late nineteenth century.

## The New Romantics

The origins of scientific criminology, emerging in the decades after Mayhew was producing his four-volume study, were steeped in notions of degeneracy. Cesare Lombroso's theories, which became popular in the 1870s and 1880s, legitimated the control, surveillance and control of habitual criminals and the 'weak-minded'. This punitive approach directed but did not completely dominate early criminological theory. Many people working in the nineteenth-century criminal justice system were infused with Christian notions of reformation and rehabilitation. Police Court Missionaries were sent by the Methodist Church to aid defendants in the magistrates' courts; Reformatories and Industrial Schools were established for children who had been criminalized, or who were vulnerable, and were usually run or funded by churches and faith communities; and penal reformers were often involved in religious organizations (Vanstone 2004). Of course, religious-inspired theories, laden with heavy moral overtones, could be equally or even more punitive and damaging, but they did at least allow for the possibility of reformation (usually focused on straightening out wayward youth). Many modern criminologists, although they tend to be more secular as a group, have adopted a similar approach. The work of Tony Parker (1994), for example, is emblematic of an intention to produce a better future for people who have had a bad start in life; the works of Shadd Maruna (2001), Fergus McNeil and Beth Weaver (2010) and Stephen Farrall (2002), and all of the other desistence experts, all attempt to explain rather than condemn the actions of offenders. They all place considerable emphasis on the possibility of reform, of good coming from bad, of lives being 'remade'. Other social scientists have played an active part in the criminal justice system as parole board members (criminologist Anne Worrall), discharged prisoner aid society leaders (crime historian Graeme Dunstall), as magistrates (criminologist Rod Morgan) and in other roles (albeit working through an imperfect system) that make a difference to defendants' and prisoners' lives. This is evidence of a strong strand of rehabilitative hope that has run through criminology for the last 150 years, a redemptive impulse which encourages some criminologists to recover the good in lives which are troubled or 'ruined'.

This chapter argues that historians of crime are perhaps even more susceptible to this tendency to want to 'repair lives'. But why? After all, they cannot influence the lives they study – those people are beyond help. The lives they study can, however, be interpreted and re-interpreted in order to reveal details which show another side to those deemed criminal, vagrant or weak. Historians hold the power to bring a perspective to the lives they study which rescues them from the 'enormous condescension of posterity' (Thompson 1963: 12). Recently many historians have adopted a life-course cradle-to-grave approach to the study of criminality which has significantly increased the ability to understand andre-interpret the lives (rather than episodes of criminality within a person's life) of people whose biographies would otherwise be neglected, forgotten or ignored. This approach is holistic and takes in all of the features of a person's life, not just their criminal careers, and does so from the time they were born until the time they died. For example, a study of drug addiction in America from the 1920s to the 1960s used long qualitative interviews to chart how people fell into addiction and how they survived the process, despite the adverse impact drug use had on their family lives and employment prospects (Courtwright and Des Jarlais 1989). The researchers could well have illustrated their interviews with photographs from Marc Asnin's photographic essay on the decline of 'Uncle Charlie' from familiar family member to multiple-addicted shell of a man: 'Uncle Charlie says he never had a friend. That no one listened then, and no one listens now. After thirty years of photographing him, I am the last guy standing, the only constant in Charlie's life. My uncle was born into dysfunction . . . but he survived. Through it all, he survived' (Asnin 2012: 401).

Like Uncle Charlie, the people interviewed by Courtwright and Des Jarlais are survivors. Hamish Maxwell-Stewart's work with Lucy Frost (1997) has examined the lives of transported convicts, many of whom survived their experiences in the penal colony and went on to thrive in their new homes (see http://foundersand-survivors.org). Godfrey, Cox and Farrall's *Criminal Lives* (2007) charted every significant event in the lives of habitual offenders in the nineteenth and twentieth centuries. They showed how persistent offenders in north-west England survived the criminal justice system and turned their lives around. The whole-life, or bio-graphical, or life-course approach (for it has many terms; see Godfrey 2011, 2015) really forces historians to see periods of offending as unusual and secondary in the lives of most offenders. It emphasizes the humanity of the subject under study – the criminal – and encourages a sympathetic and empathetic response. This does not make the biographical method better history than other forms of enquiry (see Richardson and Godfrey 2003; Godfrey and Richardson 2004) and, indeed, it can actually lead a researcher to downplay or ignore the experiences of some offenders who do not desist from crime, but it does indulge the desire to repair the lives of historical offenders.

## How do crime historians repair lives?

There are now quite a large number of researchers using whole-life biographi-cal methods (Turner 2009; Chamberlain 2012; Cox et al. 2014; Williams 2014; and projects such as the Leverhulme Trust-funded *Aftercare*). Using data collected from various sources, it is possible to re-construct a chronological series of events which occurred in one person's life (marriage, birth of children, death of relatives and so on), and their work careers and their various changes of addresses (which charted changes in employment status, or type, as well as the addresses at which people resided throughout their lives), and also a full offending history, with details of punishment and so on.[3] This information makes it possible to calculate, for individual offenders, the progress of their criminal careers, their periods of incar-ceration, their employment careers, and life events such as marriage and the death of parents. It shows the interplay between criminal episodes and other parts of life, and also shows that criminal careers were often much shorter than was assumed by the public and the media. It also facilitates an assessment of the impact of wars and significant changes in the local and national economy (which, of course, affected people across England and Wales, but which may have impacted differentially on ex-offenders). Critically, therefore, it illustrates how socio-economic policies impacted upon individual lives. The biographical methodology also produces interesting and compelling life-stories of people who were subject to the criminal justice system in the nineteenth and twentieth centuries which can engage the aca-demic and also non-professional audiences (Cox et al. 2015). The following three examples illustrate the kinds of stories that emerge with this methodology:

1   Ellen Whaling was born in 1838 in County Tipperary, Ireland. When she was a teenager, she was possibly (the records are imperfect) imprisoned in Cheshire for

concealing the birth and subsequently the death of her baby. As inmate No. 1042, aged 23, she entered Prestwich County Lunatic Asylum in Cheshire, a single woman with no children. When she was released 12 years later, she was convicted for a string of assaults and drunkenness. These minor crimes resulted in short periods of imprisonment in Knutsford House of Correction, but when she was convicted on an indictable offence (the robbery of 10 shillings from the person of Robert Allmark), she was sentenced to seven years' penal servitude at Knutsford Sessions. On reception at Millbank Prison, she was described as having a sallow complexion, grey hair, blue eyes, 5 ft ½ inch, spare build, with a long face. She had lost the roof of her mouth, which caused an impediment in her speech. There were two vaccination marks on her right arm, a scar on her left leg from a dog bite, a small cut mark on her left eyebrow and several teeth missing. She had palpitations of the heart and had suffered from syphilis for 15 years (which explains the condition of her mouth). She did, however, have a healthy heart and a sound mind, so was adjudged to be of fair health. In 1881, she was released from penal servitude on licence, and for the next two years she worked as a domestic servant when she could find work, and she was periodically convicted of indecency and drunkenness in Chester, Manchester and Liverpool. She was probably sleeping rough at times and was certainly roaming around the north-west of England with poor prospects. In July 1883, she was convicted at Liverpool Sessions of stealing a purse at Widnes and given five years penal servitude followed by another five years of police supervision.[4] In 1886, she was again released on licence to a Discharged Prisoners Aid Society, but was quickly back before the courts (this time for uttering counterfeit coins, for which she received two months' gaol). In 1891, aged 50, she was back in Prestwich County Lunatic Asylum, where she remained until she died. She had endured a difficult start to her life and a sad end.

2    William John Stinton moved out of his widowed mother's house in St Pancras, London to establish a new home with his wife Hannah Eliza. Aged 27 in 1868, Eliza gave birth to their son John, and Samuel followed two years later. In 1874, another son was born to the couple and William became a house painter. The family lived in Grebe Street, St Pancras and, if the regular birth of children is an indication, they seemed happy. Something must have gone badly wrong with the relationship by 1879, because John was charged with the murder of his wife. Eventually tried at the Old Bailey for manslaughter, he was convicted and sentenced to ten years' penal servitude. Over the next few years, the petitions he made to the Secretary of State from prison threw a little light on the turbulent relationship between himself and his wife. He alleged that his wife had been a drinker, very provocative towards him, and made other remarks that indicated that there had been a long history of arguments between the couple. His grounds for mitigation of his sentence were refused. He then wrote a series of letters pleading for his 11-year-old son, who was now in a Dr Barnado's Home, not to face emigration to Canada. After some time, the Wanderers' Home agreed that they would look after the boy until William was released from prison. That happened on 27 April 1887

when he was licensed to the St Giles Christian Mission in Holborn. Before release, however, the prison Medical Officer had noted that William had a blue line on his gums, indicating that he was suffering from lead poisoning (possibly from the lead in the house-paint he used). The disease must have taken a grip, for two years later he was a blind inmate of Camberwell House Asylum. He died in the asylum aged 53 and never had the chance to be reunited with his son.[5] His was a story of three ruined lives.

It is not just tales of misery, madness and recidivism that interests crime historians, however. Indeed, it is the recovery of good lives from the ruins of a poor start in life that has come to consume a certain section of the crime history community. For researchers who want to investigate the mechanisms that encouraged rehabilitation, the life-histories of people such as Mary Haydock are very important:

3    Mary Haydock from Bury, Lancashire ran away from her life as a domestic servant in the late eighteenth century. Dressed as a boy, she stole a horse, but was quickly caught and indicted for trial in August 1791. She was sentenced to seven years' transportation and was carried to Australia on the *Royal Admiral* in October 1792. She married Thomas Reibey, a free settler to Sydney, and the couple were granted farm land on the Hawkesbury River, where Thomas and Mary lived and farmed following their marriage. The Reibeys established a business on the river, which was so successful that it allowed them to buy up several farms on the Hawkesbury River, where they traded in coal, cedar, furs and skins. Indeed, as the company expanded and they took on partner, the business traded internationally. When Thomas died in 1811, Mary became sole carer for the children and manager of various business enterprises. Her businesses thrived and she acquired considerable wealth, which she was happy to spend on philanthropic works, investing in charities and supporting religious enterprises. Mary recovered her name to such an extent that she became a well-known Sydney resident and is now celebrated as an early Australian citizen on the $20 bill. Convict iconography is not depicted on the banknote, but she remains an example of a life which could easily have been ruined by her court-imposed sentence. Many transported people did not cope well in their new lands and again ended up in trouble or became destitute (see Godfrey and Cox 2008). However, Mary's recovery from an unfortunate start in life illustrates that, for some at least, reform was a possibility.

Biographies like Mary's are vital to criminologists investigating onset into, and desistence from, a life of offending. They provide evidence to support theories of desistence which emphasize the importance of forming a meaningful relationship, gaining some financial capital (usually through employment) and finding a purpose in life. Since Mary's life features all of those factors and since, unlike many other ex-convicts, she manages not to commit any further offending, her story lends some credence to these theories (supported by further historical work using biographical research methods: see Godfrey et al. 2007, 2010).

The ability to survey the whole life-course allows historians to explain why the lives of individuals may have taken particular directions. The focus for crime historians has been to examine why some people ended up in court and what happened to them after punishment. The lives of the poor can then be contextualized; their 'moral failings' and hereditary weaknesses' revealed as prejudicial labels for people with low financial and social capital who were unable to respond to the inequalities of the prevailing socio-economic system. Biographical methods can transform how lives are seen and therefore how evidence for changing social policy can be formed and promoted. Is this not what crime historians have always attempted to do; indeed, has not this theoretical and methodological approach been the dominant drive for 'history from below' for the past 40 years or so? In the 1970s and 1980s, historians such as Douglas Hay, Edward P. Thompson and Raphael Samuel all brought a human focus to the huge economic and legal changes that swept through eighteenth- and nineteenth-century society. Studies published in the last 15 years, for example, by Shore (1999), Brown (2003), Davies (2009), Rogers (2014) and many other social and crime historians, all seem to have continued this tradition. The analysis of the whole life-course of individuals and the representation of those lives in ways which humanize the poor and disadvantaged, and make visible the challenges which shaped their lives is, in essence, an attempt to retrospectively 'rescue' lives.[6] With the possibility of many more biographies of the poor and vulnerable becoming available, it is likely that biographical research methodologies and the tradition of producing human-focused work will continue to inform crime history to a considerable extent, and to enable the redemptive impulse to be used to rescue thousands of eighteenth- and nineteenth-century lives.[7]

## Ruin-fatigue

Commercial organizations such as Ancestry and Find My Past have published enormous amounts of personal data on criminals, prisoners, paupers, workhouse inhabitants, victims of crime and so on dating (mainly) from the nineteenth century onwards. Additionally, the Old Bailey Online website contains details of all trials carried out at London's Central Criminal Court between 1674 and 1913, nearly 200,000 criminal trials or, to put it another way, details of over a million defendants, victims and witnesses, all available for free public perusal. The Old Bailey data is currently being added together with biographical data from records of transported convicts (in the Founders and Survivors database), from the records of licensed British convicts (1853–1914) and from other extant un-digitized record sets to form the Digital Panopticon (www.digitalpanopticon.org). This is a huge amount of biographical data and detail about prisoners and ex-convicts that will be available from 2017. Each of the biographies constructed by Godfrey et al. (2007, 2010) using digital resources taken from existing disparate websites and from archived criminal records took about a day each to prepare (sometimes longer). Since then, the large-scale digitization of criminal records, and their availability on a number of websites, has altered the research landscape considerably.

The liquidity of digitally enabled biographical research methods means that thousands of life-stories can be put together from easily available online resources in a fraction of that time. Many tens, even hundreds, of life-histories could be accessed and constructed in a single day using the Digital Panopticon website. This is biographical research on an industrial scale. That this data 'recovers' and pieces together the lives of the most dispossessed and criminalized in society is remarkable. We will know more about eighteenth- and nineteenth-century prisoners than we do about prisoners serving time today.

Online digitized data has the power to transform crime historical research – liquefying historical research. The scale of digital data and the speed with which it can be accessed have engendered new forms of crime history which have the capacity to shift the theory and practice of history with a rapidity not encountered before. Whereas traditional forms of historical enquiry use data for academic research, liquid crime history is also very much concerned with the production of data for the general public. This democratization of data allows all viewers to interpret the data for themselves and to re-interpret what the academic experts have posited. However, the speed and scale of these more liquid forms of criminological and historical enquiry raise some interesting ethical questions for those historians who have used the biographical method to analyse, recast and 'rescue' ruined lives. For example, the paintings of ruined buildings hanging in art galleries provoke contemplation of entropy, decay, fading glories, mortality and a whole host of concepts which no doubt intrigue the viewer. How would viewers perceive an art gallery which had thousands (maybe tens of thousands) of similar images on its walls? Surely they would be overwhelming in the same way as thousands of digitally rendered biographies would be? Do the websites which reveal a wealth of biographical data on thousands of 'ruined lives' risk engendering 'ruin-fatigue'? Might compassion and understanding dry up when confronted with this avalanche of misery? Will web-surfers flick through digitalized life after digitized life until they find cases which suit their theoretical position; will researchers and students search for cases which are interesting, pathetic or funny rather than those which are typical (or atypical)? How will the new digital entrepreneurs protect the interests of those offenders and ex-offenders who appear on the websites (or the rights of their descendants; see Richardson and Godfrey 2003)? What safeguards are there against overfamiliarity breeding contempt? Can the liquidity and speed of the new ways of accessing biographical data digitally be used to produce ethical and progressive research? These are all issues that the new digital entrepreneurs will have to consider.

## Conclusion

Troubled lives are a mainstay of modern popular culture. The media are replete with stories of people who have fallen from grace and also with tales of dysfunctional families. Historians take the high road but travel in the same direction, as this chapter has shown. Even if we want to use digital online evidence of people's poor start in lives to explain onset into criminality or to show that poor life situations can prolong criminal careers, we cannot guarantee that the data we use is not also used for prurient entertainment. The more that we democratize our data by placing it online, the greater risk there is that people will access many hundreds of 'ruined lives' without understanding the social and political context which has shaped those lives – and which explains why and how people found themselves in terrible situations. Indeed, website visitors might just ignore some stories, those of ex-offenders that viewers find beyond the pale, for example (it is all very well to sympathize with minor offenders who suffered disproportionately harsh punishments, but some may have little sympathy for those imprisoned for sexual offences or offences against children). For those who remade their lives after serving sentences for rape, for example, sympathy and empathy may be hard to find. The explanatory essays that accompany some websites certainly help to reduce that risk, as does the use of online data in teaching modules, in academic articles and in genealogical research. Biographical methodologies encourage more rounded and nuanced appreciations of people's lives, and the new liquid forms of digital history provide and utilize a huge amount of data for academics, journalists and genealogists to popularize more empathetic portrayals of the poor and vulnerable. The thousands of digital online biographies risk ruin-fatigue, but because they are rich in detail, they should demonstrate that categories such as 'the criminal classes', 'the underclass' and the 'criminal families' belie a considerable amount of differentiated experience. From the huge number of digital lives, the individual will emerge. Ultimately the new liquid forms of historical enquiry will reveal that the lives of offenders and ex-offenders were as full of joy as misery, as much rehabilitation as recidivism, and that they were also full of family relationships, employment, social life and so on. It will show that criminality was not embedded within the whole life-course of most offenders or within criminal families, nor was it due to 'criminal genes' in some way. The more opportunities that can be provided for academics, museum curators and website designers to use biographical data, the greater the chance of undermining easy assumptions about the lives of the poor and the less chance of ruin-fatigue. Historians are finding more and more routes to public engagement and, given the public fascination with stories of ruined lives, biographical research and liquid crime history could provide a route for greater public understanding of the ways in which people overcome difficult circumstances to lead successful lives.

## Notes

1 I am grateful for the comments of Ruth Lamont, Zoe Alker and Lucy Williams on an earlier draft of this chapter.
2 There are, of course, many other strands that combine to form the discipline of criminology – some which are more scientific, cultural, administrative and so on.
3 The most important sources of further information on our sample of offenders were: census returns from the 1841 to 1911 Censuses (providing details of the residence, family status and occupation of each person we searched for); online birth, marriage and death indices (detailing if and when our offender was married and had children, and when he or she died); military records (mainly referring to the First World War, including service records – which, in turn, included disciplinary breaches – medal indices and pensions details); court records (listing charges, whether or not they were found guilty,

some details of the offence they had been charged with and any sentence imposed). Importantly, these documents also recorded the antecedent criminal history of each person appearing before the courts); British Library nineteenth-century newspapers online; *The Times* digital archive; and *The Guardian* digital archive (listing trial reports, as well as commentaries about particular offenders – in a few cases – and public opinion about crime and habitual offending); TNA (national archives) records. These records included: Home Office records such as criminal registers (HO26 and HO27), which preserve details of offenders from 1805 to 1892; Metropolitan Police records, including habitual criminal registers (MEPO 6), which contain details of criminals as defined by sections 5–8 of the Prevention of Crimes Act 1871; and Prison Commission records such as prison registers (PCOM 6), which contain details of all prisoners held at various English prisons from 1856 onwards.

4  Since the 1860s, there had been attempts to keep a watchful eye over released convicts, at least for the period they were released on licence. The 1869 Habitual Offender Act and the Prevention of Crime Act of 1871 extended this power by giving the sentencing judge the power to order a set period of police supervision for persistent offenders. On release from prison, supervisees were required to report to the police and inform them every fortnight of where they were residing. If any person under supervision re-offended, consorted with thieves and prostitutes, or could not prove they were making an honest living, they could be imprisoned for up to a year. Police supervision was finally abandoned in the 1930s.

5  Stinton's story is one of many ruined lives: his, his wife's and his sons, some of whom may have ended up in institutions similar to those analysed by Alker, Cox, Godfrey and Shore. They are currently tracing the lives of children institutionalized in the early to late nineteenth century for a Leverhulme Trust-funded study. Upon release, some of these children, many incarcerated for playing truant or committing petty thefts, were discharged to the armed forces. The 14 and 15 year olds released during the First World War period quickly found themselves fighting for their lives on the Somme, at Ypres and on the Western Front. Most died – more ruined lives.

6  Although there is no concept of finding beauty in flawed lives or objects in the West, the Japanese aesthetic tradition of Wabi-sabi, which stresses the acceptance of imperfection, asymmetry and flawed human nature, has been an important element of Japanese and Chinese philosophy (Powell 2004). Allied to Wabi-sabi, and perhaps more analogous to the attempts of crime historians to recover ruined lives, Kintsugi is a philosophy that considers the flawed or imperfect in a way but does not attempt to hide the imperfection; indeed, the repair is a visible addition (or beautification) of the flaw. It celebrates longevity and resilience by acknowledging that over the lifetime of an object, damage can occur and that it can be mended.

7  There are other forms of social history which are also coming to the fore – quantitative crime history, for example. It is not healthy for any one approach to become dominant, and the richer the mix of methods employed, the more likely we will produce robust and important publications in this area.

# References

Asnin, Marc (2012) *Uncle Charlie*. Rome: Contrasto.

Barnard, Edwin (2010) *Exiled: The Port Arthur Convict Photographs*. Canberra: National Library of Australia.

Bates, Kate (2014) 'Empathy or Entertainment? The Form and Function of Violent Crime in Early-Nineteenth-Century Broadsides'. *Law, Crime & History*, 4(2): 1–27.

Bauman, Zygmunt (2007) *Liquid Times: Living in an Age of Uncertainty*. Cambridge: Polity Press.

Bolze, Bernard and Jean-Marie Delarue (2013) *Prisons de Lyon: Une histoire manifeste.* Lyon: Lieux Dits.

Boym, Svetlana (2001) *The Future of Nostalgia.* New York: Basic Books.

Brinkley, David and Michael Eastman (2008) *Vanishing America: The End of Main Street, Diners, Drive-ins, Donut Shops, and Other Everyday Monuments.* New York: Rizzoli.

Brown, Alyson (2003) *English Society and the Prison: Time, Culture and Politics in the Development of the Modern Prison, 1850–1920.* London: Boydell Press.

Buckland, Gail and Harold Evans (2001) *Shots in the Dark: True Crime Pictures.* Boston: Bullfinch Press.

Chamberlain, Kerry (2012) 'Prostitution in Inter-War Liverpool'. Unpublished PhD thesis, Keele University.

Chesney, Kellow (1970) *The Victorian Underworld.* London: Penguin.

Courtwright, David and Don Des Jarlais (1989) *Addicts Who Survived: An Oral History of Narcotic Use in America, 1923–1965.* Knoxville: University of Tennessee Press.

Cox, David, Barry Godfrey, Helen Johnston and Jo Turner (2014) 'On License: Understanding Punishment, Recidivism and Desistance in Penal Policy, 1853–1945', in Vivien Miller and James Campbell (eds), *Transnational Penal Cultures: New Perspectives on Discipline, Punishment and Desistance.* Abingdon: Routledge, pp. 184–202.

Cox, David, Helen Johnston and Barry Godfrey (2015) *100 Victorian Convicts.* Barnsley: Pen and Sword.

Crone, Ros (2012) *Violent Victorians: Popular Entertainment in Nineteenth-Century London,* Manchester: Manchester University Press.

Davies, Andrew (2009) *Gangs of Manchester.* London: Milo Books.

Dillon, Brian (2011) 'Introduction', in Brian Dillon (ed.), *Ruins.* Cambridge, MA: MIT Press, pp. 10–19.

Doyle, Peter and Caleb Williams (2000) *City of Shadows: Sydney Police Photographs 1912–1948.* Sydney: Historic Houses.

Farrall, Stephen (2002) *Rethinking What Works with Offenders.* Cullompton: Willan Publishing.

Finger, Jarvis (2010) *The St. Helena Story: An Illustrated History of Colonial Queensland's Island Prison.* Brisbane: Boolarong Press.

Frost, Lucy and Hamish Maxwell-Stewart (1997) *Chain Letters: Narrating Convict Lives.* Melbourne: Melbourne University Press.

Gariglio, Luigi (2007) *Portraits in Prisons.* Rome: Contrasto.

Gatrell, Vic (1996) *The Hanging Tree: Execution and the English People 1770–1868.* Oxford: Oxford University Press.

Godfrey, Barry (2011) 'Historical and Archival Research Methods', in David Gadd, Susanne Karstedt and Steven Messner (eds), *The Handbook on Criminology Research Methods.* New York: Sage Publications, pp. 159–75.

——. (2013) *Crime in England 1880–1945: The Rough, the Policed and the Incarcerated.* Abingdon: Routledge.

——. (2015) 'The Crime Historians' Modi Operandi', in Anja Johansen and Paul Knepper (eds), *Oxford Handbook of the History of Crime and Criminal Justice.* Oxford: Oxford University Press, pp. 38–56.

Godfrey, Barry and David Cox (2008) 'The "Last Fleet": Crime, Reformation and Punishment in Western Australia after 1868'. *Australian and New Zealand Journal of Criminology,* 41(2): 236–58.

Godfrey, Barry, David Cox and Stephen Farrall (2007) *Criminal Lives: Family, Employment and Offending.* Oxford: Oxford University Press.

Godfrey, Barry, David Cox and Stephen Farrall (2010) *Serious Offenders*. Oxford: Oxford University Press.

Godfrey, Barry and Jane Richardson (2004) 'Loss, Collective Memory and Transcripted Oral Histories'. *International Journal of Social Research Methodology*, 7(2): 143–55.

Godfrey, Barry, Paul Lawrence and Chris Williams (2007) *History and Crime.* London: Sage Publications.

Hamilton, Peter and Roger Hargreaves (2001) *The Beautiful and the Damned: The Creation of Identity in Nineteenth Century Photography*. Aldershot: Lund Humphries.

Hell, Julia (2010) 'Imperial Ruin Gazers, or Why Did Scipio Weep?', in Julia Hell and Andreas Schonle (eds), *Ruins of Modernity*. Durham, NC: Duke University Press, pp. 169–93.

Hell, Julia and Andreas Schonle (2010) 'Introduction', in Julia Hell and Andreas Schonle (eds), *Ruins of Modernity*. Durham, NC: Duke University Press, pp. 1–17.

Hinkley, Jim and Kerrick James (2011) *Ghost Towns of Route 66*. Minneapolis: Voyager Press.

Hitchcock, Tim (2004) *Down and Out in Eighteenth-Century London*. London: Hambledon.

Lerner, Jesse (2007) *The Shock of Modernity: Crime Photography in Mexico City*. Madrid: Turner.

Lyon, Danny (1969) *The Destruction of Lower Manhattan*. London: Macmillan.

——. (1971) *Conversations with the Dead*. London: Henry Holt and Company.

——. (2014) *The Seventh Dog*. London: Phaidon.

Margaine, Sylvain (2012) *Forbidden Places: Exploring Our Abandoned Heritage*. Versailles: Jonglez.

Mayhew Henry (1851–61) *London Labour and London Poor* (available online at Project Gutenberg).

Maruna, Shadd (2001) *Making Good: How Ex-convicts Reform and Rebuild Their Lives*. Washington DC: American Psychological Association.

McNeill, Fergus and Beth Weaver (2010) 'Travelling Hopefully: Desistance Research and Probation Practice', in Jo Brayford, Francis Cowe and John Deering (eds), *What Else Works? Creative Work with Offenders and Other Social Excluded People*. Cullompton: Willan Publishing, pp. 36–60.

Moore, Andrew (2010) *Detroit Disassembled*. Bologna: Damiani.

Nead, Linda (2005) *Victorian Babylon: People, Streets and Images in Nineteenth-Century London*. New Haven: Yale University Press.

O'Mahoney, Bernard and Brian Anderson (2011) *Faces: A Photographic Journey through the Underworld*. Dublin: True Crime Publishing.

O'Sullivan, Niamh (2009) *Written in Stone: The Graffiti in Kilmainham Jail*. Dublin: Liberties Press.

Parker, Tony (1994) *Life after Life*, London: HarperCollins.

Payne, Christopher (2009) *Asylum: Inside the Closed World of State Mental Hospitals*. Cambridge, MA: MIT Press.

Powell, Richard (2004) *Wabi Sabi Simple*. Fairfield, OH: Adams Media.

Quennell, P. (1951) *London's Underworld*. London: Spring Books.

Richardson, Jane and Barry Godfrey (2003) 'Towards Ethical Practice in the Use of Transcribed Oral Interviews'. *International Journal of Social Research Methodology*, 6(4): 200–14.

Rogers, Helen (2014) 'Kindness and Reciprocity: Liberated Prisoners and Christian Charity in Early Nineteenth-Century England'. *Journal of Social History*, 47(3): 721–45.

Roma, Thomas and John Szarkowski (2006) *In Prison Air: The Cells of Holmesburg Prison*. New York: Powerhouse.

Romany, W. G. (2010) *Beauty in Decay*. Durham: Carpetbombingculture.

Shelley, Percy Bysshe (1826) 'Ozymandias', in *Miscellaneous and Posthumous Poems of Percy Bysshe Shelley*. London: W. Benbow.

Shesgreen, Sean (2002) *Images of the Outcast: The Urban Poor in the Cries of London*. Manchester: Manchester University Press.

Shore, Heather (1999) *Artful Dodgers: Youth and Crime in Early Nineteenth Century London.* Woodbridge: Boydell Press.

Thompson, Edward P. (1963) *The Making of the English Working Class*. London: Vintage.

Turner, Jo (2009) 'Offending Women in Stafford, 1880–1905: Punishment, Reform and Re-integration'. Unpublished PhD thesis, Keele University.

Vanstone, Maurice (2004) 'Mission Control: The Origins of a Humanitarian Service'. *Probation Journal*, 51(1): 34–47.

Williams, Lucy (2014) '"At Large": Women's Lives and Offending in Victorian Liverpool and London'. Unpublished PhD thesis, University of Liverpool.

Woodward, Christopher (2001) *In Ruins*. London: Chatto & Windus.

## Part III

# The craft and challenges of imaginative liquid criminology

# 9 'Risky' research and discretion in pursuing the criminological imagination

*Matthew Bacon and Teela Sanders*

## Introduction

Prior to, during and after their scholarly endeavours, researchers are expected to consider and address the ethical implications of their research for the participants and social worlds in question, and also such implications for themselves. For example, in the event that a research project poses a greater risk of harm than that which a person might encounter in his or her daily life, these risks must be managed by the researcher or the research cannot be conducted. Guiding principles for ethical research are that it should be designed and undertaken to ensure integrity, professionalism, quality and transparency. With significant caution against the use of covert and deceptive methods, the professional code holds fast that researchers must secure the consent of research participants. This consent must be voluntary, competent, informed and comprehending, and participants must be aware that they are free to withdraw from the research at any time without facing any repercussions. Participants must be made fully aware of what will happen to the data that they generate: where it will go and how their words and information will be used and disseminated. Other ethical issues that are central to the social researchers' ethical code include privacy, exploitation and the avoidance of harm at any costs. Now, of course, there is a whole academic sub-discipline devoted to laying out 'how to do ethical research' and discussing just what ethics are in this context (see, for example, Hammersley and Traianou 2012).

In this chapter, as well as adding to this canon of literature, we hope to offer a slightly different reflection on thinking about and doing so-called 'risky research', and the ethical dilemmas, experiences and decisions that are often made in the field by researchers who are opting for in-depth qualitative experiential methods as a means to answer their research questions. Drawing heavily on the anthropological tradition of using participant observation, ethnography and autobiographical methods to 'live alongside' participants in their own spaces and lives, we reflect on our own experiences of researching with police drug squads (Bacon 2013, 2016) and with sex workers and the broader sex industry (Sanders 2005, 2008) to discuss the real-life realities of dealing with ethics in the field.

## Ethical caution and the institution

The nature of criminological studies is that qualitative research entails morally ambiguous situations and often falls into the generic category of 'risky research'.

Criminologists inevitably work with participants who are considered 'risky' because of a combination of their behaviour and assigned criminogenic characteristics, or because the environment in which they work, play and inhabit is on the margins of society. This definition of risky research is applicable both to individuals and groups as well as organizations that deal with those we are expected to be cautious around. So organizations, services, professionals and practitioners who deal with 'risky' situations, people and places are part of the general category that falls into risky research areas. Research ethics protocols are a formal attempt to manage such risks.

Concerns about the ethical quality of research are characteristic of a society where anxieties about the unintended consequences of science and technology are increasingly common (Beck 1992). In order to ensure that ethical principles are embedded within the research process, academic researchers are now obliged to operate in accordance with prescribed ethical guidelines and to subject their research proposals to the review processes of Research Ethics Committees (RECs). This formal system of professional oversight aims to set the standards for ethical research practice by striking a balance between the potential harms and benefits of research as well as ensuring that research takes place within the law (for example, the Data Protection Act 1998 in the UK) and adheres to any national ethical frameworks such as those operated by the National Health Service (NHS) or the Prison Service. Whilst the debate and controversy that has surrounded the rise of formal, often university-level RECs over the past decade forms the backdrop to what we have to say here, there is not time to flesh out the details of such controversies (see Hammersley 2006). Needless to say that, on the one hand, whilst there has been a recognition of the need to standardize research processes and how university paid employees engage with the general public to protect them from exploitation and harm, there has been substantial criticism at the ways in which RECs have become gatekeepers that vet research topics and methods, imposing concerns around litigation and reputation rather than assessing applications for process and procedure (Hammersley 2010; Melrose 2011). For instance, Simon Winlow and Steve Hall (2012: 400) suggest that 'the cynics amongst us might regard this new bureaucratic gatekeeper as one of a growing assortment of aggressive "modernizing" or "managerialist" incursions now being made into the traditional cultures of Britain's venerable university system by neo-liberalism's relentless and controlling market ideology'.

The training that academics receive in research methods and their practical experience in conducting research was previously presumed to offer sufficient protections against unethical behaviour. Winlow and Hall (2012) argue that current procedures are transforming research ethics from a genuine social and internal dialogue into a box-ticking administrative task which cannot possibly cover the infinite complexities of social research as it is practised. Kevin Haggerty (2004) uses the concept of 'ethics creep' to describe the expansion of the ethics bureaucracy and the intensification of the regulation of practices deemed to fall within its official ambit. It marks, he argues, 'a move away from a system based on an assumption of professional competence and responsibility to one based on institutionalized distrust' (2004: 393). In other words, the current system treats researchers as unethical until they have proven their ethical credentials before a jury of their peers. Often the expertise of these peers lies significantly outside that of the research proposals being reviewed. Haggerty's analysis of the Canadian ethics review process reveals that the culture of Research Ethics Boards is cautious and conservative, and that members 'will occasionally feel compelled to render decisions that are patently unjust, unethical, and divorced from common sense in an attempt to appear consistent or to avoid violating the formal guidelines' (2004: 411). In conclusion, Haggerty (2004: 412) submits that an unfortunate consequence of these developments will likely be that researchers will opt out of 'the uncertainty and delays associated with qualitative, ethnographic, or critical scholarship which do not fit easily into the existing research ethics template'.

## Discretion in risky research

As Elizabeth Murphy and Robert Dingwall (2001: 347) make clear, 'given the diversity and flexibility of ethnography, and the indeterminacy of potential harm, a prescriptive approach may be positively unhelpful. It can fail to protect participants and, perhaps even more important, may deflect researchers from the reflective pursuit of ethical practice'. Some degree of autonomy in decision making is a good thing. In fact, research by its very nature is discretionary in the sense that it involves the exercise of choice or judgement in response to the dictates of situational exigencies. When conducting research in the field, researchers routinely exercise discretion and operate in conditions of low visibility with relatively little supervision. Moreover, discretion is logically necessary as broad ethical principles and terms such as 'consent', 'harm' and 'risk' require interpretation in unpredictable fact situations. As Ronald Dworkin (1977: 39) opines, 'discretion, like a hole in the doughnut, does not exist except as an area left open by a surrounding belt of restriction. It is therefore a relative concept'. In such conditions, ethical research practice largely depends upon the integrity of the researcher and the ongoing interrogation of the types of responsibilities that they might owe to others. Research is not ethical just because the existing rules have been followed or the Ethics Committee has determined that it is so. RECs operate *before* any research takes place. Reviews of ethics applications are based on prospective accounts of what will be done and hypothetical scenarios that the researcher has explained in 'lay' language in order to express quite complex social and personal situations in a manner that appears to be 'the least risky' for administrators or academics not based in the same discipline to understand. The actual conduct of research is not monitored. Writing in 'discretion' as a leading principle of engagement with participants in the field during a long-term ethnographic investigation would not meet the tick-box requirements that RECs impose or would not be adequate as a method on which to rely in order to make decisions about a researcher's behaviour. Yet, as our case studies demonstrate, discretion is a guiding principle which undercuts, informs and enables researchers to conduct effective ethnographic studies.

To understand more about how the principle of discretion works, we can draw on police studies literature and make a comparison between the criminal and the criminological investigator. Like police detectives, the discretion of the criminologist lies in how they decide to conduct the investigations they undertake, the interpretations they make that contribute to how the 'facts' are established, the ways in which they use rules to rationalize their actions, and the written accounts they give and what they leave out (Collison 1995; Ericson 1993; Hobbs 1988; Innes 2003; Maguire and Norris 1992; McConville, Sanders and Leng 1991; Skolnick 2011). In his seminal essay on rules and policing, Richard Ericson (2007) integrates and advances existing knowledge to illustrate that the police have various orientations towards rules depending on both the type of rule in question and the pragmatic circumstances faced. When actually engaged in police work, he suggests that officers 'are variously ignorant of potential applicable rules, sidestep troublesome rules they think may be applicable, break rules if such action is deemed necessary to get the job done and use rules creatively to accomplish desired outcomes' (2007: 394). Reflecting on his covert study of the police, Simon Holdaway (1983: 14) makes the valid point that ultimately it is the individual researcher who will make the decision, accept the risks and live with the consequences. The issue of whether a risk should be tolerated depends partly on why people are prepared to take it.

We would argue that the 'use of rules' in social science research is much the same. David Smith and Jeremy Gray (1983: 171) submit a convenient way of summarizing their analysis of the relationship between police rules, procedures and practices which can be applied to the context of research ethics. 'Working rules' are those that are internalized by researchers to become guiding principles of their conduct. Such rules include 'do no harm', obtain consent, ensure privacy and prevent misrepresentation. They are deeply ingrained within academic culture, shared basic assumptions that provide researchers with coping strategies and frames of reference for how and why research should and can be done in any situation. 'Inhibitory rules' are those which are not internalized, but which researchers take into account when deciding how to act and which tend to discourage them from behaving in certain ways in case they should be caught and the rule invoked against them. The requirement to operate in accordance with prescribed ethical guidelines and to submit research proposals for ethical approval are inhibitory rules. Researchers comply with these rules because they are embedded into the terms and conditions of research funding opportunities and because non-compliance can result in them being disciplined or fired by their respective universities. 'Presentational rules' are ones that exist to give an acceptable appearance to the way that social research is carried out. These are the rules that are used when constructing submissions to the REC so that the applicant 'says the right things' and 'ticks the right boxes' in order to gain approval.

The following sections consider a selection of the ethical issues that were encountered during our fieldwork endeavours and how they were managed – they are presented in the first-person singular.

## Engaging with and managing potential harms

When performing research involving human participants, there is always the chance that some harm could befall a member of the research process in some way. At the very least, 'being researched can create stress and provoke anxiety, especially if the research is believed to be evaluating one's work, one's life and oneself' (Hammersley and Atkinson 2007: 214). This is particularly true when the research is dealing with sensitive topics. Apart from the inconvenience, interruption and imposition of the research, the police were unlikely to be exposed to any harm greater than or in addition to those encountered in their normal working lives. Perhaps the main risk posed by the research was that I might observe officers engaging in informal practices, professional misconduct or corruption and decide to inform their supervisors or senior officers. However, besides the informal practices that are characteristic of the occupational culture, these behaviours were not observed. Police officers did not always act in accordance with policy and procedure, but I never witnessed them act in breach of the law or use excessive force. I was told stories about such practices, but stories are not evidence and so there is no reason to report them. Reflecting on his own observations of policing activities, Jerome H. Skolnick (2011: 33) points out that 'it is most improbable that police would treat suspects more severely, or with less regard for their constitutional rights, in my presence than out of it. Similarly, it seems hardly reasonable to suppose that police would be more lax, less concerned with the quality of their work, or less efficient under outside observation'. On this issue, the REC *suggested* that I include the following caveat in the participant consent form: 'In the event that a research participant discloses a collateral, unreported act which categorically amounts to an illegality, breach of security or gross misconduct, the researcher may be required to identify the act to appropriate authorities.' The principle is correct, but the wording is overly legalistic and not very comprehensible. Furthermore, it would have drawn attention to such issues, which participants would probably have cast more strictly than the REC intended (for example, minor breaches of police regulations). This would have raised their suspicions and made it more difficult to access the inner world of the police and observe their backstage behaviours. So, given that it was only a suggestion, I exercised my discretion and chose not to include it in the consent form.

In the case of researching alongside drug detectives in their everyday policing activities, although I would generally choose to avoid danger at all costs, if I'm honest, I found the potentially dangerous aspects of doing fieldwork with the police the most exhilarating. Coming from an academic environment where the risk of a papercut is about as bad as it gets, the thrill of the chase and the chance of a violent altercation was a welcome break from vegetating in front of a computer screen. Most fieldwork activities did not carry much enhanced risk. For example, carrying out observations in a police station or from a police car is not especially risky. The detectives actually spent most of their time performing relatively mundane administrative duties. I appreciate, however, that a few activities did carry an enhanced risk, in particular the observation of arrests and the execution of drug warrants that involved entering premises and searching for evidence of a suspected offence. The police carried out risk assessments when I entered the field and potential risks were then minimized on a case-by-case basis by way of a number of precautionary measures, such as wearing the necessary safety equipment and only going near arrestees after they had been properly secured.

Only once did I consciously stay clear of potential harm when accompanying the uniformed branch in order to observe the policing of the night-time economy. During a shift with the response team, the police officer I was partnered up with responded to an emergency call from a nightclub in the centre of a town in the north of England where there had been a violent incident involving a group of young men. As we approached the venue, the officer told me a story about a colleague who had been 'knocked out by a drunken idiot' the previous week; he said it was not an uncommon occurrence. This information got me rattled. The door staff pointed us down a nearby street, where we saw three men exchanging shirts with each other. 'It's so we don't recognize them.' He turned off the engine, got out of the car and went over to 'have a word' and find out what was going on. I stayed in the car. The potentially drunken idiots were all much bigger than me and I was not willing to take a punch for research purposes. A word was all that it required and nothing 'kicked off', but I felt like I had let the officer down by not providing him with back-up. When we were discussing the event afterwards, he said 'it would have been nice to have some support but you need to put safety first'. After that he kept referring to me as 'a safe pair of hands'. Fearfulness aside, however, the decision was justified on the grounds that I am not a trained police officer and could have put him in danger had I accompanied him. Not being skilled in the art of clairvoyance or the owner of a genuine crystal ball, these circumstances could not possibly have been foretold to the REC in the paper-pushing stage of the research process. Doing research 'in situ' means you have no idea what is going to happen and have to respond to the dictates of situational exigencies.

Another foreseeable but highly unlikely risk was that during observations, I could have been identified by criminals or their associates and mistakenly thought to be a police officer or involved with the police in some other way. On this point, the most 'at risk' I ever felt was in a courtroom in a city in the south of England. The detectives had come to watch one of their targets get 'sent down'. He was given eight years' imprisonment for possession of an illegal firearm and possession with the intent to supply heroin. Seated in the public gallery, I noticed some of the local 'gang members', recognizing them from case files and 'mug shots' on the walls of the police station. But instead of watching the court proceedings, they were watching us, intently. 'They already know who we are, they're just trying to intimidate us' explained the detective sitting next me. I was intimidated. When we left the courtroom, one of them squared up to the investigating officer and uttered a string of profanities that need not be repeated here. The detective waited for him to finish and then turned and walked away. 'He's just trying to look hard in front of the others.' It worked. From then on, I kept looking over my shoulder when walking the streets alone. To minimize this risk of mistaken identity, the REC recommended that I spend no time in the research settings when fieldwork was not being carried out. In practice, however, this was impractical, as I often had to spend the night in the police service areas. So I discussed the situation with my supervisors and decided to minimize contact with the areas to the amount which was necessary and promised that I would remain cautious and alert at all times.

In the course of researching within sex markets, there have been some occasions when harm to myself or to participants was possible, producing occasions of anxiety, confusion and instances of retreating from the research context. These anecdotes from the 'sex work field' must be caveated with a note to flag up that the majority of times and spaces through which I conducted ethnographic research within the sex industry, people and spaces have been ordinary, mundane and without any hint of danger or uncomfortableness (see, for example, Sanders and Hardy 2014). However, as in all quasi-legal activities where informal economies exist that are trading services which are considered deviant and transient, the element of risk is one of the many aspects of managing the fieldwork setting (for more details, see Sanders 2006). One such occurrence is worth repeating as a learning point and an example of how a researcher can affect the everyday happenings of an informal market. Whilst conducting a survey with street sex workers on the 'beat' in the traditionally known 'red light district' of a large city in southern England, the very presence of the research activity created ripples of anxiety in the street sex work community. Despite having the local religious welfare support group as a gatekeeper that would direct women to me whilst I was sitting in a car on a residential street waiting to conduct the short survey, such a sponsor did not make me immune from danger. The issue was not the research itself: women were happy to engage in the research and tell me about their sex work histories and needs relating to health and welfare support. The issue was the small financial remuneration that was offered to take part in the research. Following expected practice in sex work research, it was normal to offer sex workers compensation for taking part in research as this was taking time out of their working hours. The research was being conducted during the hours of 9 pm to 2 am in the dark wintery nights because this was the time that women were visible on the beat, waiting for clients to 'do business'. However, on this occasion, the financial compensation caused some difficult and dangerous circumstances. As word spread that 'easy money' could be made by doing the survey, there started to be competition for who could do the survey and obtain the quick cash.

Over the course of two evenings, various tense situations occurred. Two women had a fight outside the car as one wanted to do the survey first before she went to see her regular client at an arranged time. Another woman broke the fight up. There were various sex workers with their boyfriends hanging around waiting for their slot and it was clear that in some instances the boyfriends were controlling the activities of the women. On one occasion I saw the boyfriend snatch the money out of the participant's hand as soon as she got out of the car. On another (more upsetting occasion) a domestic violence incident happened down the street as a man was dragging a woman by her hair to my car and screaming at her to get out and earn money. The police were called. Several women revealed that the money would be used immediately to buy drugs (heroin usually) for the boyfriend and if she was lucky for her as well. On these occasions the research was terminated and the research setting was re-located away from the pressurized and volatile street sex work environment and moved to a daytime venue where women could turn up in a more relaxed environment without third parties or the overt pressure of earning cash for drugs.

As a naïve student, there were several issues going on here which were only to be revealed once in the field. The volatility of the street sex markets where many of the sex workers and their associates are motivated by chronic drug dependency meant that the presence of any possibility to get hold of immediate cash made a significant impact on the daily happenings. There was significant ethical 'fall-out' as the presence of the research activity caused distress and even violence for some sex workers. Such an experience was a real lesson about the realities of research-ing in a dynamic environment where there are 'unknowns'.

## Are you a police officer? Have you done sex work?

There are legal restrictions on how far police researchers can participate in the routine activities of policing, yet from time to time I was given the opportunity to be more of a participant than an observer and assist with some operational police work. For example, I occasionally donned a pair of rubber gloves and assisted the police in the searching of property for controlled drugs, helped fill out warrant applications and became quite proficient at taking surveillance logs. A physical appearance like mine made me something of an asset during covert operations, because I was able to make the detectives look less conspicuous. 'If [the drug dealers] see us together they'll never think I'm a cop' said a detective as we sat on a park bench pretending to read a newspaper. I even assisted the detectives and some members of a Safer Neighbourhood Team in the excavation of a large-scale cannabis factory that was discovered in a boarded-up bakery, despite the accusa-tions that I was 'only doing it to fill my pockets'. Upon reflection, in addition to the expectation that I should 'pull my weight', I believe the detectives thought they were doing me a favour by letting me get a bit of hands-on experience. At first, I was uneasy about getting my hands dirty, unsure of the legal and ethical implications, but excited by the prospect of doing police work. Sensing my inter-nal conflict, an officer once assured me that 'we're not going to put you in harm's way, mate, or let you do anything that'll get us into trouble'. I also believe the detectives were doing it to gauge my responses and joke around. This was particu-larly evident when the same officer later asked if I'd be willing to buy drugs for evidential purposes. 'I'm pretty sure I'm not supposed to do that' I replied with a slightly shaky voice. He laughed and said he was 'just pulling my leg'. Without a doubt, my readiness to participate helped develop a rapport and added another reality check to the research experience.

Although I never intentionally impersonated a police officer, members of the public occasionally mistook me for one. Given that I was usually with plain-clothed officers and wearing a bulletproof vest with the police emblem emblazoned on the front, this was an easy mistake to make. When I raised this ethical issue with the police, they said that they would explain my presence if necessary and when appropriate. For the most part, the people I encountered were so preoccupied by their deprivation or liberty or invasion of privacy that my presence went unnoticed or unquestioned. Only once did someone ask about me, when I was with the uniform branch responding to a domestic disturbance. 'Is he a cop?' asked the lady of the house. 'He's with us' said the police officer. In most situations I was not introduced at all and so people were deceived into believing I was a police officer through lack of admission. The question here is who was responsible for the field-work situation. Whilst I did not necessarily want to put police ethics over those of my academic institution, I felt it ethically unsound to impact upon police work by blowing my cover and getting informed consent from suspects, arrestees and their associates if the police deemed it not to be necessary or appropriate. This brings me on to perhaps the greatest ethical dilemma that occurred during fieldwork:

> The detectives had executed a warrant and requested that I stand guard at the front gate of the property being searched, until back-up arrived. As always, a police presence in this part of town had resulted in a small crowd of neigh-bours clustering around the scene of the crime. It was one of those estates where everybody seemed to know everybody else – or at least liked to get involved in everybody else's business. Amongst the crowd were some family members of the suspects and another suspected dealer. 'Just make sure no one comes up to the house. If you get any trouble give us a shout on this' said the drug squad sergeant as he handed me a radio. *This is above and beyond the role of a researcher.* But the squad were a few men down and clearly stressed and overstretched, so I decided to play along. *Was this another initiation ritual or a test of my allegiance?* The crowd were behaving in an orderly fashion and keeping to themselves: talking, pointing and making phone calls. *I can handle this.* Then a young girl appeared from out of nowhere, walked directly up to me and asked: 'Are you a police officer?' I panicked. *Shit.* I nodded. *Double shit.* She walked away. She stopped and stared. *Did I just illegally impersonate a police officer?* (Fieldnote)

When I returned to university later that week, I spoke with colleagues about this ethical incident. Some of them told me that under no circumstances should I have claimed to be a police officer, whereas others were of the opinion that under the circumstances I had no choice but to say yes. A problem could have arisen if a member of the public had questioned me about the police intervention. They could have provided me with sensitive information or asked me to intervene in another matter. Had any of these scenarios actually occurred, I would have imme-diately fetched a member of the drug squad. Alternatively, had I told the girl that I was not a police officer, she might have become confused. If I had told her that I was a doctoral candidate carrying out an observational study of operational police work, she would have become even more confused. If she had then told the oth-ers, it might have aggravated the situation. All things considered, I complied with a police request, was forced to make a quick decision in difficult circumstances, accepted the risks and can live with the consequences.

Much of the research conducted by Sanders has involved ethnographic methods in sex work settings – so on the street, in brothels and saunas, in strip clubs and other venues where sex workers and clients meet, including in 'virtual' environments. All of these individual arenas of interaction have often been unknown entities upon entering as a researcher, so I really only had the previous literature and 'encounters from the field' to guide my own research journey. Some of these experiences have been difficult as the personal meets the professional, and I have had to enter environments in which I would not normally put myself at certain times. For instance, observing interactions in strip clubs in the early hours of the morning whilst heavily pregnant and feeling very 'out of place'. But determined to gather the data and achieve the targets set, my 'out-of-place' physicality needed to be put aside as the deadline of both popping out a baby and calling time on the fieldwork were equally imposing. Other projects which have been closely designed to bring the participants to me (literally) have not always produced the expected response of an orchestrated environment where the researcher is in control. In a project where I interviewed men who paid for sex, the majority of participants came to my office in the university to be interviewed. The power clearly was favoured in my direction as I was in the comfort of my office, a very familiar place within the 'corridors of power' that was my institution. Yet drawing out participants' sexual stories and often being placed in the position of 'the other woman' in terms of how the married men engaged in the cathartic nature of the interview about their commercial sex lives made the comfortable space somewhat less familiar. The personal questioning the participants directed at me, the innuendos, the sexualized banter and the propositions often caught me off-guard.

Yet at the same time I was very aware that in order to research the sex industry and 'get close' to participants so as to understand them and their worlds, compromise in the research field was inevitable and was something that would frame the research encounter. Most notably, this learning point happened when I was a student, researching the indoor sex industries, spending many hours in brothels and working flats with women who were teaching me about their working and personal lives. On numerous occasions I was 'tested' by participants in terms of maintaining my confidentiality and not revealing my true 'researcher' identity to unassuming clients (see Sanders 2006). This of course involved covert behaviours and some would argue deception as I followed the requests of the sex workers and brothel owners and acted as a 'new girl' whilst sitting in the lounge with the other women: stories were created of who I was, what I was doing and when I was 'working' for the regulars who wanted to book in with the 'new girl'. I often felt at the mercy of the sex workers, as in order to gain their trust, I had to play by their rules, and when I was in their working environments, their rules became my rules. I knew on many occasions when I was put in predicaments and asked to engage in activities that may have made me turn and flee that this was about the women building up trust with me, deciphering whether I was judgemental about their lives, testing how much I would be shocked, scared and leave the environment altogether. I rarely was, and trust was built over time, as they saw I was able to work within my own professional codes, but at the same time respect their rules of engagement and not place their businesses or their identities under any pressure or exposure.

Whilst there are a range of reflections on researching the sex industry, feminist models of doing sex work research as ethically as possible, as well as dissections on the health and safety of both researchers and participants in this field (see Sanders, O'Neill and Pitcher 2009: Chapter 10), revealing anecdotes rarely permeate these academic discussions. It is in these anecdotes that we learn the complexities of ethnography in sensitive and informal economies, with hard-to-reach groups (both of elites and those considered at the margins), as it is in these 'in situ', difficult-to-anticipate events that data is often the richest and most revealing in terms of understanding how social actors engage in their worlds.

## Conclusion: negotiating restrictions to innovative research

We hope we have provided some real-life reflections on how some criminologists decide how to behave and how to negotiate research settings and relationships in their everyday engagement with participants and research spaces. We have aimed to flag up that just like other professionals who are working within a very strict set of guidelines and rules (i.e. the police), researchers who are practising ethnographic methods with sensitive topics also practise a range of discretionary practices as part of their 'working rules'. These practices arise out of certain situations, most of which cannot be foreseen or predicted, and are influenced by gatekeepers and others in the field on whom the researcher relies to carry out the research and to be kept safe. For cutting-edge and novel research to take place with organizations such as the police and sex work projects and sex workers (who are arguably over-researched), formulaic expectations about how research should be conducted are both unrealistic and naïve, out of touch with the real-life decisions of a researcher. But perhaps that is the only way it can be as ultimately for ethnographers, the lines between the personal and the professional can be somewhat blurred as we continue to invest ourselves in the processes and outcomes of the research.

In his essay on research ethics, Clive Norris (1993: 137) argues that fieldwork with the police will 'lead the researcher into a quagmire of ethical consideration. Inevitably, one is faced with contradictory and competing choices and it is impossible to satisfy them all'. Like many police researchers, Norris is supportive of what Joseph Fletcher (1966: 31) called 'situation ethics', a flexible approach to research ethics that recognizes the complexity of fieldwork and the need to judge ethical standards in a way that is attuned to the specifics of the case at hand. When addressing ethical issues, Maurice Punch (1986: 83) wisely suggests that researchers should rely on common sense, academic convention and peer control through discussion to promote understanding of the issues. We learn to become effective researchers in spaces which are often closed off from the general public through a range of methods: by formal teaching and qualifications; from doing research training during our studies; from telling stories and listening to 'tales from the field' from colleagues and experienced fieldworkers; and, most importantly, we learn as we do research. It is in the 'doing' of research in risky settings with so-called 'risky' participants that we learn the art and craft of fieldwork and how to negotiate research settings and relationships. The craft of fieldwork is learnt through 'on the job' experience and characterized by a specific set of research skills and unwritten understandings about the rules of the game. The art concerns intuition, instinctive feelings and hunches towards problem solving in a human capacity. 'Science' rarely enters the equation.

As researchers who have been crafting our own research skills for over a decade now, constantly bobbing back and forth into the research field, and always in contact with participants in some capacity, we are both left continually asking 'are we ever out of the field?' We ponder 'when does a conversational exchange become an interview?', 'when does meeting for a coffee become a participant observation activity?' and 'when does a telephone call, email, a text or Facebook message become "research" data?' Crafting a career as a criminologist in a field which is considered 'risky' (we prefer to think of these settings and topics as 'tricky' or even 'edgy') means that the field is also active, constantly re-visited, and integrated into broader social and personal relationships. Just as police detectives rely on informants who are actively involved in crime or closely associated with the criminal milieu to perform their job, researchers also need to be constantly involved in networks and contacts outside their institution and the academy in order to investigate research questions. There are often unspoken assumptions that those involved in researching 'the underworld' and criminals will invariably have contacts in such networks. As researchers, our jobs are focused on the translation process: moving from the criminal and marginalized worlds to academic reality which is vetted through the peer review process as we attempt to showcase the most convincing narratives to support our claims.

It is these negotiations, these 'working rules' which are guided by principles of discretion that create the context for ethical research entirely outside any formal ethics committee or institutional administrative surveillance. Whilst we fully take on board the principles and practices that inform REC processes such as confidentiality, informed consent, safety and anonymity, as active researchers, we are also aware that the monitoring and controlling elements of RECs can be circumvented when pursuing our criminological imaginations. RECs do not facilitate ethical research; instead, our experience demonstrates that the integrity of the researcher in adopting 'working rules' and being guided by the realities of an in situ context are what creates ethical research. Martyn Hammersley and Anna Traianou (2012) start their book on ethics with a reminder from Urie Bronfenbrenner (1952: 452), who said: 'The only safe way to avoid violating principles of professional ethics is to refrain from doing social research altogether.' We are on the same page here as we reflect on the various 'in situ' ethical dilemmas and decisions we have and will continue to have to make in the course of sex work and policing ethnographic research. Yet we firmly believe that not doing the research in a way which embeds the researcher in the setting and scenarios we have described would mean that knowledge is not created and extracted, and that there would not be the evidence excavated which can be moulded to inform policy and practice. Institutions need to trust the professionalism of their academics to make informed and accountable ethical decisions whilst working out in the field, exposed to the unknown and making human decisions. There are no guarantees in social research, paperwork or not; accountability exists in the field where researchers make the real decisions as they engage with individuals.

# References

Bacon, Matthew (2013) 'The Informal Regulation of an Illegal Trade: The Hidden Politics of Drugs Detective Work'. *Etnografia e Ricera Qualitativa*, 1: 61–80.

——. (2016) *Taking Care of Business: Police Detectives, Drug Law Enforcement and Proactive Investigation*. Oxford: Oxford University Press.

Beck, Ulrich (1992) *Risk Society: Towards a New Modernity*. London: Sage Publications.

Bronfenbrenner, Urie (1952) 'Principles of Professional Ethics: Cornell Studies in Social Growth'. *The American Psychologist*, 7: 452–3.

Collison, Mike (1995) *Police, Drugs and Community*. London: Free Association Books.

Dworkin, Ronald (1977) 'Is Law a System of Rules', in Ronald Dworkin (ed.), *The Philosophy of Law*. New York: Oxford University Press, pp. 38–65.

Ericson, Richard (1993) *Making Crime: A Study of Detective Work*, 2nd edn. Toronto: University of Toronto Press.

——. (2007) 'Rules in Policing: Five Perspectives'. *Theoretical Criminology*, 11(3): 367–401.

Fletcher, Joseph (1966) *Situation Ethics*. London: SCM Press.

Haggerty, Kevin (2004) 'Ethics Creep: Governing Social Science Research in the Name of Ethics'. *Qualitative Sociology*, 27(4): 391–414.

Hammersley, Martyn (2006) 'Are Ethics Committees Ethical?' *Qualitative Research* 2: 4–8.

——. (2010) 'Creeping Ethical Regulation and the Strangling of Research'. *Sociological Research Online*, 15(4): 16.

Hammersley, Martyn and Paul Atkinson (2007) *Ethnography: Principles in Practice*, 3rd edn. London: Routledge.

Hammersley, Martyn and Anna Traianou (2012) *Ethics in Qualitative Research: Controversies and Contexts*. London: Sage Publications.

Hobbs, Dick (1988) *Doing the Business: Entrepreneurship, the Working Class and Detectives in the East End of London*. Oxford: Oxford University Press.

Holdaway, Simon (1983) *Inside the British Police*. Oxford: Basil Blackwell.

Innes, Martin (2003) *Investigating Murder: Detective Work and the Police Response to Criminal Homicide*. Oxford: Oxford University Press.

Maguire, Mike and Clive Norris (1992) *The Conduct and Supervision of Criminal Investigations: The Royal Commission on Criminal Justice*. Research Report No. 5. London: HMSO.

McConville, Michael, Andrew Sanders and Roger Leng (1991) *The Case for the Prosecution: Police Suspects and the Construction of Criminality*. London: Routledge.

Melrose, Margaret (2011) 'Regulating Social Research'. *Sociological Research Online*, 16(2): 14.

Murphy, Elizabeth and Robert Dingwall (2001) 'The Ethics of Ethnography', in Paul Atkinson, Amanda Coffey, Sara Delamont, John Lofland and Lyn Lofland (eds), *Handbook of Ethnography*. London: Sage Publications, pp. 339–51.

Norris, Clive (1993) 'Some Ethical Considerations on Fieldwork with the Police', in Dick Hobbs and Tim May (eds), *Interpreting the Field: Accounts of Ethnography*. Oxford: Oxford University Press, pp. 123–43.

Punch, Maurice (1986) *Politics and Ethics of Fieldwork*, Beverly Hills, CA: Sage Publications.

Sanders, Teela (2005) *Sex Work: A Risky Business*. Cullompton: Willan Publishing.

——. (2006) 'Sexing up the Subject: Methodological Nuances in Researching the Female Sex Industry'. *Sexualities*, 9(4): 449–68.

——. (2008) *Paying for Pleasure: Men Who Buy Sex*. Cullompton: Willan Publishing.

Sanders, Teela and Kate Hardy (2014) *Flexible Workers: Labour, Regulation and the Political Economy of the Stripping Industry*. London: Routledge.

Sanders, Teela, Maggie O'Neill and Jane Pitcher (2009) *Prostitution: Sex Work, Politics and Policy*. London: Sage Publications.

Skolnick, Jerome H. (2011) *Justice without Trial: Law Enforcement in Democratic Society*, 4th edn. New Orleans: Quid Pro Books.

Smith, David and Jeremy Gray (1983) *Police and People in London: The Police in Action*. London: Policy Studies Institute.

Winlow, Simon and Steve Hall (2012) 'What is an "Ethics Committee"? Academic Governance in an Epoch of Belief and Incredulity'. *British Journal of Criminology*, 52(2): 400-16.

# 10 Gaining access and managing gatekeepers

## Undertaking criminological research with those 'within' the system

*Kate Fitz-Gibbon*

### Introduction

At a time when criminal justice systems internationally are facing new challenges surrounding the cost, openness and effectiveness of justice, the interaction between those within the system and those researching their operations is increasingly important. For criminologists, a better understanding of the experiences and perceptions of the professionals operating at all levels of a justice system may yield valuable insights into the practice and operation of the law. By directly engaging those involved in the delivery of justice, criminologists can seek not only to illuminate the 'hidden' decisions and processes of the law, but also to examine the influences and views of these institutional gatekeepers. The need to achieve both is apparent in light of the evolution of processes of criminal justice decision making and an abundance of reform over the past three decades across Western justice systems. In particular, there are two features of contemporary criminal justice systems that must be taken into account in qualitative criminological research. First, in the post-9/11 climate, justice is increasingly achieved behind a wall that can be seen as impenetrable to the public and inaccessible to the researcher – a trend which presents unique barriers and challenges to those researching the decisions and operations of closed systems of justice. Second, legislators, advocates and legal professionals at all levels are increasingly required to consider the interests of those previously thought to be outside the bounds of law, such as women, children, the marginalized and the racialized. The extent to which this leads to a meaningful change in practice and access to justice, however, remains a highly contested area of inquiry. Within this liquid climate, criminologists will arguably not be able to fully understand the decisions made in, or the impact of, the criminal justice system in practice if they do not penetrate the barriers and engage the gatekeepers to 'look' inside.

To illuminate how and why criminologists should engage with criminal justice gatekeepers, this chapter examines both the process and potential outcomes of such research. The first section considers issues surrounding access and how the difficulty of gaining access to institutional gatekeepers has changed over the last two decades. The second section builds on access to explore the value of managing working relationships with these gatekeepers both during and beyond the life of the research. The third section highlights the need for, and benefits of, interviews with those people who work within the criminal justice system, particularly with reference to the increasingly non-transparent operation of several Western criminal justice systems, law reform processes and the plausibility of policy transfer between comparable criminal justice systems.[1] Throughout this chapter, the experiences and views of those who have undertaken criminological research with institutional gatekeepers are drawn upon to examine the value of, and need for, qualitative interviews with those engaged in the delivery of criminal justice.

The police are often described as the gatekeepers of the criminal justice system (Australian Law Reform Commission 2010; Hartman and Belknap 2003); however, when applying this term to criminological research, gatekeepers exist at every level of the justice system. This aligns with the definition provided by Angela Dwyer and Hennessey Hayes (2011: 109) that 'gatekeepers are individuals in the field from whom access to research participants must be requested'. Within the context of criminological research, this can include police, prosecutors, judicial clerks and officers, correctional staff, parole officers and institutional ethics committees.

At each level of the criminal justice system, gatekeepers play a key role in either opening the system up or actively excluding researchers from accessing those who operate within the system. As noted by Carla Reeves: 'These people can help or hinder research depending upon their personal thoughts on the validity of the research and its value, as well as their approach to the welfare of the people under their charge' (2010: 317). The decision on the part of the gatekeeper to 'help or hinder' research can be further influenced by a range of factors, including the power dynamics between the researcher and their subject, the currency of the research and appetite for an inquiry of that focus, as well as the perceived resource strain that involvement in the research would cause for its target respondents. In making these decisions, gatekeepers can be categorized as internal and external, or formal and informal (Davies and Peters 2014; Reeves 2010). For the purposes of this chapter, the gatekeepers of the criminal justice system are considered formal and are examined here according to the part of the system within which they operate – police, prosecution and courts.

A central issue of concern between an institutional gatekeeper and a researcher are considerations of power. Who holds power? How can power be misused or influential in the research process? How do power dynamics influence a person's willingness to participate in research? While criminologists often find themselves engaged in research involving vulnerable populations, such as victims of crime and prisoners (Noaks and Wincup 2004; Richards 2011; Richards and Bartels 2011), a reflection on accessing and managing gatekeepers involves consideration of how researchers can effectively engage with those most empowered within the system. This is described by Kelly Richards (2011: 68) as researching 'up' and refers to research that directly engages those in official positions of power, such as police officers, legal practitioners (defence and/or prosecution) and judicial officers. The lessons from criminological research that involves engaging with those more powerful than the researcher have been subject to much less scrutiny than comparable research examining vulnerable subjects (Lumsden and Winter 2014). For this reason, this chapter adds important insight into how and why, in the current penal climate, criminologists must not only engage those working in the criminal justice system, but must also consider the subsequent power dynamics of doing so.

## Gaining access

Criminologists have long recognized (and often lamented) the difficulty of gaining access to those who operate 'within' the criminal justice system (Ashworth 1995; Baldwin 2008; McGovern 2011; Pierce 2002).[2] Writing 20 years ago, Andrew Ashworth described the difficulty that researchers face in accessing members of the justice system, in this case judicial officers:

> Research into why judges and magistrates do what they do has long been advocated as a prerequisite of the successful development of sentencing policy, but sentencers in many countries seem to resist research. Apart from the irony that judges sometimes berate academics for not understanding practice when it is the judge who bar the way to research by means of observation and interview, the social importance of sentencing is a powerful argument in favour of careful research. More ought to be known about the motivation of judges and magistrates. Such knowledge would assist in the formation of sentencing policy, and it might also help to extend a form of accountability into this sphere of public decision-making. (Ashworth 1995: 263)

Mirroring Ashworth's depiction, and writing a decade later, Geraldine Mackenzie (2005: 2) argues that 'there is little interchange between those writing about sentencing theory, and those involved in its actual practice, despite the importance of one to the other'.

As identified by Ashworth and Mackenzie, the resistance from those within the system has led to something of a traditional dichotomy in criminological, socio-legal and law scholarship between those who work within (the 'insiders') and those who sit outside (the 'outsiders') the daily operation of the criminal justice system. The consequential operational knowledge gap that inevitably arises between the insiders and outsiders of the criminal justice system has been recognized in past research (Bibas 2006; Fitz-Gibbon 2014a) and is well captured by Stephanos Bibas:

> A great gulf divides insiders and outsiders in the criminal justice system. The insiders who run the criminal justice system – judges, police, and especially prosecutors – have information, power, and self-interests that greatly influence the criminal justice system's process and outcomes. Outsiders – crime victims, bystanders and most of the general public – find the system frustratingly opaque, insular, and unconcerned with proper retribution. (Bibas 2006: 911)

While Bibas does not include the researcher within his descriptors of the 'outsider', for the purposes of this chapter, it is argued that the researcher (at least at the outset of the research process) is an 'outsider' when undertaking fieldwork with those working within a criminal justice system.[3] However, criminologists, through accessing gatekeepers and engaging them in research, can play an important role in bridging the divide between the insiders and outsiders of the criminal justice system.

In recent years there has been a noticeable shift; increasingly, criminologists are gaining access in order to examine the system from the views of those within. This includes the emergence of a body of criminological research drawing on interviews with legal professionals (for example, Bartels 2009; Beyens et al. 2013; Darbyshire 2011; Erez and Rogers 1999; Fitz-Gibbon 2013, 2014a; Jaremba and Mak 2014; Mackenzie 2005; Pierce 2002; Walsh and Douglas 2012) and police officers (for example, Fleming 2011; Gill 2015; McGovern 2011; Skinner 2005). This 'opening up' of the justice system to research is undoubtedly to the benefit of both parties; those working within the justice system and those seeking to undertake research that aims to understand the ways in which justice is administered enhance understandings of its operation and improve the effectiveness of the delivery of criminal justice.

This is not to suggest that access has become easy as such – engaging criminal practitioners in research continues to require the researcher to overcome a series of barriers including institutional ethics (likely both at the university and justice system level) and institutional gatekeepers themselves. Beyond formal mechanisms, in accessing gatekeepers, criminologists are at the whim of the willingness and interest of the individual professional to participate in the research. This stage of recruitment can result in a negative response due to a range of influencing factors, including the busy schedule of the criminal justice practitioner, a reluctance to engage with academia, disorganization or miscommunication on the part of the gatekeeper, and concerns surrounding confidentiality and anonymity (Fitz-Gibbon 2014b; Mackenzie 2005; McGovern 2011). For this reason, while attempts at access may have become more fruitful for criminologists, the approval process for undertaking qualitative research within justice institutions continues to require the researcher to navigate a long and winding path.

## Managing gatekeepers

Once access to gatekeepers has been achieved, there are many ways in which the criminological researcher can utilize and manage that relationship. Gaining access to gatekeepers should be viewed as merely a first (albeit important) step in the research process. As argued by Chad Trulson, James Marquart and Janet Mullings:

> Getting access means that the researcher gets 'in the door' or gets permission to conduct the research. Maintaining access means that the researcher gets what is needed. Importantly, while getting access means that the researcher gets in the door, getting in the door does not ensure that the researcher will be privy to the necessary 'data' to make the research successful. (Trulson, Marquart and Mullings 2004: 453)

Good management of relationships with gatekeepers can also have the added benefit of ongoing research access beyond the initial project, as well as the opportunity to utilize gatekeepers to assist in respondent recruitment and participation. Once the data collection phase of the research has been undertaken, Julie Davies and Eleanor Peters (2014: 39) have noted that gatekeepers can also perform an 'output' role in that they may seek to influence or suppress research findings and, in some cases, apply 'politically motivated pressure' to the interpretation and presentation of the research findings. Each of these issues, which can arise as part of negotiating the researcher–gatekeeper relationship, extends far beyond questions of access.

Once access has been negotiated, there are many ways in which research with legal practitioners can be completed; for example, by disseminating a survey, a structured questionnaire, a semi-structured interview, an in-depth case study interview or through observational research (Noaks and Wincup 2004). Compounding the range of options available, several of these methods can also be conducted on a one-on-one basis between the interviewer and the respondent or in a group format, such as through focus group research (Noaks and Wincup 2004). While it is not the intention of this chapter to examine the strengths and weaknesses of each methodological approach, the relationship between the researcher and the institutional gatekeeper raises important issues related to the time-intensive nature of fieldwork, the negotiation of power relations and the allocation of resources. Each of these issues requires consideration when a researcher is deciding on which methodological approach to adopt.

For the purposes of the remainder of this chapter, the value of conducting qualitative interviews with gatekeepers who operate within the justice system is focused on. This is not to undermine the value of other methodological approaches, which can often be used in conjunction with interviewing or as a valuable alternative, but rather this is done for the purpose of focusing the discussion.

## The research benefits of engaging with the gatekeepers of criminal justice

'Interviewing also allows one to discover worlds that may forever be closed to direct observation, allowing one to hear people report their perspectives and describe their behaviour' (McBarnet 2009: 152). This quote from Doreen McBarnet captures the essence of why criminologists should not shy away from engaging in research with gatekeepers of the criminal justice system despite the aforementioned hurdles. At a time when justice systems worldwide are undergoing significant reform and becoming increasingly non-transparent, it is essential that criminologists adopt qualitative research methods that allow for a detailed examination and analysis of the actions, behaviour and views of those engaged in the delivery of justice.

Highlighting the value of this approach, Jenny Fleming (2011: 23) has argued that the 'capacity to sit where the other person is sitting and to see the world through their eyes is essential', a perspective that is arguably best gained through research methods which directly engage those operating within the area of the justice system under study. Beyond Fleming, the value of interviewing those responsible for the delivery of criminal justice has been widely recognized by criminologists and legal scholars (for example, Davis 2005; Fitz-Gibbon 2014b; Hartman and Belknap 2003; Nelken 2010; Partington 2005; Richards 2011; Ward and Wasby 2010).

This body of research has argued that interviewing gatekeepers provides an opportunity to see inside the criminal justice system and better understand the experiences of the decision makers of justice. As described by Fleming:

> [Interviewing] allows the researcher to enter the field, and is a practicable way to glean a subject's knowledge, opinions, interpretations, accounts, experiences and understandings that form part of the 'social reality' the researcher is trying to capture . . . Police make sense of their world better than most researchers and their 'voice' and perceptions about how things work greatly assists our understanding . . . If we are to understand how police officers approach and negotiate complex problems, we must ask them. (2011: 19)

Building on this, and writing specifically on interviewing judges, Jason Pierce (2002: 139) argues that the interviewing process also has benefits for those within the system, as it provides judges with 'the unique opportunity to discuss, outside of an actual legal dispute, the judicial process and their decision making'. In this respect, interviews with members of the judiciary are beneficial to criminologists as they can offer detailed insight into the reasoning and 'personal approaches' underpinning the work of the judiciary (Jaremba and Mak 2014). Urszula Jaremba and Elaine Mak describe this as an opportunity to go 'behind the scenes of the formal law', arguing:

> Qualitative interviewing has brought us in the middle of the judicial environment, and has allowed us to learn what it really means to be a judge. It made it possible to identify what and how judges really think, and how they work. It facilitated looking behind the scenes of the formal law and indicating those factors which influence the daily judicial decision-making, which normally would go unnoticed. (Jaremba and Mak 2014)

This is particularly valuable given that judicial deliberations are not accessible and, in some cases, a judge's statements on sentence are not made publicly available, particularly in those involving a sexual offence and/or vulnerable victim. As argued by Kelly Richards:

> Criminologists should pay more attention to the views of policy makers, legislators and other people in positions of power. Interviewing elites can be very useful given that it allows the researcher access to data that may be impossible to obtain by using any other method. (2011:68)

This is particularly central to criminal jurisdictions such as England and Wales, where sentencing judgments are not publicly accessible or, in many cases, may only be available for research purposes if the researcher covers the transcription costs and approval for access is gained from the presiding judge. This illustrates an additional layer of gatekeeping. While there are inevitable costs associated with undertaking interviews, including in some cases travel and audio transcription fees, without the ability to analyse judicial comments on sentence and understand the decision making behind judicial deliberations, it is difficult, if not impossible, for a researcher to gain a clear understanding of how sentencing decisions are made and with what impact.

Through interviews with judges, research can also illuminate 'the human face of judging' (Mackenzie 2005: 12) and gain a better understanding of how legislation is brought to life in practice. This methodological approach to research is also valuable to improving community understandings of the decisions made by the judiciary and the process of judging. These are important gains given that the body of research on public confidence finds that the more informed members of the community are about judicial processes and the sentencing exercise, the more likely they are to support the length of sentences imposed (Roberts 2003).

Interviews have also been used by law reform bodies and commissions, which often draw upon the results of consultation processes with relevant legal practitioners to inform discussion papers, final reports and drafts of proposed reforms.[4] Reflecting on his role as Law Commissioner for England and Wales, Martin Partington (2005: 139) notes the value of consulting those within the system to 'fill gaps in knowledge by deliberately engaging with people or other agencies or groups with special knowledge or experience in the current operation of the law and how it might develop'. Building on these sentiments, the final three sections of this chapter examine the value of qualitative research interviews with legal practitioners in the context of an increasingly non-transparent justice system in the period following the implementation of law reform and in relation to gauging the viability of crime and justice policy transfer.

### *Non-transparent justice and researching the criminal courts*

The importance of criminological research that accesses and engages institutional gatekeepers is crystallized when considering the increasingly non-transparent justice systems of the UK, the US and Australia. The principle of open justice is a key element of the rule of law and is described by Lord Bingham (2010: 8) as the principle 'that all persons and authorities within the state, whether public or private, should be bound by and entitled to the benefit of laws publicly made, taking effect (generally) in the future and publicly administered in the courts'. While previously considered a hallmark of a 'just' criminal justice system, over the last two decades, concerns relating to privacy, the rights of vulnerable persons and national security have seen the introduction of a range of reforms that serve to 'close' the criminal justice system.[5] While these reforms have often been introduced for valid reasons relating to the efficiency of justice and the need to protect vulnerable victims and offenders,[6] they have led to a situation where now some 'key decisions are made out of mind, sight and analysis of those outside the criminal justice system' (Fitz-Gibbon 2014b).

Within this climate, the criminological researcher's ability to access and maintain a working relationship with gatekeepers becomes paramount. Research which bridges this gap ensures that the courts, as well as the views and experiences of those within them, are not entirely impenetrable by those outside the system. Interviews can cast a light on the reasoning, motivations and processes behind 'hidden' decisions of justice that impact on charge, trial, conviction and sentencing – such as plea bargaining, in camera court rulings and submissions on sentence.

The need for criminologists to engage those within the system is particularly important in the post-9/11 climate, where threats to the open justice principle have increased and are largely justified on the basis of national security (McLachlin 2014). For example, in 2014 the Court of Appeal of England and Wales in *R v Incedal* ruled that a criminal trial involving two young men charged with serious terrorism offences could be held partially in a closed courtroom, stating that 'from time to time, tensions between the open justice principle and national security will be inevitable' (at 15). The Appeal Court stated:

> Open justice must . . . give way to the yet more fundamental principle that the paramount object of the court is to do justice; accordingly, where there is a serious possibility that an insistence on open justice in the national security context would frustrate the administration of justice, for example, by deterring the crown from prosecuting a case where it otherwise should do so, a departure from open justice may be justified. (*Guardian News and Media Ltd & Ords v Incedal* [2014] EWCA Crim 1861, as cited in Bowcott 2014)

While this decision was high profile and attracted significant media coverage in the UK, it is not unique. Legislation permitting secret justice processes has been introduced in Australia[7] and Canada post-9/11,[8] and in the UK through the Justice and Security Act 2013. The 2013 Act permits the use of closed hearings (often referred to in the media as 'secret courts') in intelligence-related cases (McLachlin 2014; see also Bowcott 2013 and Zaiwalla 2013 for a critique of the use of 'secret' courts in England and Wales).

It is not the intention of this chapter to argue whether or not intelligence cases should be held in open or closed courtrooms. Instead, this chapter highlights the need for criminologists to engage with those within non-transparent justice environments in order to critically analyse the operation and attainability of justice in those settings. Through interviews with those who operate within such environments, legal practitioners' experiences and views on the administration, process and outcomes of 'secret' justice can be illuminated, while individual case details and decisions remain confidential. These are important lines of inquiry in terms of continuing to analyse the effectiveness and impact of criminal justice systems.

### Implementation problems and researching law reform

Understanding the views and experiences of those engaged in the daily operation of the law is also important, given the body of research that recognizes the gap between the law as it appears in writing and the law as it operates in practice (Bibas 2006; Fitz-Gibbon 2014a; Hunter 2008; Terpstra and Fyfe 2015). Focusing on the operation of the justice system post-law reform, this has been described by Rosemary Hunter (2008) as the 'implementation problem' – the gap between the aims and intentions underpinning law reform and the impact of its operation in practice. The notion of 'implementation problems' has been studied extensively in relation to the apparent success or failure of feminist law reform targeted at improving sexual assault and homicide laws for female victims and offenders (see, for example, Fitz-Gibbon 2014a; Hunter 2008; Smart 1989).

In the context of this chapter, the importance lies in how criminological research can engage with legal professionals to better understand why implementation problems occur and how they may be negated before, during or after law reform. In this context, interviews with criminal justice practitioners allow criminological researchers to go beyond an analysis of how the law *should* operate and justice *should* be achieved, to understand what actually occurs in practice and with what impact. This analysis must take into consideration the inevitable dependence on the decision making and actions of those within the system to uphold the intentions of Parliament and law reform bodies. As described by Jan Terpstra and Nicholas Fyfe, the operation of the law post-implementation of law reform is 'often dependent on the joint actions of large numbers of semi-autonomous actors, each having their own interests, agendas and victims, that may or may not be in line with the policy mandate' (Terpstra and Fyfe 2015: 14).

The importance of the actions of individual decision makers post-reform reveals an additional reason for why criminologists should undertake research that directly engages with legal practitioners. By asking legal practitioners their views on the need for reform, the impact of reform and current gaps in legal practice, criminologists can illuminate how those engaged in the implementation of the law perceive its reform. These responses are important on an individual respondent basis to understand how those individuals may act to either promote the intentions of reform or circumvent the original goal of the law reform package. Furthermore, when analysed together, they also allow researchers to examine the collective thinking and responses to reform of those within the system.

Related to this notion of implementation problems is what Andrew Ashworth (1995: 262) conceptualized as the 'drag coefficient'; which is described by Geraldine Mackenzie (2005: 4) as the extent to which the behaviours and actions of individual judicial officers 'can slow down change in sentencing law and blunt its effectiveness'. While Ashworth and Mackenzie were both focused on the application of the drag coefficient in sentencing, this notion can be extended to all actors within a criminal justice system who have the power to influence the operation and outcomes of crime and justice policies. In attempting to avoid or minimize the impact of the 'drag coefficient', it has been suggested that 'radical reforms' be avoided in favour of more 'incremental reform' that is less likely to challenge the status quo of those within the system (Hunter 2008: 7). Similarly, feminist legal scholars who have long sought to reform the law's response to violence against women have argued that advocates should focus their attention outside of doctrinal reform (Smart 1989). However, there is also an important role to be played by criminologists who, in examining the system from an insider's perspective, can illuminate the reasons why criminal justice practitioners may actively push back against law reform. Such research can provide an evidence base for how professionals could be better integrated into the reform process to increase the likelihood of successful integration.

Both of these concepts relate back to a wider body of research that recognizes the role legal practitioners can play in resisting change within the system, if that change is perceived to be out of step with the existing legal culture(s) (Fitz-Gibbon 2014a; Friedman 1994; Hunter 2008; Horney and Spohn 1991).[9] The consequence of this is captured by Lawrence Friedman (1994: 130), who argues law reform which is out of sync with the values of the prevailing legal culture is 'doomed to failure'. For this reason, interviews with legal professionals provide an opportunity not only to understand the framework and structure of the law (as can be achieved through document and policy analysis), but also to gain an insight into the culture of the law. In this way, this approach allows researchers to understand how an individual's views and experiences of the need to maintain and protect that status quo may impact on their willingness to adapt to new legislation and adopt new reforms.

### Policy transfer and understanding comparative criminal justice

Related to this examination of implementation problems is the value of criminological research with legal practitioners in researching the operation of criminal justice policy across comparative jurisdictions. Criminological research has long examined the tendency for policy transfer to occur between comparable jurisdictions, such as the UK, the US, Australia and European countries (for example, Jones and Newburn 2002; Muncie 2001; Newburn 2002; Terpstra and Fyfe 2015).[10] This body of research has recognized the need to understand the context within which the policy was implemented, the key role played by those within the jurisdiction that stands to inherit the policy, as well as the requirement to examine the original justifications underpinning the policy. Each of these lines of inquiry seeks to better understand whether a policy adopted in one context can be applied to create meaningful and desired reform in a comparative jurisdiction.

Policy transfer, and the effectiveness of adopting similar responses to similar problems from one jurisdiction to another, is not always straightforward. As David Nelken argues in his examination of comparative criminal justice:

> It is misleading to assume that modern criminal justice systems all face the same 'problems' even if they deal with them in different ways. 'Problems' – and 'solutions' – are perceived and constructed differently within different cultures. (2010: 46)

Problematically, despite recognition of the difficulties in meaningfully transferring policy from one jurisdiction to another, there is a lack of empirical research to date to support and inform policy transfer in the area of crime and justice. On this note, Trevor Jones and Tim Newburn argue:

> Policy formation is underresearched. International links in policy formation in this area have not been subject to empirical scrutiny. As a consequence, not only do we lack the necessary data, but the means by which such questions might be investigated have not been spelled out in any detail. (Jones and Newburn 2002: 113)

These issues can arguably each be addressed through criminological research that engages those involved in the delivery of crime and justice policy to understand its operation, need and impact. Interviews conducted with those within the jurisdiction in which a policy originated, as well as with those where it has and/or will be transferred, can illuminate differences in practice from the view of those directly engaged in the delivery of the law. For this reason, the notion of policy transfer provides a further justification for why criminologists must engage institutional gatekeepers in order to conduct this type of qualitative research and why they should not be deterred by the initial difficulties of gaining and negotiating access.

## Conclusion

This chapter has examined why criminologists must engage with those operating within the criminal justice system to better understand their inner workings and the impact of their operation. While achieving access to criminal justice gatekeepers can be fraught with difficulty and time-intensive, gaining and maintaining these working relationships is of significant value to the criminological researcher. It should be of comfort to those seeking to undertake qualitative research within the criminal justice system that access to police, legal counsel and judges is increasingly being achieved across a range of crime and justice research areas, including with the police, judicial officers and legal counsel. This method of criminological inquiry is particularly important in the current environment of crime and justice policy where decisions and processes are becoming increasingly non-transparent. By accessing and engaging gatekeepers in research, criminologists can bridge the gap between the insiders and outsiders of the justice system and play a key role in improving the understanding of 'closed' justice practices as well as ensuring accountability and integrity of the system.

This chapter also highlights why research that engages those within the criminal justice system can be used to improve processes and outcomes of law reform and policy transfer. By understanding the views, experiences and motivations of those working within the criminal justice system, criminologists are better placed to illuminate why law reforms and policy transfers may, or may not, be realized as intended in practice. While these may appear to be ambitious outcomes for criminological research, researchers are undoubtedly more likely to achieve them by directly engaging the system than working outside the walls of justice.

## Notes

1 This chapter draws on the author's own experience completing over 150 semi-structured face-to-face interviews with members of the Australian, English and American criminal justice systems. This includes interviews undertaken with legal practitioners, members of the judiciary, policy stakeholders and police officers examining the operation of the law of homicide, reform of the partial defences to murder and the impact of sentencing reform in Australia and the UK. The results of these interviews have been examined in several publications, including Fitz-Gibbon (2013, 2014a).

2 Within this, access is defined widely to encompass 'access to the environment, to knowledge, to participants and to their trust' (Flynn 2011: 47).

3 See also Flynn (2011) for a discussion of how researchers can move between being an 'outsider' and 'insider' during the data collection process.

4 See, for example, recent law reform inquiries undertaken by the Law Commission (2003, 2005), the Ministry of Justice (2008) and the Victorian Law Reform Commission (2004).

5 'Hidden' justice processes that arise in criminal and civil law cases include plea bargaining (also referred to as negotiated case resolutions) and closed courts to allow for vulnerable witness testimony (often used in cases involving children and/or sexual assault victims).

6 For example, in Canada the privacy rights of victims of sexual assault are protected under section 486.4 of the Criminal Code (1985), and section 111 of the Youth Criminal Justice Act (2002) protects the privacy rights of young victims and witnesses in cases involving an accused youth.

7 For example, National Security Information (Criminal and Civil Proceedings) Act 2004 (Commonwealth).

8 See McLachlin (2014) for a discussion of Canadian anti-terrorism reforms.

9 It is recognized that no single 'legal culture' exists and that this is an ever-changing phenomenon across time and place. For an extended examination of legal cultures, see Friedman (1994).

10 'Policy transfer' is defined by Newburn (2002: 165) as 'the way in which ideas, ideologies, practices and policies are transported from one jurisdiction to another'. For the purposes of this chapter, the transfer of crime and justice policies and practices are largely focused upon. See also Dolowitz and Marsh (1996).

## References

Australian Law Reform Commission (2010) *Family Violence – A National Legal Response*. ALRC Report 114, Canberra: Australian Government.

Ashworth, Andrew (1995) 'The Role of the Sentencing Scholar', in Chris M.V. Clarkson and Rod Morgan (eds), *The Politics of Sentencing Reform*. Oxford: Clarendon Press, pp. 251–65.

Baldwin, John (2008) 'Research on the Criminal Courts', in Roy D. King and Emma Wincup (eds), *Doing Research on Crime and Justice*, 2nd edn. Oxford: Oxford University Press, pp. 375–98.

Bartels, Lorana (2009) 'Suspended Sentences – A Judicial Perspective'. *Queensland University of Technology Law and Justice Journal*, 9: 44–63.

Beyens, Kristel, Sonja Snacken and Dirk van Zyl Smit (2013) 'Trust in (Implementation of) Sentencing: Belgium and Elsewhere', in Tom Daems, Dirk van Zyl Smit and Sonja Shacken (eds), *European Penology?* Oxford: Hart Publishing, pp. 271–92.

Bibas, Stephanos (2006) 'Transparency and Participation in Criminal Procedure'. *New York University Law Review*, 81(3): 911–66.

Bingham, Tom (2010) *The Rule of Law*. London: Penguin.

Bowcott, Owen (2013) 'What are Secret Courts and What Do They Mean for UK Justice?'. *The Guardian*, 14 June.

——. (2014) 'Key Elements of Secret Terror Trial Can Be Heard in Public Court Rules'. *The Guardian*, 13 June.

Darbyshire, Penny (2011) *Sitting in Judgment: The Working Lives of Judges*. Oxford: Hart Publishing.

Davies, Julie T. and Eleanor Peters (2014) 'Relationships between Gatekeepers and Researchers: The Experiences of Conducting Evaluations into Parenting Programmes in Community and Penal Settings', in Karen Lumsden and Aaron Winter (eds), *Reflectivity in Criminological Research: Experiences with the Powerful and the Powerless*. London: Palgrave Macmillan, pp. 35–46.

Davis, Ian (2005) 'Targeted Consultations', in Brian Opeskin and David Weisbrot (eds), *The Promise of Law Reform*. Sydney: Federation Press.

Dolowitz, David and David Marsh (1996) 'Who Learns What from Whom: A Review of the Policy Transfer Literature'. *Political Studies*, 44: 343–57.

Dwyer, Angela and Hennessey Hayes (2011) 'Getting Lost in the Field: The Unpredictable Nature of Fieldwork with Young People', in Lorana Bartels and Kelly Richards (eds), *Qualitative Criminology: Stories from the Field*. Sydney: Hawkins Press, pp. 106–15.

Erez, Edna and Linda Rogers (1999) 'Victim Impact Statements and Sentencing Outcomes and Processes: The Perspective of Legal Professionals'. *British Journal of Criminology*, 39(2): 216–39.

Fitz-Gibbon, Kate (2013) 'The Mandatory Life Sentence for Murder: An Argument for Judicial Discretion in England'. *Criminology and Criminal Justice*, 13(5): 506–25.

——. (2014a) *Homicide Law Reform, Gender and the Provocation Defence: A Comparative Perspective*. London: Palgrave Macmillan.

——. (2014b) 'Overcoming Barriers in the Criminal Justice System: Examining the Value and Challenges of Interviewing Legal Practitioners', in Karen Lumsden and Aaron Winter (eds), *Reflectivity in Criminological Research: Experiences with the Powerful and the Powerless*. London: Palgrave Macmillan, pp. 247–58.

Flynn, Asher (2011) 'Breaking into the Legal Culture of the Victorian Office of Public Prosecutions', in Lorana Bartels and Kelly Richards (eds), *Qualitative Criminology: Stories from the Field*. Sydney: Hawkins Press, pp. 47–57.

Fleming, Jenny (2010) 'Learning to Work Together: Police and Academics'. *Policing*, 4(2): 139–45.

——. (2011) 'Qualitative Encounters in Police Research', in Lorana Bartels and Kelly Richards (eds), *Qualitative Criminology: Stories from the Field*. Sydney: Hawkins Press, pp. 13–24.

Friedman, Lawrence M. (1994) 'Is There a Modern Legal Culture?' *Ratio Juris*, 7(2): 117–31.

Gill, Martin (2015) 'Senior Police Officers' Perspectives on Private Security: Sceptics, Pragmatists and Embraces'. *Policing and Society*, 25(3): 276–93.

Hartman, Jennifer L. and Joanne Belknap (2003) 'Beyond the Gatekeepers: Courts Professionals' Self-reported Attitudes about and Experiences with Misdemeanour Domestic Violence Cases'. *Criminal Justice and Behaviour*, 30(3): 349–73.

Horney, Julie and Cassia Spohn (1991) 'Rape Law Reform and Instrumental Change in Six Urban Jurisdictions'. *Law and Society Review*, 25: 117–53.

Hunter, Rosemary (2008) *Domestic Violence Law Reform and Women's Experience in Court: The Implementation of Feminist Reforms in Civil Proceedings*. New York: Cambria Press.

Jaremba, Urszula and Elaine Mak (2014) 'Interviewing Judges in the Transnational Context'. *Law and Method*, online ahead of print, DOI: 10.5553/REM/.000003.

Jones, Trevor and Tim Newburn (2002) 'Learning from Uncle Sam? Exploring U.S. Influences on British Criminal Control Policy'. *Governance: An International Journal of Policy, Administration and Institutions*, 15(1): 97–119.

Law Commission (2003) *Partial Defences to Murder: Summary Paper*. Consultation Paper No. 173. London: Law Commission.

——. (2005) *A New Homicide Act for England and Wales?* Consultation Paper No. 177. London: Law Commission.

Lumsden, Karen and Aaron Winter (2014) 'Reflexivity in Criminological Research', in Karen Lumsden and Aaron Winter (eds), *Reflectivity in Criminological Research: Experiences with the Powerful and the Powerless*. London: Palgrave Macmillan, pp. 1–20.

Mackenzie, Geraldine (2005) *How Judges Sentence*. Sydney: Federation Press.

McBarnet, Doreen (2009) 'Whiter than White Collar Crime' in Simon Halliday and Patrick Schmidt (eds), *Conducting Law and Society Research: Reflections on Method and Practices*. Cambridge: Cambridge University Press, pp. 152–62.

McGovern, Alyce (2011) 'Negotiating Access to the NSW Police Media Unit: A Personal Research Experience', in Lorana Bartels and Kelly Richards (eds), *Qualitative Criminology: Stories from the Field*. Sydney: Hawkins Press, pp. 51–9.

McLachlin, Beverley (2014) 'Openness and the Rule of Law: Remarks of the Right Honourable Beverley McLachlin (Chief Justice of Canada)'. Presentation at the Annual International Rule of Law Lecture, London.

Ministry of Justice (2008) *Murder, Manslaughter and Infanticide: Proposals for Reform of the Law: Consultation Paper CP19/08*. London: Ministry of Justice.

Muncie, John (2001) 'Policy Transfers and 'What Works': Some Reflections on Comparative Youth Justice'. *Youth Justice*, 1(3): 27–35.

Nelken, David (2010) *Comparative Criminal Justice*. London: Sage Publications.

Newburn, Tim (2002) 'Atlantic Crossings: 'Policy Transfer' and Crime Control in the USA and Britain'. *Punishment and Society*, 4(2): 165–94.

Noaks, Lesley and Emma Wincup (2004) *Criminological Research: Understanding Qualitative Methods*. London: Sage Publications.

Partington, Martin (2005) 'Research', in Brian Opeskin and David Weisbrot (eds), *The Promise of Law Reform*. Sydney: Federation Press.

Pierce, Jason L. (2002) 'Research Note: Interviewing Australia's Senior Judiciary'. *Australian Journal of Political Science*, 37(1): 131–42.

Reeves, Carla L. (2010) 'A Difficult Negotiation: Fieldwork Relations with Gatekeepers'. *Qualitative Research*, 10(3): 315–31.

Richards, Kelly (2011) 'Interviewing Elites in Criminological Research: Negotiating Power and Access and Being Called "Kid"', in Lorana Bartels and Kelly Richards (eds), *Qualitative Criminology: Stories from the Field*. Sydney: Hawkins Press.

Richards, Kelly and Lorana Bartels (2011) 'The Story Behind the Stories: Qualitative Criminology Research in Australia', in Lorana Bartels and Kelly Richards (eds), *Qualitative Criminology: Stories from the Field*. Sydney: Hawkins Press, pp. 1–10.

Roberts, Julian (2003) 'Public Opinion and Mandatory Sentencing: A Review of International Findings'. *Criminal Justice and Behaviour*, 30(4): 483–508.

Skinner, Tina (2005) 'Researching People in Power: Practice, Analysis and Action', in Tina Skinner, Marianne Hester and Ellen Malos (eds), *Researching Gender Violence: Feminist Methodology in Action*. Cullompton: Willan Publishing, pp. 44–65.

Smart, Carol (1989) *Feminism and the Power of Law*. London: Routledge.

Terpstra, Jan and Nicholas R. Fyfe (2015) 'Mind the Implementation Gap? Police Reform and Local Policing in the Netherlands and Scotland'. *Criminology and Criminal Justice*, 15(5): 527–44.

Trulson, Chad R., James W. Marquart and Janet L. Mullings (2004) 'Breaking in: Gaining Entry to Prisons and Other Hard-to-Access Criminal Justice Organisations'. *Journal of Criminal Justice Education*, 15(2): 451–78.

Victorian Law Reform Commission (2004) *Defences to Homicide: Final Report*. Victoria: Victorian Law Reform Commission.

Walsh, Tamara and Heather Douglas (2012) 'Lawyers' Views of Decision Making in Child Protection Matters: The Tension between Adversarialism and Collaborative Approaches'. *Monash University Law Review*, 38(2): 181–211.

Ward, Artemus and Stephen L. Wasby (2010) '"Get a Life!": On Interviewing Law Clerks'. *The Justice System Journal*, 31(2): 125–43.

Zaiwalla, Sarosh (2013) 'Secret Courts: Justice Conducted Behind Closed Doors is Not Justice at All'. *The Guardian*, 19 August.

# 11 The politics of doing imaginative criminological research

*Kerry Carrington and Ashleigh Larkin*

## Introduction

One of the defining characteristics of criminology is its lack of a stable referent. Crime has no singular unifying or universal essence. It is a signifier of historically and culturally contingent designations of deviance. Crime and criminality are thus variably represented as labels, offences, acts, stigmas, symbols, creations of social control, legal fictions, markers of non-belonging or badges of resistance. This inherit instability of criminology's referent is now more pronounced than ever before as the editors to this volume remind us in their introduction. This chapter examines how the politics of criminological research has been melded by the shifts in intellectual currents from deviance theories, critical, feminist and now southern criminologies. This chapter argues that choice of method for doing imaginative critical scholarship has blossomed, especially with the creation of the Internet and the instantaneous global production and dissemination of knowledges. Method is now largely a practical and not a political matter, shaped only by the criminological imagination. However, the politics of research remains deeply enmeshed in the shaping and scoping of research topics which are still seldom transparent except in reflexive research designs. What research questions attract funding, what theories shape the research framework, what is worthy of study and what is not all invariably involve some form of political calculation. The chapter concludes with some case studies of imaginative criminological research using online methodologies.

## Deviance theorists and the politics of research

Debates about the politics of knowledge in criminology have been a constant feature of the discipline since the publication of the pioneering work of deviance theorists in the 1960s. Deviance theory was enormously popular within the social sciences at the time. One of the reasons for that popularity was the appeal of its critique of a criminological positivism that reified subjects as objects, muted their voices, abstracted their everyday realities into data, and overlooked wider questions of the politics of crime control and their power effects. Deviance theorists commenced what critical and feminist criminologists took up with gusto, rocking the foundations of criminology's claim to produce objective scientific knowledge and questioning the possibility of separating the political effects of knowledge from its production.

Deviance theory was characterized by a pluralism that promoted a range of theoretical perspectives. Among these were naturalism, labelling theory, symbolic interactionism, phenomenology, transactionalism and ethnomethodology. While these perspectives are distinguishable – more in emphasis than approach – they nevertheless shared a fundamental scepticism of criminology's epistemological claim to be a science. Deviance theory was part of a larger epistemological project that questioned the positivist constructions of crime causality (Taylor, Walton and Young 1973: 140). What constituted crime or deviance was now a contested proposition and not a pre-given. This radically changed the face of discipline from the 1960s onwards. The politics of criminological research reversed from asking which individuals are deviant to focusing on to whom they are deviant and why. They explored how deviance is constructed by social rules or legal norms, and how social reaction to behaviour labelled 'deviant' can have amplifying effects (Taylor, Walton and Young 1973: 140).

Chief among the early critics of criminological positivism was David Matza, whose main purpose was to correct the positivist portrait of juvenile delinquency in the now-classic text *Delinquency and Drift* (1964). Positivism asserted the primacy of the criminal actor over the criminal act, elevating the criminal science of causation over the vagaries of criminal law and philosophical belief in free will (Matza 1964: 3): 'Positivism, blessed with the virtues and prestige of science, has little concern for the essence of phenomenon it wishes to study' (Matza 1964: 8). Criminological positivism extinguished agency, subjectivism and any sense that the commission of crime or deviance had any natural element of agency. In adopting a methodology that he called naturalism, Matza made a conscious effort to view the world through the phenomenon being studied. He re-directed research towards the complex relation between beliefs and actions and the construction of meaning in interaction. He argued that delinquent values are held intermittently and may even overlap with the values of conventional society. He based this insight on a study where he interviewed 100 boys committed to a training school. When shown images of offending behaviour, only two per cent of the boys approved of the criminal acts (Matza 1964: 49) This led Matza to argue that 'beneath the surface difference lies an obscured similarity' (1964: 62). This is what he called a 'picture of drift' (1964: 50). With Gresham Sykes, Matza then developed this insight into a theory of techniques of neutralization, leaving a legacy of tools for critical scholars that are still in use to this day (Sykes and Matza 1957).

One of the main strengths of deviance theory is that it problematized crime, questioning the possibility of its measurement, when its very definition was socially constructed in interaction (Young 1998: 274). Deviance theory had its limitations, however. It overly narrowed the focus of critical analysis to an interaction between a delinquent and a social audience, and the effect of that social reaction on an individual's behavior. It drew attention to rule breakers and rule makers, but largely left out the politics of crime control. Stanley Cohen muses that the 'nuts, sluts, and perverts of criminology and social pathology text-books – could emerge from their dark closets into the sociological daylight' (Cohen 1988: 5). Deviance theory failed to adequately appreciate history, social structure and the wider structural analysis of social power and political change. Ian Taylor, Paul Walton and Jock Young once famously pointed out that 'in a study of deviancy as in the study of society at large, what is required is a sociology that combines structure, process and culture in a continuous dialectic' (Taylor, Walton and Young 1973: 171). They criticized Matza for lapsing into a subjectivism and thus an inability to connect meaning, beliefs and actions to the wider politics of society which shape these. At worst, subjectivist relativism equated truth with an individualist production of meaning. Truth was about taking sides with the underdog. The predictable politics of deviance research became rescuing the underdog from being unfairly labeled. This is a problem that plagued early feminist standpoint studies of female crime and victimization too, with truth always being on the side of women regardless of the context.

## Feminist criminologies and the politics of research

Debates about the politics of knowledge in feminist criminology mirrored the debates in feminist theory more widely (Gunew 1990). Different perspectives developed in feminist theory. The main distinctions were drawn between feminist empiricism, standpoint feminism and post-colonial, postmodern and poststructuralist feminisms (Punch 1998: 141–2). Feminist empiricism aimed to correct the masculine bias of the methodologies of the human sciences, but accepted its modernist knowledge claims of causality and universality. Standpoint feminism rejected masculinist research methods while aiming to construct feminist ways of knowing based largely on experience (Stanley and Wise 1983; Grosz 1989). Postmodern and poststructuralist feminisms rejected the epistemological assumptions of modernity – that truth can be impartial, ahistorical or universal. Influenced by the work of Michel Foucault, they argued that knowledge is a necessary partial, unstable interpretive and very much the product of power.[1] Poststructuralist feminists consequently sought to produce limited ways of knowing which accept multiplicity and fallibility as defining characteristics of epistemology (Carrington 2002). Post-colonialists criticized the concept of an essential woman, stressing the enormous historical, cultural and ethnic variations among women as a group.

As a result of this chequered history, there is no single feminist approach to doing imaginative criminological research and a fair amount of contention about how to do feminist research (Carrington 2002). There are, however, a number of distinguishing features of feminist research that have spawned several decades of imaginative criminological research.

First, feminist research methodologies that questioned the separation of objectivity from subjectivity led to a plethora of creative feminist research on victims. These feminists saw science as a method that had no means of tapping into 'the world of emotions, feelings, political values; of the individual and collective unconsciousness; of social and historical particularity' (Harding 1986: 245). Scientific 'methods cannot convey an in depth understanding of, or feeling for those being researched and that they often ignore sex or gender differences or look at them without considering mediating variables' (Gelsthorpe 1989: 90). Hence, one of the major contributions of feminist criminology has been to problematize the social, criminological and legal construction of victims that sieve out feelings and experiences. This has spawned a great deal of imaginative criminological research on women as victims and survivors of violence, the limitations of criminal justice responses to female victims of male violence, and the problematic way in which female victims are treated in a masculinist criminal justice system (Barbaret 2014; Carmody and Carrington 2000; Powell 2010; Renzetti 2013; Smart 1989; Walklate 2007). It also helped to create and sustain an internationally successful journal, *Violence Against Women*, edited by Claire M. Renzetti, which produces eight volumes of imaginative research per annum and now ranks in the top-cited journals in the world.

Second, for many feminist scholars, the process of doing research is fundamentally important in designing any research project, elevating reflexivity as a characteristic of good research. Questions about process are especially significant in field research where there are significant power differentials between the subjects of research and those who research them. By consciously reflecting on the role of the researcher, the particularities of power and the muddiness of the research process, which is often concealed in criminological research, feminist criminologists promote transparency around the research process (Davies 2000: 83). Reflexivity is now widely accepted as a routine practice of good criminological research.

Third, in order to rectify the historical neglect of gender, feminist criminology has been focused on making women visible locally and globally (Barbaret 2014: 3). As women's voices have been historically repressed and disqualified (Gunew 1990; Harding 1986), the object of feminist research has been to make visible the formerly invisible knowledges and experiences of women. For some, this led to the adoption of feminist standpoint methodologies as an antidote to the phallocentricism of criminology. The choice of topic for these feminist researchers then tended to be the study of women as gendered subjects – 'that is asking how patterns of crime, penal policies, crime prevention and community safety strategies, ideologies of law and order, or indeed criminological theories affect women' (Hudson 2000: 185). The problem with standpoint feminist methodologies is that they equate women's experience with truth and then run the risk of lapsing into a naïve essentialism (Harris 1990). Truth becomes a product of women's voices, of being heard, of speaking out. If only it were so simple. Moreover, feminist standpoint methodologies which assume that there is a commonality among women, and a universal subjectivity among men, run the added risk of constructing fictive unities among cohorts of diverse criminological subjects (Carrington 2002). For example, women who are the most vulnerable to criminalization in Australia are Indigenous. They share very little in common with the overwhelming majority of white women, who never come into contact with the criminal process (Carrington 2002). As studies of female offending in the UK, the US and Australia have repeatedly shown, women in prison and girls in detention are from the most marginalized sections of the population (Carlen 1988; Carrington and Pereira 2009; Chesney-Lind and Pasko 2004; Sharpe 2012).

A fourth characteristic of feminist criminological research has been an historical preference to use qualitative methods over quantitative or experimental methods, aligning the latter with phallocentricism (Carrington 2002). Qualitative methods were regarded as superior research instruments that could capture the richness of the meaning of everyday life and every woman's experiences of criminal justice. This is the case with respect to some research projects, such as those which seek to understand and interpret the world from the framework of reference of female survivors, victims or offenders. Nevertheless, why should feminist research not be able to use the power of data, for example, to highlight reliable facts such as that almost half of all homicides in Australia today are due to family violence, that Indigenous girls comprise three-quarters of female detainees and that less than five per cent of sexual assault cases end up with a conviction? As feminist criminology is an avowedly both a 'political and intellectual' enterprise (Naffine 1995: 28), surely the choice of method should reflect the priorities of that project. Hence, method should be a practical matter and not an ideological choice.

Lastly, feminist research in criminology has been increasingly influenced by intersectionalism. Intersectionality is as much as a political project as it is a corrective methodological tool to the masculinist biases of criminological research. It is an approach that is global in outlook and that pursues alliances, but respects differences based on a vision of a shared humanity. Power is re-imagined, gender becomes only one axis of power, and the subject woman is deconstructed. She is no longer a timeless, placeless, universal category of history, politics, society and culture (Carrington 2015: 19). Choice of method is then not necessarily a political question, pre-empted by a feminist standpoint, but a practical matter of how to produce a persuasive answer to the research question within the limits of the episteme. These imaginative but pragmatic feminist researchers engage with the politics of knowledge production, fully cognizant of its power effects. All research is inescapably political as all knowledge has power effects. The politics of research is embedded in doing research that makes visible that which was invisible – the gendered aspects of criminalization, victimization and criminal justice, and the local and global dimensions of these. Of course, what research gets funded, what does not, what is published and what is not, and who decides all these things still remains inherently political.

## Critical criminologies and the politics of research

'Critical criminology is the criminology of late modernity' (Young 2002: 252), emerging at a time when a constellation of diverse social forces and historical events questioned the moral legitimacy of the prevailing social order, the apparatuses of social control and the science that legitimated it (Cohen 1988: 4–6). As one of the most state-dominated of the social science disciplines, criminology was among those sciences regarded as colluding with the systems of repressive social control (Taylor, Walton and Young 1973), casting aside the politics of research in the quest to cosy up to the powers that be to leverage that next research grant (Carrington and Hogg 2002: 1). Criminology was trapped in a relationship of subservience to the status quo and bondage to state-defined definitions of criminality (Garland 1994; Cohen 1988). Critical criminology changed all that. It was in some sense a creature of the politics of late modernity – of feminist, countercultural and civil rights movements, of anti-colonial struggles, of anti-psychiatry movements and prison abolitionism (Carrington and Hogg 2002: 2). As Jock Young, a leading exponent of critical criminology, argued, 'critical criminology in this age of the gulag and the punitive turn is massively needed – it is the counter voice to neoliberalism and conservatism' (Young 2002: 259).

A diverse array of imaginative criminological studies emerged under the banner of radical, critical or new criminology that challenged state-based definitions of crime and positivist approaches to conducting criminological research (e.g. Stuart Hall and Tony Jefferson's classic text *Resistance through Rituals* and Stuart Hall et al.'s *Policing the Crisis*). Critical criminology took aim at what was variously referred to as administrative, correctionalist or positivist criminology that was 'individualistic in focus, technicist in outlook, and minimalist in theory – its aim was the social engineering of the "maladjusted" individual into the ranks of the consensual and contented society' (Young 2002: 253). Those engaged in the mindless production of statistical analyses were famously lambasted by Young as 'datasaurs' (Young 2011).

By the late 1990s, a central tension emerged between the conflicting political projects in which critical criminologists were often involved on a day-to-day basis and the abstract ambition of a critical criminology which ultimately sought the radical transformation of social relations to reduce inequality, crime and victimization (Taylor, Walton and Young 1973: 270). Ironically, but inevitably, a programme of such ambition made little room for everyday local politics – or indeed the study of crime at all (Carrington and Hogg 2012). If the essential structure of the Western capitalist order was the root problem, it made little sense to differentiate amongst the various forms of government – liberal, social democratic, autocratic – to work with existing political agents for progressive ends, however limited. Reform was adaptation and co-option, leading to the adoption of an outright oppositional or abolitionist posture to the agents of social control (courts, prisons and the justice system), spurning any research collaboration as reformist. This political stance unnecessarily narrowed the scope for imaginative criminological research. Research projects driven from this pessimistic outlook became captives of a negativism – always looking for more examples of criminalization, oppression and repressive social control (Brown 2013). Frustration with idealist frameworks of critical criminology spawned a large body of innovative work in realist criminology that wrestled with law and order politics, and took both the victim and the crime problem seriously (for example, Brown and Hogg 1992; Hogg and Brown 1998; Currie 1985; Lea and Young 1984; Matthews and Young 1986; Walklate 1992).

## Southern criminology and the politics of research

Southern criminology is an intellectual, political and empirical project concerned with how issues of vital criminological research and policy significance abound in the Global South, with important implications for global security and justice. Yet much of criminology historically – as a theoretical, political and empirical project – overlooks the distinctive contributions of the Global South (Carrington, Hogg and Sozzo 2016). The Global North is used here as a metaphor for the 'Western' world and the Global South as a metaphor for the countries and continents (not all from the Global South) outside that 'Western' world. Like social sciences more generally (Connell 2007), the hierarchical production of criminological knowledge privileges theories, assumptions and methods based largely on empirical specificities of the Global North. The purpose of southern criminology is not to dismiss the conceptual and empirical advances that criminology has produced over the last century or to cast negative aspersions on northern criminology, but to de-colonize and democratize the toolbox of available criminological concepts, theories and methods (see Carrington, Hogg and Sozzo 2016).

In a hierarchy of global social science, southern theorists from Asia, Africa, Australia and Latin America have all too rarely been regarded as relevant within the canons of knowledge produced in the metropole (Connell 2007: 44). The 'metropolitan gaze', as Raewyn Connell (2007) coins it, is particularly evident in the field of criminology because traditions in criminological theory have for the most part had their roots in the traditions of classical thinking from eighteenth-century Europe (e.g. Beccaria 1764). Sociological approaches to criminology have also derived from classic Chicago School studies in America, and Émile Durkheim's concept of anomie and structuralist accounts of the role of crime and punishment in early twentieth-century Europe (Garland 1994). Critical criminologies, referred to above, were also originally based on studies of the criminalization of working-class kids and drug takers in the metropolis of the Global North (e.g. Hall and Jefferson 1975; Cohen 1980). Likewise, deviance theories referred to at the beginning of this chapter emerged from innovative research of deviance theorists in North America beginning with the works of Howard S. Becker (1963), Gresham Sykes and David Matza (1957) and David Matza (1964) (see Carrington 2015 for an extended analysis of southern criminology). What these bodies of research have in common is that the problem of social order in the large cities of the Global North is their main empirical referent.

There is, of course, nothing wrong with adopting global perspectives, theories and gleaning insights from research conducted in the Northern Hemisphere (Carrington and Hogg 2012). The main problem is that criminological theories based on studies of the Northern Hemisphere do not necessarily transplant well to the vast continents of the Southern Hemisphere (Australia, South America, the Asia Pacific Rim, and South Africa) shaped by distinctly different patterns of settlement, political economy, religion, society, culture, crime, violence and social control (Carrington 2015). In these countries and continents, crime and violence is not even necessarily primarily an urban phenomenon, disrupting one of the major assumptions embedded in criminological theory for over a century. A growing body of criminologists dispute this and have undertaken original research on rural crime and crimes on the periphery to correct this preoccupation with urban crime (Carrington, Donnermeyer and DeKeseredy 2014; DeKeseredy and Donnermeyer 2013; Hogg and Carrington 2006).

Southern criminology aims to correct the metropolitan biases of the discipline, renovate the theoretical and methodological approaches to the study of crime, globalize criminological theory and research, push the boundaries of the discipline beyond the jurisdictional limits of the nation state and thus shift its empirical referent away from an instinctive bias on the Global North (Carrington, Hogg and Sozzo 2016). Southern criminology does not privilege place-based theories of crime. Nor does it privilege any one social variant over another (e.g. class, gender, race, the metropolis, or the urban). The southern is a metaphor for the other, the invisible, the marginal and the power relations embedded in the 'periphery–centre relations in the realm of knowledge' (Connell 2007: viii). It is an emergent project, coinciding with the rise of liquid modernity, the erosion of stable referents, rapid globalization, the radical Islamization of parts of the globe, a post-9/11 world preoccupied with risk and national security, the exponential explosion of the cyber-world, and a world increasingly more unequal and divided than in the past. This is a criminology that inquiries into the possibilities for global justice, that has the courage to be critical and the boldness to envision the ideas, institutions and programmes necessary for creating a just world. It aims ambitiously to transform and re-imagine the criminological project in the twenty-first century and to connect southern scholars and criminologists with northern scholars to re-imagine a truly global criminology premised on a conception of a 'shared humanity' and a just society.

We are back to where we began. Just as crime and criminality have no stable referent, nor does the critical label in criminology anymore (Carrington and Hogg 2012). It is no longer sufficient to define being critical as simply being feminist, radical or oppositional. Nor is it solely a northern discourse with an empirical referent situated in one of the sprawling cities of the Global North. It is a transnational dialogue of intersectional discourses – a body of scholarship constantly re-inventing its boundaries, its focus, its allies and its objects and subjects of inquiry, across the Northern and Southern Hemispheres.

## Doing imaginative criminological research using online methodologies

We are on the cusp of major transformations in the production and dissemination of social science research – paper-based surveys will disappear as will much face-to-face real-time empirical research. It is now possible to conduct ethnography, surveys, interviews and all sorts of discourse and content analysis using online methodologies. The invention of the Internet and the widespread global take-up of mobile phones, Facebook, Twitter and social media have resulted in online interactions becoming a routine part of everyday life. As a result, the parallel worlds of reality and cyber-reality are becoming increasingly blurred (Murthy 2008), with there being no clear distinction between online and offline behaviour (Hallett and Barber 2014). Consequently, many of us live in a parallel world of unbounded cyberspace and bounded reality, saturated with opportunities for the criminological imagination to go to work. There are several important ways in which digital technologies assist with the creation of imaginative criminological research.

First, the emergence of social media platforms such as Twitter and Facebook provides a unique social and cultural space where participants construct meaning through interaction with others online. This has opened up a whole new cyber-world of everyday interactions to study. YouTube videos, for example, provide a way of observing social behaviour and conducting ethnographic research on the social construction of meaning (Bredl, Hunniger and Jensen 2014). Online performances provide researchers with a valuable resource though which to collect unique data about deviance, crime, culture and sociality not otherwise easily explored (Fielding, Blank, and Lee 2012).

Second, in addition to providing access to new ways of behaving, the emergence of the Internet and social media technology has provided new ways for people to engage in deviant or criminal behaviours (Bluett-Boyd et al. 2013). These include a host of e-crimes, such as e-hacking, e-invasion of privacy, e-pornography, e-scams, cyber-stalking, cyber-bullying, e-victim grooming, e-drug markets, e-commercial sex markets, email-order brides, e-fraud and e-romance scams (Grabosky 2007; Lee et al. 2013:39).

Third, the Internet opens up a host of new online methods for studying sensitive issues such as victimization, crime and violence, and for accessing difficult marginalized populations. There is a growing body of research that uses the Internet to complement traditional research methods (Fielding, Blank and Lee 2012; Hallett and Barber 2014; Hesse-Biber and Griffin 2013; Murthy 2008). There are many advantages of using the Internet to conduct research. Online research is a speedy, cost-effective and practical way of reaching a wide range of audiences across geographical boundaries (Liamputtong and Ezzy 2005: 233). Online research is increasingly replacing paper-based surveys and face-to-face data collection instruments (Liamputtong and Ezzy 2005: 229–31). Online methods also have the advantage of preserving the anonymity of respondents through the provision of generic links to online surveys. Anonymity encourages frank, honest reporting, particularly on sensitive issues like crime victimization and violence (Liamputtong and Ezzy, 2005: 235). This is why online research methods are especially useful to criminologists. Other advantages of online methods include: increased participation rates, the collection of information on the powerful and elite, and access to marginalized populations (Fielding, Blank and Lee 2012; Hallett and Barber 2014; Hesse-Biber and Griffin 2013).

There are also some disadvantages associated with online research. Most of these revolve around issues of sampling to control for, or at least take into account, population biases (Hesse-Biber and Griffin 2013; Hooley, Wellens and Marriott 2012). It is almost impossible for instance to achieve a representative sample which limits the generalizability of the research conclusions (Hesse-Biber and Griffin 2013; Hooley, Wellens and Marriott 2012). This limitation only affects those wishing to conduct inferential statistical analyses. In any case, it is possible to recruit purposive samples of socio-demographic populations through online surveys as approximately three-quarters of households in Australia have Internet access (Australian Bureau of Statistics 2010: Cat. 1318.3), and the reach of the Internet is now almost global. Another problem with the Internet is validating the reliability of sources of information publicly available through the Internet. Images can be Photoshopped, video clips staged and information distorted. We now turn to examples that illustrate the innovativeness of online technologies in doing creative criminological research.

## Imaginative criminological research, new technologies and cyber-methods

There are hundreds of thousands of YouTube videos featuring instances of physical violence reproduced online, with the number of uploads increasing exponentially each year (Carrington 2013, 2015). There are hundreds of Facebook pages with thousands of likes dedicated to documenting and in effect glorifying violence. We contrast several studies to illustrate how social media platforms have been used to incite and reward performances of violence in the parallel real world. We then contrast two other studies that draw attention to the problematic way that the Internet and social media can be used to criminalize, vilify and undermine social democratic values.

The first study considered here is by Michael Salter and Stephen Tomsen (2012), who through 2010 analysed several dozen *Felony Fights* clips featuring physical violence between men that had been uploaded to YouTube (Salter and Tomsen 2012: 312). They analysed both the videos and the corresponding viewer comments to determine how YouTube was being used as a platform to encourage and reward specific performances of masculinity and violence. Some of the videos that were included in the study had received hundreds of thousands of views and had thousands of viewer comments. The authors specifically examined how the men in the fight videos were using violence to establish their masculine identity and to engage in protest masculinity as their status as ex-criminals prevented them from successfully engaging in hegemonic masculinity. However, it was the fight participants' criminal status that enhanced their ability to successfully engage in violence (Salter and Tomsen 2012: 312). The comments posted by the online viewers provided clear evidence that some performances of violent masculinity were encouraged and rewarded over others, and it was clear that the online audiences gained voyeuristic pleasure in watching criminalized men engage in physical violence against each other.

Through the course of their analysis, the authors found that viewers of the online videos encouraged some performances of violent masculinity while rejecting others. For example, the study found that 'judging for the popularity of some clips on YouTube, viewers have an open preference for a clear winner and an excessive display of aggression, particularly where at least one combatant sustains serious injury' (Salter and Tomsen 2012: 314). This can be contrasted with videos that featured the combatants predominantly engaging in wrestling, where the participants quickly became exhausted. These were less popular, as the voyeuristic interests of the viewers were not met (Salter and Tomsen 2012: 314). This study provides a clear example of how social media provides a rich source of authentic research data for imaginative criminological analysis.

Another piece of original analysis using social media was undertaken by Ashleigh Larkin (2013), one of the authors of this chapter. She undertook a study of physical violence between girls that was filmed, uploaded and shared online. This project studied 60 fight videos featuring physical altercations between young women that had been predominantly uploaded to Facebook and YouTube. Like Salter and Tomsen (2012), this study analysed both the uploaded videos and the online viewer comments. This project was able to include verbal comments made by both the fight participants and the audience to the altercation while the physical fight was taking place in the analysis, in addition to the comments posted by the online viewers. Real-time information about girls' fights could not have been accessed using any other research method. The original data was then subject to thematic analysis, which led to an analysis into which performances of violence were encouraged and rewarded by participants, bystanders and online viewers. Further, examining videos of real physical altercations between young women and using online videos as a source of research data allowed detailed descriptions to be drawn about their character.

The key findings of this study were that young women were not rejecting a feminine gender performance in favour of a masculine one in order to successfully engage in violence with other. Rather, the young women were blurring the gender dichotomy as they were adhering to a feminine gender performance while at the same time engaging in brutal and masculine fighting techniques. Again, this is information that could not be accessed using more traditional or real-time offline research methodologies. The project concluded that in order to gain a more nuanced understanding of why videos of young women's violence are proliferating over social media, more research collected both online and offline data would be beneficial in order to interpret and analyse the social and cultural context in which this occurs.

Nicole Bluett-Boyd et al. (2013) undertook a study of the role of communication technologies in the commission of sexual violence against young people. The project used a mixed method approach combining focus group and semi-structured interview data to study how communication technologies and social media platforms were used in the proliferation of sexual violence. The authors concluded that there were three main ways of social media-enhanced opportunities for the sexual harassment of young people. First, they argued that communication technologies blurred the distinction between young people's online and offline interactions, and made young people more accessible as targets of sexual violence. For instance, it was easier for perpetrators to integrate themselves into the young person's online life by doing things like sending Facebook friend requests to both the victim and the victim's offline friends. Second, communication technologies provided perpetrators with a forum where sexual predators could record acts of sexual violence using communication technologies and subsequently threaten to distribute these recordings over social media. Finally, the perpetrator could use social media and other communication technologies to remain in contact with the victim, creating an abusive relationship by threatening to release photos or videos of the sexual violence online. Hence, they conclude that one victimization online can lead to repeat victimization online.

Social media platforms can also be used to criminalize, vilify and undermine social democratic freedoms. Two recent studies, one by Lee and his colleagues (2013) and the other by Milivojevic and McGovern (2014), draw attention to this problematic dimension of social media. Murray Lee and his colleagues (2013) undertook a study that explored how young people engaging in sexting have been criminalized in a number of jurisdictions across the world under pornography and child sexual assault legislation. Sexting involves the transmission of sexually explicit or naked images to others via Facebook, mobile phone or the Internet. The authors are careful to distinguish sexting from sexual harassment, arguing that sexting between consenting adults is not a crime and can indeed even be a 'pleasurable' pastime. They acknowledge that while teen sexting can be harmful if it involves the transmission of embarrassing lurid photos of ex-girlfriends, for instance, most instances of teen sexting are harmless and consensual. However, when young people engage in sexting, they are susceptible to criminalization under child pornography and sexual assault legislation that prohibits the dissemination of images of people under the age of 18. Lee et al. (2013) argue that the emergence of teen sexting online fed into a politicized discourse about social media and new technologies being used to promote pornography and paedophilia. This political context made it impossible to have a rational debate about the unintended consequences of charging young people with serious criminal offences. Anyone who did was seen as siding with paedophilia. They point out that the criminalization of trivial acts of sexting has been net-widening and raises cause for concern. Finally, 'sexting involving young people has become framed as a problem in the regulation of child sexuality' (Lee et al. 2013: 45). Like other studies, Lee et al. (2013) illustrate the importance of theorizing and researching interactions through social media in contemporary criminological research.

Sanja Milivojevic and Alyce McGovern (2014) undertook a study that examined how social media platforms can be used in the production of the discourses of crime, blame and punishment in the digital age. The authors took as their case study the social media discourse over the disappearance, abduction and subsequent murder of Melbourne journalist Jill Meagher after a night out with friends on 22 September 2012. The Facebook campaign all began as a well-intentioned page urging the public to 'Help find Jill Meagher'. YouTube and Facebook were initially used to broadcast CCTV footage of Meagher in the immediate aftermath of her disappearance. Images of a suspect last seen with Meagher captured on CCTTV were widely disseminated to the public, who in turn re-tweeted and shared the images millions of times. The image of the suspect was recognized by other women who allege he had attacked them, and a few days later, on 27 September 2012, Adrian Riley was charged with Meagher's murder. Following his arrest, two more Facebook pages emerged seeking justice and retribution for Jill Meagher, calling for the reintroduction of the death penalty and for the offender to be hung (Milivojic and McGovern 2014: 23). These Facebook sites were used to publicly shame, vilify and promote vigilantism, which undermines the presumption of innocence – a central tenet of criminal law fundamental to a social democratic society. Milivojevic and McGovern argue that the case highlights the urgent need for criminologists to engage with the power of social media to define agendas, to exercise undue influence over criminal investigations and to conduct 'trial by social media'. Ultimately they 'call for more audacious and critical engagement by criminologists and social scientists in addressing the challenges posed by new technologies' (Milivojevic and McGovern 2014: 22).

This study also considered issues surrounding the validity and reliability of online research methods in terms of how to accurately study an online platform upon which users are sharing 'over four billion individual pieces of content' (Milivojevic and McGovern 2014: 24). The authors suggest that researchers needed to be clear about where they start collecting data from and what they are trying to capture in order to ensure the collection of valid data (Milivojevic and McGovern 2014: 24). Despite these issues, they argue that ignoring the use of social media platforms and communication technologies would prevent criminological research from keeping up with the way in which social behaviour is increasingly governed in the twenty-first century.

Here we have briefly explored five studies that have used e-methodologies as their focus for conducting contemporary criminological research on conduct that traverses the parallel worlds of the Internet and social reality. These studies illustrate that not only can online platforms provide researchers with access to unique ethnographic data sets, but also that these new technologies raise important wider sociological concerns about new forms of social control in the twenty-first century, such as the criminalization of sexting, the creation of new harms, new anxieties and new forms of vigilantism.

## Conclusion: the politics of the criminological imagination

While the politics of criminological research has shifted with changes in intellectual currents from deviance theories, critical, feminist and now southern/liquid criminologies, choice of method for doing imaginative critical scholarship has blossomed. Digital technologies have removed many of the obstacles while multiplying the opportunities for doing imaginative studies of crime and social control that challenge the hegemony of knowledge production. This has a democratizing effect on knowledge production and dissemination. It also embodies the prospect of disrupting the centre–periphery relations of power that have dominated the production of knowledge in the social sciences for well over a century, which have until now have privileged the Global North (Carrington, Hogg and Sozzo 2016). E-methodologies provide a means of doing research that does not reproduce the Global northern hegemony. Doing imaginative criminological research is dislodged from geographical boundedness. Once-taken-for-granted boundaries and empirical referents melt and become liquefied. The conditions of liquid criminology align well with the political project of southern criminology to disrupt the dominance of centre–periphery power relations. Here 'southern' is used as a metaphor for the other, the formerly invisible and formerly unknowable. It is not meant as an exclusionary identifier – to exclude scholars from the Global North from being part of this epistemological break with place-based criminologies that instinctively bias the metropolitan thinking of the Global North.

Pat Carlen reminds us that all good research should be driven by a 'criminological imagination' to think the unthinkable, to represent the unrepresentable, to shift the boundaries and imagine a more just criminal justice system (Carlen 2010). She also astutely notes that criminological knowledge, critical, feminist or otherwise, is subject to the risk of falling into what she calls the 'discursive abyss' of being absorbed by other discourses over which the author has no control (Carlen 2010). This discursive abyss has accelerated exponentially with the creation of digital technologies that enable the rapid global production, dissemination and re-tweeting of information and discourse. While loss of authorship and ability to control discursive and power effects of knowledge is one consequence, we argue that these new technologies characteristic of liquid modernity have also widened the possibility for both conducting imaginative criminological research and challenging Global northern dominance.

## Note

1 Michel Foucault once observed: 'Truth isn't outside power, or lacking in power . . . truth isn't the reward of free spirits, the child of protracted solitude, not the privilege of those who have succeeded in liberating themselves. Truth is a thing of this world: it is produced only by virtue of multiple forms of constraint. And it induces regular effects of power' (Foucault in Rabinow 1984: 72–3).

## References

Australian Bureau of Statistics (2010) *Household Use of Information Technology, Australia, 2010–11.* Available at: www.abs.gov.au/ausstats/abs@.nsf/Latestproducts/ 4E4D83E02F39FC32CA25796600152BF4?opendocument.

Barbaret, Rosemary (2014) *Women, Crime and Criminal Justice.* London: Routledge.

Beccaria, Cesare (1764) *On Crimes and Punishments.* London: Printed for E. Newbery, at the Corner of St Paul's Church-Yard.

Becker, Howard S. (1963) *Outsiders: Studies in the Sociology of Deviance.* New York: Free Press.

Bluett-Boyd, Nicole, Bianca Fileborn, Antonia Quadara and Sharnee Moore (2013) 'The Role of Emerging Communication Technologies in Experiences of Sexual Violence a New Legal Frontier'. Australian Institute of Family Studies. Available at: www.aifs. gov.au/institute/pubs/resreport23/index.html.

Bredl, Klause, Julia Hunniger and Jakob Linaa Jensen (2014) *Methods for Analyzing Social Media.* London: Routledge.

Brown, David (2013) 'Mapping the Conditions of Penal Hope'. *International Journal for Crime, Justice and Social Democracy,* 2(3): 27–42.

Brown, David and Russell Hogg (1992) 'Law and Order Politics – Left Realism and Radical Criminology', in Roger Matthews and Jock Young (eds), *Issues in Realist Criminology.* London: Sage Publications, pp. 136–76.

Carlen, Pat (1983) *Women's Imprisonment: A Study of Social Control.* London: Routledge & Kegan Paul.

——. (1988) *Women, Crime and Poverty.* Buckingham: Open University Press.

——. (2010) *A Criminological Imagination: Essays on Justice, Punishment, Discourse.* Farnham: Ashgate.

Carmody, Moira and Kerry Carrington (2000) 'Preventing Sexual Violence?'. *Australian and New Zealand Journal of Criminology*, 33: 341–61.

Carrington, Kerry (1993) *Offending Girls: Sex, Youth and Justice.* Sydney: Allen & Unwin.

——. (2002) 'Feminism and Critical Criminology: Confronting Genealogies', in Kerry Carrington and Russell Hogg (eds), *Critical Criminology: Issues, Debates and Challenges.* Cullompton: Willan, pp. 114–42.

——. (2013) 'Girls and Violence: The Case for a Feminist Theory of Female Violence'. *International Journal for Crime, Justice and Social Democracy*, 2(2): 63–79.

——. (2015) *Feminism and Global Justice.* London: Routledge.

Carrington, Kerry and Russell Hogg (2002) 'Critical Criminologies', in Kerry Carrington and Russell Hogg (eds), *Critical Criminology: Issues, Debates and Challenges.* Cullompton: Willan, pp. 1–14.

——. (2012) 'History of Critical Criminology in Australia', in Molly Dragiewicz and Walter S. DeKeseredy (eds), *Routledge Handbook of Critical Criminology.* New York: Routledge, pp. 46–60.

Carrington, Kerry and Margaret Pereira (2009) *Offending Youth: Sex, Youth and Justice.* Annandale: Federation Press.

Carrington, Kerry, Joseph F. Donnermeyer and Walter S. DeKeseredy (2014) 'Intersectionality, Rural Criminology and Re-imagining the Boundaries of Critical Criminology'. *Critical Criminology*, 22: 463–77.

Carrington, Kerry, Russell Hogg and Máximo Sozzo (2016) 'Southern Criminology'. *British Journal of Criminology*, 56(1): 1–20.

Carrington, Kerry, Maryanne Dever, Russell Hogg, Jenny Bargen and Andrew Lohrey (1991) *Travesty! Miscarriages of Justice*, Sydney: Pluto Press.

Chesney-Lind, Meda and Lisa Pasko (eds) (2004) *Girls, Women and Crime: Selected Readings*, Thousand Oaks, CA: Sage Publications.

Cohen, Stanley (1980) *Folk Devils and Moral Panics: The Creation of Mods and Rockers.* Oxford: Martin Robinson.

——. (1985) *Visions of Social Control.* Cambridge: Polity Press.

——. (1988). *Against Criminology.* New Brunswick, NJ: Transaction Books

Connell, Raewyn (2007) *Southern Theory: The Global Dynamics of Knowledge in the Social Science.* Sydney: Allen & Unwin.

Currie, Elliott (1985) *Confronting Crime.* New York: Pantheon Books.

——. (2013) 'The Sustaining Society', in Kerry Carrington, Matthew Ball, Erin O'Brien and Juan M. Tauri (eds), *Crime, Justice and Social Democracy.* Basingstoke: Palgrave Macmillan, pp. 3–15.

Davies, Pamela (2000) 'Doing Interviews in Prison', in Victor Jupp, Pamela Davies and Peter Francis (eds), *Doing Criminological Research.* London: Sage Publications, pp. 82–96.

DeKeseredy Walter and Joseph Donnermeyer (2013) 'Thinking Critically about Rural Crime: Toward the ~Development of a New Left Realist Perspective', in S. Winlow and R. Atkinson (eds), *New Directions in Crime and Deviancy.* London: Routledge, pp. 206–22.

Fielding, Nigel G., Grant Blank and Raymond M. Lee (eds) (2012) *The Sage Handbook of Online Research Methods.* Thousand Oaks, CA: Sage Publications.

Garland, David (1994) 'Of Crimes and Criminals: The Development of Criminology in Britain', in Mike Maguire, Rodney Morgan and Robert Reiner (eds), *The Oxford Handbook of Criminology.* Oxford: Oxford University Press, pp. 17–68.

——. (2013) 'Forward', in Kerry Carrington, Matthew Ball, Erin O'Brien and Juan M. Tauri (eds), *Crime, Justice and Social Democracy*. Basingstoke: Palgrave Macmillan, pp. ix–xi.

Gelsthorpe, Lorraine (1989) *Sexism and the Female Offender*. Aldershot: Gower.

Grabosky, Peter (2007) *Electronic Crime*. Upper Saddle River, NJ: Pearson Education.

Grosz, Elizabeth (1989) 'The In(ter)vention of Feminist Knowledges', in Barbra Caine, Elizabeth A. Grosz and Marie M. de Lepervanche (eds), *Crossing Boundaries: Feminisms and the Critique of Knowledges*. Sydney: Allen & Unwin, pp. 92–104.

Gunew, Sneja (1990) *Feminist Knowledge: Critique and Construct*. London: Routledge.

Hall, Stuart and Tony Jefferson (eds) (1975) *Resistance through Rituals: Youth Subcultures in Post-War Britain*. London: Hutchinson.

Hall, Stuart, Charles Critcher, Tony Jefferson, John Clarke and Brian Roberts (1978) *Policing the Crisis: Mugging, the State and Law and Order*. London: Macmillan.

Hallett, Ronald E. and Kristen Barber (2014) 'Ethnographic Research in a Cyber Era'. *Journal of Contemporary Ethnography*, 43(3): 306–30.

Harding, Sandra (1986) *The Science Question in Feminism*. Ithaca: Cornell University Press.

Harris, Angela P. (1990) 'Race and Essentialism in Feminist Legal Theory'. *Stanford Law Review*, 58: 581–616.

Hauztinger, Sarah (2010) 'Criminalising Male Violence in Brazil's Women's Police Stations: From Flawed Essentialism to Imagined Communities'. *Journal of Gender Studies*, 11(3) :243–51.

Hesse-Biber, Sharlene and Amy J. Griffin (2013) 'Internet-Mediated Technologies and Mixed Methods Research: Problems and Prospects'. *Journal of Mixed Methods Research*, 7(1): 43–61.

Hogg, Russell and David Brown (1998) *Rethinking Law and Order*. Sydney: Pluto Press.

Hogg, Russell and Kerry Carrington (2006) *Policing the Rural Crisis*. Annandale: Federation Press.

——. (2013) 'History of Critical Criminology in Australia', in Walter S. DeKeseredy and Molly Dragiewicz (eds), *Routledge Handbook on Critical Criminology*. London: Routledge, pp. 46–60.

Hooley, Tristram, Jane Wellens and John Marriott (2012) *What is Online Research? – Using the Internet for Social Science Research*. London: Bloomsbury Academic.

Hudson, Barbara (2000) 'Critical Reflection as Research Methodology', in Victor Jupp, Pamela Davies and Peter Francis (eds), *Doing Criminological Research*. London: Sage Publications.

Ibitissam, Bouachrine (2014) *Women and Islam: Myths, Apologies, and the Limits of Feminist Critique*. Lanham, MD: Lexington Books.

Larkin, Ashleigh (2013) 'Fighting like a Girl . . . or a Boy? Investigating Uploaded Fights between Young Women and Performances of Femininity on Online Social Media'. Honours dissertation, School of Justice, Faculty of Law, Brisbane: Queensland University of Technology.

Lea, John and Jock Young (1984) *What is to Be Done about Law and Order?* Harmondsworth: Penguin, pp. 169–89.

Lee, Murray, Thomas Crofts, Michael Salter, Sanja Milivojevic and Alyce McGovern (2013) '"Let's Get Sexting": Risk, Power, Sex and Criminalisation in the Moral Domain'. *International Journal for Crime, Justice and Social Democracy*, 2(1): 35–49.

Liamputtong, Pranee and Douglas Ezzy (2005) *Qualitative Research Methods*. Oxford: Oxford University Press.

Matthews, Roger and Jock Young (eds) (1986) *Confronting Crime*. London: Sage Publications.

Matza, David (1964) *Delinquency and Drift*. New York: John Wiley.

Maxfield, Michael and Earl Babbie (2005) *Research Methods for Criminal Justice and Criminology*, 4th edn. Los Angeles: Thomson Wadsworth.

Milivojevic, Sanja and Alyce McGovern (2014) 'The Death of Jill Meagher: Crime and Punishment on Social Media'. *International Journal for Crime, Justice and Social Democracy*, 3(3): 22–39.

Murthy, Dhiraj (2008) 'Digital Ethnography: An Examination of the Use of New Technologies for Social Research'. *Sociology: The Journal of the British Sociological Association*, 42(5): 837–57.

Naffine, Ngaire (1995) 'Sexing the Subject of Law', in Margaret Thornton (ed.), *Public and Private: Feminist Legal Debates*. Melbourne: Oxford University Press, pp. 18–39.

———. (1997) *Feminism & Criminology*. Sydney: Allen & Unwin.

Powell, Anastasia (2010) *Sex, Power and Consent: Youth Culture and the Unwritten Rules*. Melbourne: Cambridge University Press.

Poynting, Scott, Greg Noble, Paul Tabar and Jock Collins (2004) *Bin Laden in the Suburbs*. Sydney: Federation Press.

Punch, Keith (1998) *Introduction to Social Research: Quantitative and Qualitative Approaches*. Los Angeles: Sage Publications.

Rabinow, Paul (1984) *The Foucault Reader*. Harmondsworth: Penguin.

Renzetti, Clair M. (2013) *Feminist Criminology*. London: Routledge.

Salter, Michael and Stephen Tomsen (2012) 'Violence and Carceral Masculinities in Felony Fights'. *British Journal of Criminology*, 52: 309–23.

Sharpe, Gilly (2012) *Offending Girls: Young Women and Youth Justice*. London: Routledge.

Smart, Carol (1989) *Feminism and the Power of Law*. London: Routledge.

Stanley, Liz and Sue Wise (1983) *Breaking Out: Feminist Consciousness and Feminist Research*. London: Routledge & Kegan Paul.

Sykes, Gresham and David Matza (1957) 'Techniques of Neutralisation: A Theory of Delinquency'. *American Sociological Review*, 22: 667–70.

Taylor, Ian, Paul Walton and Jock Young (1973) *The New Criminology*. London: Routledge.

Walklate, Sandra (1992) 'Appreciating the Victim: Conventional, Realist or Critical Criminology', in Roger Matthews and Jock Young (eds), *Issues in Realist Criminology*. London: Sage Publications, pp. 102–18.

———. (2011) 'Reframing Criminal Victimisation: Finding a Place for Vulnerability and Resilience'. *Theoretical Criminology*, 15: 175–92.

———. (ed.) (2007) *Handbook on Victims and Victimology*. Cullompton: Willan Publishing.

White, Rob (1990) *No Space of Their Own: Young People and Social Control in Australia*. Sydney: Cambridge University Press.

Young, Jock (1998) 'Breaking Windows: Situating the New Criminology', in Paul Walton and Jock Young (eds), *The New Criminology Revisited*. London: Macmillan, pp. 14–46.

———. (2002) 'Critical Criminology in the Twenty-First Century', in Kerry Carrington and Russell Hogg (eds), *Critical Criminology: Issues, Debates and Challenges*. Cullompton: Willan Publishing, pp. 251–74.

———. (2011) *The Criminological Imagination*. Cambridge: Polity Press.

# Conclusion

## Revisiting 'liquid criminology' – politics, poetics, pitfalls and promises

*Michael Hviid Jacobsen and Sandra Walklate*

### Introduction

The notion of 'liquid criminology', quite contrary to the gradual success and increasing use of its sibling notion of 'liquid sociology', has not yet really caught on in contemporary criminology circles. Looking at the Internet for hits, one will be disappointed to discover that only very few criminologists so far have actually written on or even considered the viability of the idea of 'liquid criminology'. This is quite surprising – especially since the interplay, mutual exchange and open-ended import-export of ideas, perspectives and theories between the disciplines of criminology and sociology in particular have always been prevalent. The idea of 'liquid sociology' is obviously closely associated with the work of Zygmunt Bauman (see Davis 2013) who in his seminal book *Liquid Modernity* suggested that we are currently leaving the 'solid modernity' of the nineteenth and twentieth centuries behind and entering a time described as 'liquid modernity' (Bauman 2000). Contrary to solid modernity, liquid modernity heralds a new social habitat in which the securities, certainties and predictabilities of the past are giving way to liquefied, unpredictable and precarious lives lived in a society that is increasingly dismantling everything solid and lasting. This situation challenges and puts a strain on the discipline of sociology, which can no longer rely uncritically on its conventional theories and methods originally developed to study a radically different social environment than the present state of affairs. In many ways, criminology – like sociology – was a golden child of solid modern society sharing with that discipline a quest for control, structure, calculability, security, transparency, predictability, territoriality, stability and not least of all, social order (Bauman 1991).

Today's society – as compared to that of solid modernity – in many respects looks very different indeed with relentless pressures of individualization, globalization, consumerism and a host of other processes now increasingly shaping and transforming the social landscape in new and previously unknown ways. This also informs and affects the world of crime, its causes and its consequences, and how we try to comprehend and perhaps even counter it. This does not mean, however, that the criminology of the past is deemed either outdated, irrelevant or unable to account for the phenomenon of crime, but it does suggest that we seriously and soberly contemplate what we have achieved so far and carefully consider where we are heading from here. A the end of the day, it also urges us to consider (and perhaps even reconsider) what we are doing, how we are doing it, why we are doing it and, not least, for whom we are doing it. As Bauman stated in interview, 'the challenge we face now is not trivial at all: the parameters of the "crime phenomenon" need to be urgently re-thought' (quoted in Daems and Robert 2007: 99).

Although Bauman himself neither directly described nor ever paid any tribute or allegiance to the concept of 'liquid sociology', his work has always suggested the need to move sociology beyond the confines of and to critically explore the boundaries of the already known, and this necessity has become all the more pertinent and pronounced by the advent of liquid modernity. As the late Mike Presdee rightly observed in *Cultural Criminology and the Carnival of Crime*, the rational liberalism so closely associated with solid modernity may be unable to account for many aspects of contemporary life (Presdee 2000: 157–8). The 'carnival of crime' is today perhaps more carnivalesque than ever before, and although crime is obviously still 'crime', the way we approach, understand, react to and attempt to counter it can no longer rest or rely on ideas, theories or methods developed under the auspices of solid modernity. The reasons why people commit crime and the way they do it is not a solid, fixed or unchanging thing. Thus, the 'seductions of crime' mentioned by Jack Katz (1988) in liquid-modern settings are therefore not necessarily the same as in industrialized, panoptic and rational solid modernity. Liquid modernity is most of all about flux – the fact that things cannot hold their shape for long – and this means that changing social formations, changing figurations, changing relationships, changing ethnic compositions, changing political agendas, changing moral sentiments, changing attitudes and changing forms of interaction are now becoming the new background variables for criminological research. Moreover, this is intimately coupled with the rise of a society of fear (Bauman 2006, 2007) and with an increasing acceleration of everything social (Rosa 2015), as well as with the appearance of new forms of crime: crimes mediated and made possible through information technologies; new patterns of consumption and new types of social expectancy; transnational and globalized networks of criminal offenders and transnational initiatives to control and counter crime. All of this, as well as much more (too much to mention here), highlights the fact that we need to tune criminology and make it more relevant and responsive to the contemporary social scene. Hence, we need a 'liquid criminology' to better understand what is going on.

So, these liquid modern times might benefit from a more liquid kind of criminology able to capture, highlight and critically assess the many what's, when's, why's, who's and how's of the contemporary crime scene. As was pointed to in our introduction to this collection, Jock Young's last book, *The Criminological Imagination*, put the contemporary criminological imagination under considerable scrutiny. Charging the discipline with the 'crime' of being dominated in its theories and methods by the most atypical society in the world, he laid down a serious challenge to the discipline and its capacity to make sense of crime in its current global context (Young 2011). If Young's assessment of the state of the discipline captures the essence of its contemporary dilemmas, it is important that those engaged with the discipline respond to Young's challenge. The contributions in this collection, either implicitly or explicitly, offer the tentative beginnings of such a response.

One focus of this collection has been the concept of the 'imagination'. How does imagination inform how we think about and practise criminology (see the chapter by Carlen in this volume; see also Carlen 2010)? How might conventional research methods, so intimately connected with the kind of criminology vehemently critiqued by Young, be used imaginatively and thereby generate better understandings of crime (see the chapters by DeKeseredy, Westmarland, and Petherick and Ferguson in this volume)? What kinds of less conventional data sources available to us in the contemporary world can be used imaginatively and in the interests of those with whom we are researching (see the chapters by Carrabine, O'Neill, McGarry and Godfrey in this volume)? What kinds of imaginative practices are then demanded of us in gaining access to data and ensuring ethical practice if we follow these less conventional paths? What political questions lie behind such imaginings (see the chapters by Godfrey, Bacon and Sanders, Fitz-Gibbon, and Carrington and Larkin in this volume)? Each of the contributions to this volume offers valuable insights into different ways of responding to these kinds of questions. None of these insights is bound by the conventional criminological canons associated with the 'bogus of positivism' imbued with the 'nomothetic impulse' (Young 2011; see also the postscript to this volume by Ferrell). They each start with the question: if the contemporary world and ways of living in this world are characterized by liquidity, might there be some mileage in exploring the features of a 'liquid criminology'? In framing the possibility for practising criminology informed by liquidity in the introduction to this book, we also posited the view that this kind of criminology raises epistemological as well as practical challenges for the discipline. In drawing on the work of Raewyn Connell (2007), Katja F. Aas (2012) and Boaventura de Sousa Santos (2014), we suggest, in agreement with them, that this epistemological challenge focuses attention on how to render the knowledge production process within criminology more democratic and inclusive (see also Carrington, Hogg and Sozzo 2016).

Of course, observing that social research of any kind – and thus also criminology – suffers from the presumptions of a 'democratic bias' is not new. Quite some time ago, Johan Galtung (1967) made this observation about social surveys. This observation was taken further in feminist-informed work to render the voices of women much more audible in proposing research 'by women, with women, for women'. Arguably, however, there is another dimension to democracy in the context of the discussion here. Aspiring to a democratic epistemology involves not just having the right kinds of samples of the relevant groups of people or making sure that their voices are heard. Nor does it mean that we should be concerned only with seeking definitive answers to equally definitive questions. In fact, a democratic epistemology requires that we are just as concerned with asking the right questions than with finding the right answers, because, as Bauman once stated, 'questions are hardly ever wrong; it is the answers that might be so' (Bauman 1999: 8). Criminologists should therefore perform the role of 'problem raisers' rather than 'problem solvers'

(Taylor, Walton and Young 1973). Obviously, a democratic epistemology also demands that we think about whether or not we are not only asking the right questions of the right people, but also considering whether or not the questions we are asking are *conceptually informed* in such a way that both the act of asking and the practice of listening make sense for those participating in the research. Consequently, each of the chapters in this collection has differently opened up the 'black box' (Latour 1987) of criminological research, not to enable us to operationalize particular research techniques better (this is not a 'how to do book'), but to enable us to consider different ways of engaging in research in a meaningful and democratically informed way. This, without doubt, raises the thorny question of politics both within and outside of the discipline.

## The politics of 'liquid criminology'

The so-called 'politics of criminology' is a recurring theme within the discipline. Raising the spectre of politics both within and outwith the discipline in no way implies a position 'against method' (Feyerabend 1975), nor does it suggest that criminologists should be taking sides, but it does suggest the need for deep reflection on such questions as: how do we know things, in knowing things whose knowledge counts and, in the light of answering these two questions, what is to be done on the basis of these answers? Here is not the place to engage in an in-depth exploration of the extensive literature and debates that thinking about questions such as these has generated. It is sufficient at this juncture to observe that asking them implies putting much of the criminology to which Young (2011) refers in its place: geographically, culturally, conceptually, methodologically and ethically. Put simply, that version of doing criminology does not travel well despite claims otherwise. This does not mean throwing the 'baby out with the bathwater' but it does mean thinking hard and reflectively about context, culture, specificity and imagination. As an example, and one that Sandra Walklate (2007: 176–7) has used before, it implies valuing different kinds of 'knowing' well illustrated in the following extract taken from Robert M. Pirsig's (1976) well-read book *Zen and the Art of Motorcycle Maintenance*. In reflecting on the problems of motorcycle repair, he has this to say:

> 'Remove side cover plate' in that wonderful technical style that never tells you what you want to know . . . This isn't a rare scene in science or technology. This is the commonest scene of all. Just plain stuck . . . What you're up against is the great unknown, the void of all Western thought. Traditional scientific method has always been at the very best 20-20 hindsight. It's good for seeing where you've been . . . but it can't tell you where you ought to go unless where you ought to go is a continuation of where you were going in the past. Creativity, originality, inventiveness, intuition, imagination – 'unstuckness' in other words- are completely outside its domain. (Pirsig 1976: 262–3)

The clue to the political challenge in the quote above lies in the questions of what might be understood as science and scientific practices, either continuing with what has gone on before or using other sources of inspiration for how we might solve problems looking to move forwards: unstuckness. Foregrounding creativity, inventiveness, intuition and imagination, all of which are present in the contributions in this volume, is a real political challenge for those committed to more conventional ways of doing criminology. Such liquidity is uncontrollable and this characteristic is considered anathema to more conventional understandings of science. Moreover, this political challenge of what counts as knowledge, alongside the question of whose knowledge counts, carries with it other considerations too, one of which returns us to the seminal question once posed by Howard S. Becker (1967): 'Whose side are we on?'

The democratic epistemology within which we have situated the potentialities that emerge from a liquid criminology implicitly demands a commitment to social justice. This demand in some respects takes us beyond the question of whose side we are on (as Becker pointed out all those years ago, as social scientists we are all on somebody's side) in a partisan sense. This epistemology is more than merely giving voice to the oppressed, the deviant or, as Bauman (2004) might say, the wasted. It requires that we need to ask questions relating to the distribution of power, wealth, inequality, opportunity and authority in our contemporary liquid-modern societies (Georgoulas 2012). It also requires a commitment to democracy throughout the entire research process. This knowledge co-production process challenges not only who might be considered as 'the expert', but also what might be considered as findings, who owns them and what might be done on the basis of them. All of this can and will be differently interpreted and acted upon in the light of the interests of those parties involved. All of this involves political decisions of one kind or another. Thus, liquid criminology, by implication, eschews not only traditional concepts of what counts as science, but also the conventional separation of facts from values that have so dogged more positivistic orientations within the discipline.

All of the chapters in this collection illustrate how it is possible to pursue imaginative, fluid and democratically oriented work and to retain principled approaches to such work conducted in the search for knowledge with integrity. Yet such work still retains a commitment to engaging with a public criminology in which as criminologists they 'play their part in imagining and building the kinds of civic institutions that can bring the light of public reason to problems about which they – like many of their co-citizens – care so passionately' (Loader and Sparks 2011: 147). Liquid criminology is therefore also necessarily a 'public criminology' – a criminology concerned with and committed to taking its knowledge outside the stuffy ivory towers of the academic world and to willingly engage with a variety of publics (such as research subjects, private and public organizations, research units, politicians, the media and so on) concerned with the phenomenon of crime. Just like 'public sociology', which has recently served as an inspirational source for discussing and reconsidering sociology's relationship to the world outside of academia (see, for example, Agger 2007; Brewer 2013; Burawoy 2004; Jacobsen 2008), the idea of 'public criminology' should therefore be seen as a golden opportunity for the discipline of criminology to reconsider and indeed strengthen its engagement with a multitude of publics, thereby making its knowledge claims relevant to and accessible for larger proportions of liquid modern society (see e.g. Currie 2007; Ruggiero 2012).

## The poetics of 'liquid criminology'

Besides being concerned with politics in a new, inclusive, democratic and in many ways heretofore unprecedented manner, a 'liquid criminology' is also concerned with the poetics of practising, doing, learning, living and imagining criminology. Once upon a time, most criminological literature was indeed a pleasurable and inspirational read. Taking a glance at some of the classics of the discipline, it becomes obvious how the purpose was not merely to report empirical 'facts', to describe 'data' in a detached manner, to indulge in ingenious 'methodological' manoeuvres or to provide lengthy and self-promoting discussions of 'findings' as compared to those of colleagues. Rather, the purpose of the classics was often to provide a 'perspective' on crime – its roots, its rhythms and routes as well as its repercussions. The shift from 'scholarship' to 'research' so readily apparent also in other social science disciplines has had an impact not only on the way academic practitioners conceive of their work as a 'career', but also on the way they manage that career and the way their write and communicate about their subject matters. Thus, today – for large proportions of the outpourings of the discipline of criminology – the read is no longer necessarily so pleasurable. A lot of criminological knowledge is now reported in an unnecessarily standardized and technicalized way that leaves little or no room for poetic expressions, not to mention the possibility of presenting anything resembling or approximating a 'perspective'. This tendency is exacerbated by the rise of the 'journal indus-try' by way of which careers in criminology, as well as in most other scientific disciplines, are now made. Journal publication, or writing your PhD thesis in a 'journal-based manner', has now become the apex of academic achievement, making the development or presentation of a more comprehensive 'perspective' the odd man out or a waste of time. Catering for the demands for easily acces-sible, quickly readable and instantly digestible pieces of work now dominate the way in which criminology is being conducted and consumed to the detriment of the discipline. This – obviously subjective experience – does not mean that there are no pearls of wisdom to be retrieved from the treasure trove of the discipline. However, it does suggest that we need to consider whether there are other more creative, more readable and perhaps even more desirable ways of reporting what we know about the workings of the world of crime.

More than half a century ago, C. Wright Mills (1959) in his seminal book *The Sociological Imagination* famously warned against the advancing tendencies or the monstrous Scylla of 'grand theorizing' on the one side and the equally dae-monic Charybdis of 'abstracted empiricism' on the other. In his view, both of these camps represented ideas about science, how to conduct it, how to report it and how to use it, which let down the great promises made by the classics of the discipline. Later, but in a similar vein, Stanislav Andreski (1972) stated that much of what passed as 'social science research' was in fact closer to a kind of 'sorcery' which through the camouflage of quantification, a smokescreen of excessively technical jargon and a subtly underplayed ideological stance lured its readers and stakeholders into believing that it was in fact 'science'. He even went as far as suggesting that 'pretentious and nebulous verbosity, interminable repetition of platitudes and disguised propaganda are the order of the day, while at least 95 per cent of research is indeed re-search of things that have been found long ago and many times since' (1972: 11). Andreski also chastised those 'worshippers of methodology' who hunted down, 'like a vicious hunting pack', anyone who dared to write and communicate their research in a comprehensible, impressionistic or even interesting and poetic manner, showing at least some sense of cultural refinement (1972:117), just as he warned against the dangers of any captivating yet disingenuous talk about the search for scientific objectivity or value-neutrality.

Is Andreski's caustic critique of the state of social science in general in the early 1970s in any way whatsoever relevant to a critique of the status of criminological research in the twenty-first century? Obviously, there will be different answers to this question. Whereas some will claim that this is an over-dramatized or outdated description of the state of play in criminology, others will doubtlessly sense that it is not entirely off-target. In his classic *In Search of Criminology*, Leon Radzinowicz mourned the widespread tendency in criminology to make the communication of research difficult to understand. He observed how 'jargon, padding, overelaborated statistical data, hunting for far-fetched hypotheses, pretentiousness and repetitiveness are the deadly sins' and provocatively recommended that the volume of what was at the time being produced in criminology could with advantage be reduced (Radzinowicz 1961: 178). What Radzinowicz stated more than half a century ago still has some merit when looking at contemporary criminology – a discipline that has been documented to privilege quantitative methods and statistical analysis at the expense of other, read qualitative, types of research (see e.g. Tewksbury, DeMichele and Miller 2005; Tewksbury, Dabney and Copes 2010). Bruce DiChristina's (1995: vii) teasingly rhetorical question 'should any research method be granted privileged status in criminology?' is therefore still as relevant and as pertinent today as when it was first posed two decades ago. Thus, at the moment – and perhaps as a signifier of liquid modernity – we are witnessing the increasingly visible contours of a counter-tendency to the reign of positivism in criminology especially spearheaded by exponents of 'cultural criminology' who argue for a re-orientation of the discipline's understanding and appreciation of what counts as 'methods', 'data', 'science' and 'evidence' (see Jacobsen 2015b). As anticipated quite some time ago:

> We see emerging not simply a reconceptualization of field research, but radically new ways of living and knowing as criminologists and sociologists, ways of living and knowing which are at the same time more clear and more mysterious, closer than earlier methods to subjects of study and at the same time never close enough. We see, in place of a vain search for scientific objectivity, a dangerous poetic for criminology and sociology, an artistry

and an artistic intensity in research and reporting that emerges somewhere beyond the careful constraints of courthouse criminology and arid academic discourse. (Ferrell and Hamm 1998: 14–15)

One of the many consequences of this cultural criminological counter-tendency is that we are experiencing an expanding and exciting interest in imaginative or poetic ways of approaching the discipline of criminology (see e.g. Barton et al. 2007; Carlen 2010; Frauley 2015; Jacobsen 2015a) – a tendency that is obviously indebted particularly to the legacy of Jock Young. In the second chapter of *The Criminological Imagination*, entitled 'Closing Down the Imagination', Young started out by showing the mindboggling gobbledygook characterizing so much of the so-called 'mainstream criminology' that is mesmerized as well as enslaved by the promises of positivism. Examples abound that testify how criminologists – using incomprehensible language, obfuscating mathematical formulae, excessively simplified explanatory models and downright gibberish – often construct quite dubious 'truths' about crime issues, their causes and their consequences (Young 2011: 10–23). Young's ambition was to revitalize the criminological imagination in order to install a sense of critical understanding of their work in the minds of criminologists and also to make the discipline relevant to non-criminologists. However, this criminological imagination – just like the sociological imagination – is not merely about the ability to integrate an understanding of structural and historical developments with individual-centred experiences and levels of life, which Mills (1959) saw as one of the main analytical promises of the sociological imagination. It is also about trying to imagine and locate criminology as part of a broader social and cultural mentality that allows for some much-needed leeway to propose new theories, new methods, new and alternative sources of knowledge as well as thinking and communicating in new, surprising, provocative and perhaps even previously untested ways. As Zygmunt Bauman once stated on the often neglected or overlooked possibilities of sociology, something which also obviously pertains to the discipline of criminology:

> When repeated often enough, things tend to become familiar, and familiar things are self-explanatory . . . Familiarity is the staunchest enemy of inquisitiveness and criticism – and thus also of innovation and the courage to change. In an encounter with that familiar world ruled by habits and reciprocally reasserting beliefs, sociology [and criminology] acts as a meddlesome and often irritating stranger . . . [that] defamiliarize[s] the familiar. (Bauman 1990: 15)

Obviously, it does require courage and determination to change our ways, to confront the familiar and taken-for-granted, and to defamiliarize the already well-known world of criminological knowledge. And yet, if we do not dare to do it, things will remain the same. So we need and we crave what Elliott Currie described as 'a kind of criminological imagination that is able and willing to break free of old constraints and look at the problems of crime and punishment with fresh eyes' (Currie 2002: viii). Most importantly, we need to revive the classical veneration for 'criminological craftsmanship', which, just like its sociological counterpart, in the wonderful words of Mills, amongst other things comprises 'an attitude of playfulness toward the phrases and words with which various issues are defined [that] often loosens up the imagination' (Mills 1959: 212). Moreover, in order to capture the maelstrom of liquid modernity, we should particularly remember Mills' advice to the craftsman: 'Let your mind become a moving prism catching light from as many angles as possible' (1959: 214). By doing so, we may perhaps be able not only to understand our contemporary world – including the world of crime – in a better and more comprehensible way, but also, as Mills suggested in the closing sentence of his seminal book, to 'make a difference in the quality of human life in our time' (1959: 226).

## The pitfalls and promises of 'liquid criminology'

Unfortunately, there are no easy ways and no available shortcuts to this criminological adventure. Most roads – including the roads leading to new insights and new knowledge – promise their travellers a bumpy and risky ride as they are fraught with major or minor holes, re-routings, inattentive, annoying or even aggressive fellow road users and poorly illuminated stretches of road. Add to this the many dangers lurking in the wilderness beyond the asphalted road system waiting to strike if the car should break down or run out of petrol. As a metaphor for some of the potential challenges confronting an attempt at re-imagining criminology, this admittedly simplified traffic example illustrates how internal and external obstacles as well as expected and unexpected incidents are always going to be part of the game when attempts are made to move forward.

One of the main pitfalls of a 'liquid criminology' is the fact that the notion in itself could easily be accused of indicating or connoting a less than scientific enterprise by its adversaries. Anything 'liquid' is almost by definition regarded as if it entails a dilution, diffusion or distortion of everything time-honoured and as standing as the opposite of a solid, sober, principled and proud criminology. However, by suggesting the notion of 'liquid criminology' in this book, we are neither claiming that criminology should compromise on what has so far been achieved nor that it should seek to imitate that which goes on in an increasingly liquefied society, such as constantly changing fads, superficial trends, consumerist ideologies or the aspiration for instant gratification. Rather, we are suggesting that a criminology attempting to understand and come to terms with contemporary liquid-modern society must aspire to develop understandings, draw on theories and use methods that are capable of capturing the constantly changing landscape of crime. To refrain from doing so means running the risk of irrelevance. At the end of the day, it is therefore not a matter of choosing between a 'solid' or a 'liquid' criminology. It is, however, a choice between making the knowledge of criminology relevant to and readable for a wider (also non-academic) audience or either keeping it securely stored behind locks and bolts in the ivory towers of 'Science' or understandable and usable only by the managers and the proponents of the 'bureaucratic ethos' (Mills 1959: 100–18).

Another possible pitfall relates to the criminological reception of the origins of the notion of 'liquid criminology'. Claims that criminology is and has lived a large part of its life as a parasite upon the discipline sociology are far from new and they continue to be repeated (see e.g. Cohen 1988: 4; Braithwaite 2011: 131). For some, this parasitic situation poses a problem, especially if they want to emphasize the purity, originality or superiority of one's own scientific status. For others, it is nothing but a historical fallacy, and for yet others, it remains utterly irrelevant. True, the idea of 'liquid criminology' originally comes from the idea of a 'liquid sociology' associated with the work of Zygmunt Bauman and his sociological analysis of the arrival of 'liquid modernity' (Bauman 2000). So why should criminologists adopt yet another of sociology's inventions instead of coming up with their own specialized terminology? Why should criminology incorporate or embrace the idea of 'liquidity' just because a given concept, theory or perspective appears to have proven useful or promising within a neighbouring discipline? Without purporting or wishing to intervene in the protracted, complex and intricate intellectual relationship between criminology and sociology, we do not see this as an either/or situation. The notion of 'liquid modernity' is not likely to respect academic boundaries and its analytical appeal and use has only expanded over the years (Jacobsen 2015c). Criminology might doubtlessly benefit from engaging with this notion of 'liquidity' whether as a concept describing features and dimensions of the world of crime that it studies or as a notion with relevance pertaining to its own scientific practice. The acceptance of the idea of 'liquidity' might in fact facilitate communication between sociologists, criminologists and other academic practitioners who see some analytical merit in the idea and who individually or collaboratively may try to document, test, corroborate or even falsify the notion that we are indeed living in liquid-modern times.

The final pitfall we will here mention is the one relating to the aforementioned discussions of politics and methods. According to Zygmunt Bauman towards the end of *Liquid Modernity*, 'there is no choice between "engaged" and "neutral" ways of doing sociology. A non-committal sociology is an impossibility' (2000: 216). We do agree that criminology – just like its sociology sibling – must indeed be a critical, committed and an engaged endeavour to understand the world of crime. However, in our understandable eagerness to 'escape the criminological straitjacket' (Barton et al. 2007: 209) often associated with the reign of 'value-neutral' positivism and the dominance of quantitative studies, we must be very careful not to conflate criminology with particular political stances or ideologies. While promoting an understanding of politics that is basically democratic, inclusive and public, as we mentioned above, as criminologists we must also beware becoming or parading as politicians ourselves. This would be doing a great disservice to the discipline as it would potentially detract from all the important, interesting and innovative ideas and insights that criminology can provide and would needlessly open up the flanks for criticism and castigation. At the end of the day, criminology is a science – but a science rooted in a democratic project. Moreover, although we have argued for a more poetically oriented criminology, the discipline does not necessarily need to be either cultural, creative or qualitative in order to be interesting or relevant. Many quantitative or statistically oriented studies provide indispensable knowledge about and insight into the world of crime – its causes, its careers and its consequences. However, in order to obtain a deeper sense of what is at stake in the motivations behind, experiences of and feelings involved in crime, in order to counter ingrained ideas and knowledge that we uncritically take for granted, and in order to achieve social relevance, we argue that a criminology – a 'liquid criminology' – capable of moving beyond or mixing conventional and imaginative methods and methodologies may have an important role to play.

Just as there are many potential pitfalls – and undoubtedly many more than what we have been able to propose and discuss here – to imagining and practising liquid criminology, so there are also many promises involved in this endeavour. Opening up the 'black box' of criminological research to liquidity opens the discipline up to an appreciation of the contemporary nature of people's everyday lives, and how criminology can understand such lives, in new and inventive ways. The potentialities that result provide the criminologist with an opportunity to grasp those lives as they are actually lived (rather than how they might be construed as being lived). This kind of orientation has the capacity to re-invigorate the discipline both internally and externally: internally in relation to the teaching of research methods, and externally in terms of the potential meaning and impact of research findings. It is worth saying a little more about each of these in turn.

'Creativity in the classroom', as Anders Petersen, Michael Hviid Jacobsen and Rasmus Antoft (2014) might term it, is important not only because of the obvious need to engage and enthuse students of criminology, but also because many of these students go into a range of different professional roles in which their capacity to work with, and make sense of people's lives, can be paramount to whether or not they are successful in those roles. Practising liquid criminology, drawing out the students as knowledgeable contributors to how we understand what is going on in the world, rather than viewing them as empty vessels or receptacles of established practices, is a good way to start. For example, using film, photographs, newspaper clippings, music pieces, YouTube clips, amongst a vast range of other data sources, as opposed to more tedious and conventional teaching material is not only one way of capturing the student's imagination, but also serves to constitute important sources of data for them to make sense of in relation to prescient social problems and what might be done about them (see also, *inter alia*, Jacobsen and Petersen 2016; Seymour 2014). Moreover, using the students' own life experiences as biographical data (*qua* Ross McGarry in this volume) can add both sensitivity and depth of understanding to routes into and out of crime, for example, that can be effectively put alongside other methods for exploring such issues. Further, biographies, especially victim biographies, are a massively under-explored data source for understanding how and under what conditions someone might embrace a victim identity, what that identity feels like and what that might mean for policy. From just these examples, it is possible to see that students can learn much about data, its veracity and what it may or may not tell us about the reality of people's lives by centring the questions posed by a liquid criminology.

Externally, the kind of research that a liquid criminology might promote, in centring the questions of democracy and whose knowledge counts, affords a route into working with and for the marginalized, the 'hard to reach' and those voices on the periphery of the Westocentric agenda centred by positivism, which can only open up and re-invigorate criminological understandings of social problems outwith that agenda. Given the increasing sensitivity to the rise of criminology internationally (in China, Asia and South America, for example), it is foolish to hold on to a way of thinking and doing business that is not equipped to meet these changing horizons. Returning to where we began, such developments have the potential to open an exciting Pandora's Box of delights. What it lets loose cannot be put back. Moreover, it is certainly inappropriate to think that the concepts and ways of doing business that have become so embedded within the discipline of criminology are fit for purpose on such a disciplinary global stage. The contributions in this book here offer us one way of thinking about how criminology might become better equipped to respond to such a stage, but rather than with one voice, arguably with many equally valid voices as a challenge to the nomothetic impulse so characteristic of current policy and practice.

## Conclusion

We have discussed above a range of topics relating to what we consider a 'liquid criminology', including those of politics and poetics. Moreover, we have pointed to some of the pitfalls that a re-imagination of criminology is almost destined to encounter, as well as some of the promises that it may hopefully be able to carry forward in the years ahead. In this edited volume we have deliberately refrained from providing a definition of what 'liquid criminology' is and how it should be understood or practised as something distinctive and definitive. Instead – and aided and abetted by the contributors to the volume – we have attempted to propose the idea of 'liquid criminology' as an overarching framework for showing how criminology could be re-imagined in contemporary liquid-modern times. For us, the notion of 'liquid criminology' should thus be seen as an example of what Herbert Blumer once described as a 'sensitizing concept' that – contrary to so-called 'definitive concepts' which 'provide prescriptions of what to see' – 'merely suggest directions along which to look' (Blumer 1969: 148). We do hope that we have been successful in pointing to some of the directions that criminology can decide to look along on its road ahead rather than suggesting which destinations to arrive at.

Recurrently, it has been claimed that criminology finds itself in a state of deep and acute – perhaps even permanent – disciplinary crisis (see e.g. Braithwaite 1989; Cohen 1988; Ericson and Carriere 1994; Ferrell 2009, 2015; Lea 1998). Whereas some criminologists have primarily blamed internal fragmentation, disciplinary dilution or collegial ignorance for this situation and its severity, others have attributed the postulated 'crisis of criminology' to the fragmenting forces of globalized late modernity and the accompanying disruption of stable and incremental scientific development, policy pressures and continuous government cutbacks on resources or other external sources of detrimental influence on the discipline. It has even been suggested that this crisis climate has paved the way for what Massimo Pavarini once described as 'a situation of crisis of identity so profound that we may have serious doubts about [criminology's] survival as presently constituted' (Pavarini 1994: 43). The apparently widespread acceptance of this situation has meant that claiming a 'criminological crisis' is not seen as a surprising, preposterous or earth-shattering proposition (Barak 2009: 7). As is evident, there are many different causes, expressions and consequences of the much-publicized 'crisis of criminology'. Looking at the discipline of criminology from a helicopter view, however, we are not so sure that criminology as such finds itself in a state of crisis. In fact, in some countries, for example, Denmark, from which one of us is writing, criminology is currently experiencing an unprecedented revival with the opening of new university programmes, the establishment of research units and academic communities, the organization of conferences and seminars, increasing political attention as well as a general rise in research initiatives and public interest in criminology. Without neglecting the important fact that the situation may look very different in other parts of the world, any suggestion of a general 'crisis of criminology' needs qualification and to take into consideration the fact that criminology in many places is in fact very much alive and kicking. Perhaps the aforementioned developments do not so much warrant the distinct label of a 'crisis', but should rather be seen as 'challenges' that criminology will necessarily have to confront and take on. These challenges may in fact prove to be the main reasons why criminology does not suffer from stagnation or ossification, but is continuously kept on its toes and asked to prove its worth. Moreover, these challenges are not isolated or exceptional to the discipline of criminology, but may be the – for some deplorable, for others delightful – consequence of the so-called 'postmodern turn' having affected and infected so many social sciences throughout the last few decades (see e.g. Susen 2015), a 'turn' which has made the discussion of scientific achievements, academic status and authority and not least public relevancy a permanent state of affairs. So perhaps this is a perpetual situation of most of the social scientific disciplines struggling to claim and maintain their status as 'scientific'.

We are of the opinion that there are no obstacles without options for overcoming them. We see the current situation as one in which criminology is standing at the crossroads between succumbing to or overcoming the challenges it confronts. We regard this more as a situation of possibility than as one of doom. Let us therefore end this conclusion with the spot-on observation made by Jock Young in his endeavour to rescue the criminological imagination: 'We must constantly be aware of the inherent creativity of human culture and of the rush of emotions and feelings which characterizes the human condition and the capacity for imagination which this demands and engenders' (2011: 224). This capacity of imagination is required, perhaps more so than ever before, in liquid times like ours.

## References

Aas, Katja F. (2012) '"The Earth is But One But the World is Not": Criminological Theory and its Geopolitical Divisions'. *Theoretical Criminology*, 16(1): 5–20.

Agger, Ben (2007) *Public Sociology: From Social Facts to Literary Acts*. Lanham, MD: Rowman & Littlefield.

Andreski, Stanislav (1972) *Social Science as Sorcery*. London: Penguin.

Barak, Gregg (2009) *Criminology: An Integrated Approach*. Lanham, MD: Rowman & Littlefield.

Barton, Alana, Karen Corteen, David Scott and David Whyte (eds) (2007) *Expanding the Criminological Imagination: Critical Readings in Criminology*. Cullompton: Willan Publishing.

Bauman, Zygmunt (1990) *Thinking Sociologically*. Oxford: Blackwell.

——. (1991) *Modernity and Ambivalence*. Cambridge: Polity Press.

——. (1999) *In Search of Politics*. Cambridge: Polity Press.

——. (2000) *Liquid Modernity*. Cambridge: Polity Press.

——. (2004) *Wasted Lives*. Cambridge: Polity Press.

——. (2006) *Liquid Fear*. Cambridge: Polity Press.

——. (2007) *Liquid Times – Living in an Age of Uncertainty*. Cambridge: Polity Press.

Becker, Howard S. (1967) 'Whose Side are We on?' *Social Problems*, 14(3): 239–47.

Blumer, Herbert (1969) *Symbolic Interactionism: Perspective and Method*. Englewood Cliffs, NJ: Prentice Hall.

Braithwaite, John (1989) 'The State of Criminology: Theoretical Decay or Renaissance?'. *Australian and New Zealand Journal of Criminology*, 22: 129–35.

——. (2011) 'Opportunities and Dangers of Capitalist Criminology', in Stephan Parmentier, Lode Walgrave, Ivo Aertsen, Jeroen Maesschalck and Letizia Paoli (eds), *The Sparkling Discipline of Criminology*. Leuven: Leuven University Press, pp. 131–50.

Brewer, John D. (2013) *The Public Value of the Social Sciences – An Interpretive Essay*. London: Bloomsbury Publishing.

Burawoy, Michael (2004) 'Public Sociology: Contradictions, Dilemmas and Possibilities'. *Social Forces*, 82(4): 1603–18.

Carlen, Pat (2010) *A Criminological Imagination: Essays on Justice, Punishment, Discourse*. Farnham: Ashgate.

Carrington, Kerry, Russell Hogg and Máximo Sozzo (2016) 'Southern Criminology'. *British Journal of Criminology*, 56(1): 1–20.

Cohen, Stanley (1988) *Against Criminology*. New Brunswick, NJ: Transaction Publishers.

Connell, Raewyn (2007) 'The Northern Theory of Globalization'. *Sociological Theory*, 25(4): 368–85.

Currie, Elliott (2002) 'Preface', in Kerry Carrington and Russell Hogg (eds), *Critical Criminology: Issues, Debates, Challenges*. Cullompton: Willan Publishing, pp. vii–ix.

——. (2007) 'Against Marginality: Arguments for a Public Criminology'. *Theoretical Criminology*, 11: 175–90.

Daems, Tom and Luc Robert (2007) 'Crime and Insecurity in Liquid Modern Times: An Interview with Zygmunt Bauman'. *Contemporary Justice Review*, 10(1): 87–100.

Davis, Mark (ed.) (2013) *Liquid Sociology: Metaphor in Zygmunt Bauman's Analysis of Modernity*. Farnham: Ashgate.

De Sousa Santos, Boaventura (2014) *Epistemologies of the South: Justice against Epistemicide*. Boulder, CO: Paradigm Publishers.

DiChristina, Bruce (1995) *Method in Criminology: A Philosophical Primer*. New York: Harrow & Heston.

Ericson, Richard and Kevin Carriere (1994) 'The Fragmentation of Criminology', in David Nelken (ed.), *The Futures of Criminology*. London: Sage Publications, pp. 89–109.

Ferrell, Jeff (2009) 'Kill Method: A Provocation'. *Journal of Theoretical and Philosophical Criminology*, 1(1): 1–22.

——. (2015) 'Manifesto for a Criminology Beyond Method', in Michael Hviid Jacobsen (ed.), *The Poetics of Crime: Understanding and Researching Crime and Deviance through Creative Sources*. Farnham: Ashgate, pp. 285–302.

Ferrell, Jeff and Mark S. Hamm (1998) 'True Confessions: Crime, Deviance and Field Research', in *Ethnography at the Edge: Crime, Deviance and Field Research*. Boston, MA: Northeastern University Press, pp. 2–19.

Feyerabend, Paul K. (1975) *Against Method*. London: Verso.

Frauley, Jon (ed.) (2015) *C. Wright Mills and the Criminological Imagination: Prospects for Creative Inquiry*. Farnham: Ashgate.

Galtung, Johan (1967) *Theory and Method of Social Research*. London: Allen & Unwin.

Georgoulas, Stratos (ed.) (2012) *The Politics of Criminology: Critical Studies on Deviance and Social Control*. Münster: LIT Verlag.

Jacobsen, Michael Hviid (ed.) (2008) *Public Sociology*. Aalborg: Aalborg University Press.

——. (ed.) (2015a) *The Poetics of Crime: Understanding and Researching Crime and Deviance through Creative Sources*. Farnham: Ashgate.

——. (2015b) 'Towards the Poetics of Crime: Contours of a Cultural, Critical and Creative Criminology', in Michael Hviid Jacobsen (ed.), *The Poetics of Crime: Understanding and Researching Crime and Deviance through Creative Sources*. Farnham: Ashgate, pp. 1–28.

——. (2015c) 'Introduktion: Velkommen til den flydende moderne verden – Zygmunt Baumans samfundskritiske samtidsdiagnose [Introduction: Welcome to the Brave New Liquid World – Zygmunt Bauman's Critical Diagnosis of the Times]', in Zygmunt Bauman, *Fagre flydende verden* [*Brave New World of Liquidity*]. Copenhagen: Hans Reitzels Forlag, pp. 7–52.

Jacobsen, Michael Hviid and Anders Petersen (2016) 'Contours of a Cinematic Criminology – Distillation, Dramatization, Distortion and Anecdotal Data', in Caroline Joan S. Picart, Michael Hviid Jacobsen and Cecil Greek (eds), *Framing Law and Crime: An Interdisciplinary Anthology*. Madison, NJ: Rowman & Littlefield/Fairleigh Dickinson University Press, pp. 401-32.

Katz, Jack (1988) *Seductions of Crime: Moral and Sensual Attractions in Doing Evil*. New York: Basic Books.

Latour, Bruno (1987) *Science in Action: How to Follow Scientists and Engineers through Society*. Cambridge, MA: Harvard University Press.

Lea, John (1998) 'Criminology and Postmodernity', in Paul Walton and Jock Young (eds), *The New Criminology Revisited*. London: Macmillan, pp. 163–89

Loader, Ian and Richard Sparkes (2011) *Public Criminology*. London: Routledge.

Mills, C. Wright (1959) *The Sociological Imagination*. New York: Oxford University Press.

Pavarini, Massimo (1994) 'Is Criminology Worth Saving?', in David Nelken (ed.), *The Futures of Criminology*. London: Sage Publications, pp. 43–62.

Petersen, Anders, Michael Hviid Jacobsen and Rasmus Antoft (2014) 'Creativity in the Classroom: The Poetics of Pedagogy and Therapeutic Shock in Teaching Sociology', in Michael Hviid Jacobsen, Michael S. Drake, Kieran Keohane and Anders Petersen (eds), *Imaginative Methodologies in the Social Sciences*. Farnham: Ashgate, pp. 197–216.

Pirsig, Robert M. (1976) *Zen and the Art of Motorcycle Maintenance*. London: Corgi.

Presdee, Mike (2000) *Cultural Criminology and the Carnival of Crime*. London: Routledge.

Radzinowicz, Leon (1961) *In Search of Criminology*. London: Heinemann.

Rosa, Hartmut (2015) *Social Acceleration: A New Theory of Modernity*. New York: Columbia University Press.

Ruggiero, Vincenzo (2012) 'How Public is Public Criminology?'. *Crime, Media, Culture*, 8(2): 151–60.

Seymour, Julie (2014) 'The Methodological Imagination: Using Art and Literature in Social Science Methods Teaching', in Michael Hviid Jacobsen, Michael S. Drake, Kieran Keohane and Anders Petersen (eds), *Imaginative Methodologies in the Social Sciences*. Farnham: Ashgate, pp. 217–34.

Susen, Simon (2015) *The 'Postmodern Turn' in the Social Sciences*. London: Palgrave Macmillan.

Taylor, Ian, Paul Walton and Jock Young (1973) *The New Criminology: For a Social Theory of Deviance*. London: Routledge & Kegan Paul.

Tewksbury, Richard, Matthew DeMichele and J. Mitchell Miller (2005) 'Methodological Orientations of Articles Appearing in Criminal Justice's Top Journals: Who Publishes What and Where'. *Journal of Criminal Justice Education*, 16(2): 265–79.

Tewksbury, Richard, Dean A. Dabney and Heith Copes (2010) 'The Prominence of Qualitative Research in Criminology and Criminal Justice'. *Journal of Criminal Justice Education*, 21(4): 391–411.

Walklate, Sandra (2007) 'Risk and Criminal Victimization: Exploring the Fear of Crime', in Kelly Hannah-Moffat and Pat O'Malley (eds), *Gendered Risks*. London: Routledge-Cavendish, pp. 165–82.

Young, Jock (2011) *The Criminological Imagination*. Cambridge: Polity Press.

# Postscript
## Under the slab

*Jeff Ferrell*

## Introduction

This postscript is in part a postmortem, noting as it does the death of criminological method – or at least the death of what many once imagined criminological method to be. For those steeped in positivist ideologies, criminological method seemed a guarantor of detached objectivity, a foundation for comprehensive understanding, and a guard against the subjective and the unpredictable. Over the past few decades, a combination of intellectual critiques and evolving global circumstances have conspired to destroy, for all but the truest of believers, this sense of criminological method and its merits. Many of us have instead begun to imagine method as more a fluid process of engagement with a world that is itself increasingly ill-defined and adrift – that is, to see method as more a tentative orientation than a set of technical certainties. In this sense the death of criminological method is at the same time its re-birth. In this new life, criminological method is mobilized, animated by openness and innovation, and attuned to features of liquid social life largely excluded from its earlier incarnation: the spectral and the interstitial, the visual and the autoethnographic. In this new life, criminological method holds perhaps the possibility of revitalizing criminology itself.

## Unstable circumstances

The contemporary world is beset by instability and social uncertainty for people of all sorts. In Europe, the US and elsewhere, millions remain jobless year after year, drifting between accommodations and doubling up in those they find, moving back in with parents, sleeping under bridges or in train stations. Those who can find jobs of necessity find too many of them; in place of a single occupation, they now negotiate a shifting maze of temporary and seasonal work, freelancing and outsourced identity, with the only certainty being long-term uncertainty. Meanwhile, millions more who are displaced by war crimes or ecological failure or ongoing neocolonialism leave behind family and community in desperate journeys towards something else, anything else, crowding leaky boats to cross the Mediterranean, setting out by foot from Eastern Europe or the Middle East, or riding atop freight trains north through Mexico. For these and others, old social and spatial stabilities of neighbourhood, community and career crumble; even for those more settled and less desperate, the daily news of such happenings, mixed with the global flow of mediated identities and immediate entertainments, creates other sorts of uncertainty and concern. Underlying all of this are still other layers of instability associated with the shock waves of late capitalism, economic failure and structural inequality. Contracting empires leave behind ruins of all sorts, some of them architectural, others social and organizational, and all of them disconnected from the assurances that once sustained them. Growing economic inequality generates unthinkable wealth for the few, but remands the rest to a loose archipelago of abandoned shopping malls, undependable social services, inadequate health care, temporary housing, off-the-books economy and cheap diversions.

Any number of concepts can help us understand this world of pervasive instability and serial dislocation – anomie, alienation and liquid modernity certainly come to mind – but I find it particularly useful to think in terms of drift (Ferrell 2012a). Drift suggests ongoing movement without benefit of a map, a radical uncertainty as to identity or destination, and a sense of being cut loose and caught up in currents beyond one's own making. The collective experience of drift in turn seems to create not some stable common ground, but rather a sort of shifting sand trod by more and more people, from jobless college graduates to impoverished pensioners, from desperate Southern Europeans to those desperately seeking Southern Europe, from Syrian refugees to battered women seeking temporary refuge. And if indeed our historical circumstances are increasingly those of dislocation and drift, the question then becomes how we as criminologists might usefully attune ourselves to such circumstances and make sense of them. That is, the methodological question echoes the circumstances in which it is asked: how to navigate our research without a procedural map, how to find a way forward when no sure destination awaits – how to orient ourselves to a world of disorientation.

This instability, and with it the demand for appropriate alternative methods, redoubles when we consider our own place in it as criminologists. For criminologists seeking to understand those who drift though the contemporary world, methods will be needed that are as fluid and episodic as are the lives of those they study. Researchers may need to approach their subjects of study less as groups or communities and more as loose federations or temporary assemblages. Writers may need narratives that are distinctly non-linear, sentences that fall into fragments, and chapters that float free of enumeration and heading. Visual criminologists and film makers may need to be concerned less with scouting locations than with embracing dislocation, may need to abandon establishing shots altogether, and may need to imagine movies *sans* central characters and fixed narratives. In all of this, it is not only the medium that's the message, but the method that's the message as well; if drift is the subject, it demands methods that avoid boxing it in and stopping it cold, lest it be made into something it's not.

That is one sort of connection between criminology, method and drift – and here is another: What if criminologists are themselves adrift? The world of academic researchers is falling apart, with universities increasingly reliant on part-time faculty who piece together a course here and there while being excluded from any meaningful investment in their university, their research or their career. Liberal education and critical thought are almost everywhere under attack, with politicians and business leaders calling for technical training, efficiency and accountability in place of long-term investigation and analysis. In such a context, criminal justice studies and statistical data analysis, with their promises of predictability and practical certainty, threaten to drive critical or humanist criminologists even further from the stability of academic career. In this emerging world, criminologists will need new methods not only to attune themselves to their subjects of inquiry, but also to attune themselves to themselves – that is, to make their way through a life whose circumstances may well be as fragile and uncertain as those who are the subjects of their research. In this sense the interplay of drift, method and criminology suggests a particular sort of potential relationship; if the appropriate methods can be found, such methods can perhaps shape new sorts of shifting commonalities between those who employ them and those who are their subject. Maybe the better we understand a world adrift, the better we understand our own lives as contemporary criminologists within it.

In my experience, there's one more thing you learn from drifters: travel light. Discard that which encumbers you, lest it drag you down as you move from place to place and shift from identity to identity. For a new generation of criminologists, this will mean no big textbooks turgid with fixed methodological procedures. No 'social science' and the accumulated weight of its staid, bureaucratic ethos. No static, singular notions of truth and quantifiable knowledge. And no slabs – definitely no slabs.

## Slabs and foundations

According to conventional criminological understanding, method is the foundation on which research is built and against which the validity of research is measured. A competent researcher constructs this methodological foundation carefully, first choosing a method that is efficient in its production of data and legitimate in its standing before the wider academic community, then deciding and developing *a priori* protocols for designing questions, collecting data, ensuring confidentiality and coding findings, and finally submitting this elaborate methodological foundation for approval by university or governmental review committees. Once completed and approved, this methodological design becomes the sturdy, steady base on which the research rests; day after day, interview after interview, survey after survey, the preset methodological protocols guarantee research consistency and guard against unintended bias or intellectual tangent on the part of the researcher. When the research is subsequently published, method re-appears as foundation again, this time establishing the evaluative basis for the findings presented and arguments made in the article or book. In this sense those traditionally trained in criminology generally see good method as a well-laid concrete slab – a level, reliable foundation for constructing research, a firm footing for investigating the social world.

Survey research and subsequent statistical analysis constitute especially solid foundational slabs. Quick and quantifiable, with preset questions and preset answer options structuring in replication and reliability, surveys flood criminology with information on subjects ranging from police procedures and domestic violence to gang membership and crime fears. Yet what survey research churns forth in quantity it forfeits in quality. Shallow in its conceptualization, abstract in its approach to the lived social world, dehumanizing and reductionist in its statistical manipulations, survey research is questionable at best – the foundation for a sort of pre-fabricated intellectual housing often thrown up with little craft or care (Ferrell 2014; Young 2004). As a foundation for research into a world adrift, survey research and statistical analysis are especially inappropriate; by the necessities of their design and execution, they constitute a uniquely wrongheaded and heavy-handed slab of methodological misdirection. Survey research generally assumes a social world defined by static, discrete and measurable factuality – degree of drug use, amount of sexual misconduct, number of victims – a factuality foreign to the fluid arrangements and emergent identities of those whose lives float with movement, uncertainty and change. Based on models of statistical probability and sampling, surveys are seldom administered to the entire population under study; instead, they are administered to a statistically representative sample of a set, knowable population. By definition, though, drifters offer no definable population and thus no possibility of accurate sampling; the lives of homeless folks, illicit migrants, sex workers and unknown others are defined by, if nothing else, a sort of sacred immeasurability. And even if survey researchers could know the precise population of homeless wanderers or international migrants – which they can't – how would they locate a sample in order to administer the survey? You can't read a survey to someone you can't find. You can't call someone without a phone or mail a survey to someone without an address. You can't elicit a response to an online survey from someone without a computer.

When researchers nonetheless attempt to lay down slabs of survey research and data analysis amidst situations shaped by emergence and ambiguity, the results are predictably disfiguring. The shifting codes of the street, and the shifting populations that do and don't abide by them, are imagined to be captured in survey answer sets or statistical summaries. The fluid, Rashomon-like ambiguity of encounters between police officers and citizens is made measurable, both in its frequency and in its characteristics. The liquidity of gang membership, and the parallel liquidity of gang identity as negotiated in various situations, is claimed to be captured in a series of summary tables. The severity of crimes committed by 'the homeless', the degree of alcohol abuse among unemployed college graduates, the scope of the underground economy – all are artificially constructed as stable structures atop the foundation of positivist method. In this way the slabs sit heavier still. The solidity of the method trumps the fluidity of the world it means to investigate; the foundation comes to matter more than the damage it does. And, in reality, these criminological edifices and the slabs on which they sit offer little place for drifters, the displaced and those in search of identity. In fact, they are engineered to exclude and erase them, to convert emergent issues and fluid populations into static data sets available for ceaseless statistical manipulation.

## Under the slab, the beach

'Sous les pavés, la plage', the Situationists wrote – 'Under the paving stones, the beach' – suggesting that lost underneath the suffocating uniformity of an administered and paved-over existence, waiting to be re-discovered, was the vital beauty of wave-like movement, fresh intellectual breezes and languid pleasure. Dig up the paving stones, disassemble the structures of technical certainty, they argued, and human possibility would re-surface. So it is with criminological method; prying up the slab foundations of positivist methodology, we are able to imagine methods more in sync with the drifting uncertainty of contemporary life, methods better able to flow with liquidities of human identity and understanding. A few of these can be suggested here – some that wait under the slab and some that were there long before it was laid.

### Before the slab

In 1923, Nels Anderson published *The Hobo: The Sociology of the Homeless Man*, one of the canonical texts in sociological criminology. Like his father, Anderson was himself a long-time itinerant worker – in fact, he hopped the last of his many freight trains to get to graduate school at the University of Chicago. Once there, he began his focused research and writing on hobos – and yet even then, as he recalled (Anderson 1923/1961: xi–xiii): 'I found myself engaged in research without the preparation a researcher is supposed to have. I couldn't answer if asked about my "methods".' What methodological instruction Anderson was offered was decidedly informal. 'Of the guidance I received at the University of Chicago from Professors Robert E. Park and Ernest W. Burgess', Anderson remembers, 'most was indirect. The only instruction I recall from Park was, "Write down only what you see, hear, and know, like a newspaper reporter".' Later, Anderson (1940: 2) modestly wondered if *The Hobo* even held up in comparison to 'better contributions of earlier date', like that of Jack London's (1907) *The Road*, a largely autobiographical work recalling London's early years of tramping and hoboing around America. And London's method, to which Anderson graciously deferred? 'Every once in a while, in newspapers, magazines, and biographical dictionaries, I run upon sketches of my life, wherein, delicately phrased, I learn that it was in order to study sociology that I became a tramp', London (1907: 85) recalled. 'This is very nice and thoughtful of the biographers, but it is inaccurate. I became a tramp – well, because of the life that was in me, of the wanderlust in my blood that would not let me rest. Sociology was merely incidental; it came afterward, in the same manner that a wet skin follows a ducking.'

The work of esteemed documentary photographer Dorothea Lange and her husband and collaborator, the economist Paul Taylor, proceeded similarly. During the 1930s, Lange and Taylor wandered the country with those whom economic and agricultural failure had forced on to the road. As Taylor noted in their 1939 book *An American Exodus*, under the heading 'Nonstatistical Notes from the Field', he and Lange purposely decided to avoid numbers and 'to place primary reliance on personal observation of people in the situation to be studied in the field close-up' (Lange and Taylor 1939/1969: 136). Describing the iconic 'White Angel Bread Line' and other on-the-spot Depression-era photos that she shot, Lange likewise recalled: 'I can only say I knew I was looking at something. You know there are moments such as these when time stands still and all you do is hold your breath and hope it will wait for you. And you just hope you will have enough time to get it organized in a fraction of a second on that tiny piece of sensitive film' (cited in Coles 1997: 149). Likewise, the pioneering photodocumentarian Henri Cartier-Bresson lived by his notion of *images à la sauvette* ('images on the run'), to be captured by the photographer in a 'decisive moment' which involved the photographer's 'simultaneous recognition, in a fraction of a second, of the significance of an event as well as the precise organization of forms which give that event its proper expression' (cited in Miller 1997: 102; see also Ferrell and Van de Voorde 2010).

Approaches like these mix the open road of intellectual and physical wandering with those little moments that emerge, unplanned and otherwise unnoticed, along that road. The collaborative drifting that results is animated by informality, sympathy, sharp awareness and a distinct disinclination to reify methodology. The approach remains emergent *in extremis*, neither a technical straitjacket nor an end in itself, but rather a careful preparation for carelessly letting go, a method by which method can be abandoned in the moment. Unlike the fetishized reifications of those who insist on slabs, this approach is fluid and supple, best perhaps when it disappears into instinct and intuition. 'We never, never talked about photography', Cartier-Bresson recalls of his time spent working with other founders of documentary photography. 'Never! It would have been monstrous, presumptuous' (cited in Miller 1997: 24). In this sense, digging up the slabs of contemporary criminological method allows us to remember, re-discover and revitalize that which was buried beneath them in the name of social scientific rigour and methodological status. It encourages us to reject a contemporary criminology that has now become precisely the sort of presumptuous monster that Cartier-Bresson disavowed – fetishizing method as something exterior to, even superior to, the worlds it aims to engage – and to re-orient ourselves to mystery and immediacy.

### Time and space, liquefied

The liquefied circumstances of the contemporary world are such that it is not only careers and communities that melt into air; time and space also dissolve away from the rigidities of the Fordist factory clock and the urban planner's grid. Because of this, criminologists need research approaches that can flow with this uncertain movement, approaches that resemble rhythmic inventions more than stationary foundations.

*Instant ethnography* (Ferrell et al. 2015), for example, recalls the photographic approaches of Lange and Cartier-Bresson by focusing on those ephemeral moments in which social life takes shape and takes on meaning. Highlighting both the instantaneity of late modern communication and the dangerous unpredictability that besets dislocated populations and fragile situations, instant ethnography attunes researchers to those emergent flashes of action and emotion that animate transgression and social control. This approach also incorporates a sociology of drifters and the dislocated, suggesting that the intensities of their ephemeral associations may require different sorts of focused attention than do the less intense, long-term associations of the sedentary. Likewise, instant ethnography responds to the illicit identities, thrill-seeking endeavours and short-term affiliations that pervade late modern life; it is meant to be a method that can put researchers inside the risky uncertainty of such circumstances and prepare them for the sort of instantaneous recognition necessary to make sense of them. *Spectral ethnography* or *ghost ethnography*, on the other hand, looks beyond the present instant to search for what is now gone or never was. To look for what never was is to invoke the criminological imagination (Young 2011) and the politics of absence; it is to trace the ghosts of exclusion, the women or immigrants or homeless folks never allowed in. To notice what is now gone is to invoke a different politics of absence; it is to record those populations who have drifted away and those arrangements that have been lost to historical change, while also accounting for the ghostly presence of these losses that lingers in our lives (Armstrong 2010; Linnemann 2015; Tunnell 2011). In this context, ghost ethnography also suggests an attentiveness to aftermaths and ruins, whether temporal, physical or emotional – a necessary attentiveness, it would seem, in a world of failing industries, lost careers, brief encounters and contracting empires.

What we might call *interstitial ethnography* promotes a sensitivity to spaces that exist in between and around the edges; it suggests as way of seeing the world glancingly, out of the corner of one's eye, with an awareness that the most important action may take place out of frame and out of focus. Those on the margins, for example, are as likely to be found moving between official urban spaces as residing in them; in the same way, they may well spend more of their lives 'between jobs' than in a single job, with this ongoing interstitial state taking on its own meanings and rituals. Likewise, drifters, immigrants and outcasts are often consigned to the back stages of social life, their lives spent as temporary labourers or service personnel hidden behind, beneath or between the official spaces of institutional life. And these interstitial states are temporal as well, characterized by waiting and hanging out on the one hand, and hurried departures and temporary occupation on the other. As Andrea Brighenti (2013: xviii, emphasis in original) argues, 'interstices *cannot be known in advance*: the interstice is not simply a physical space, but very much a phenomenon "on the ground", a "happening", a "combination" or an "encounter"'. Here the interstitial intersects with the immediate, further destabilizing any possibility of slab-like certainty. Here also is precisely the point that scholars like Robert Garot (2010) and Simon Hallsworth (2013) make about street gangs: they are not the steady organizational structures that slab researchers imagine, but rather shifting webs of identity and affiliation that form up in the immediacies of the city's margins. Hallsworth (2013: 124, 196) in this light recommends 'reading the street as rhizome' and adds: 'think fuzzy thoughts about fluid institutions that are only ever always interstitial and you are halfway there'.

Perhaps the most fluid of these approaches is, aptly enough, *liquid ethnography*. As developed by Ferrell, Hayward and Young (2005), liquid ethnography replaces ethnography's traditional focus on relatively stable, identifiable groups and spatial situations with a focus on social lives in ongoing transition; in this sense, it is as much the study of uncertainty and destabilization as it is the study of people and groups. As undertaken by various researchers, this approach has meant following the trajectory of illicit subcultures as law enforcement campaigns push them between cities and countries, and in and out of legal categories as well; tracing the careers of those labelled criminal as some sink deeper into crime, while others change course toward commercial success; and even tracking the commodity chains by which global labour continually underwrites the pleasures of First World transgression (see Redmon 2015). Where instant ethnography attends to the immediacy and intensity of liquid life, liquid ethnography in this way follows the long unwinding of drift and dislocation. Beyond this, liquid ethnography embraces the contemporary power of the image, and the spiralling overspill between social life and images of it. Liquid ethnographers investigate the politics of image production in and around alternative worlds, actively collaborate with research subjects in the production of public and scholarly images, and work to shift criminological discourse itself into the realms of video and film. In this sense, methods like liquid ethnography that move criminological researchers towards engagement with the fluidity and visuality of modern life are meant to move the discipline in that direction as well.

### *Liquid identity*

A method like liquid ethnography embodies yet another fluidity – one that perhaps most dramatically distances these newer approaches from the positivist pretensions of slab criminology. This is the liquid interplay between researcher and subjects of study; that is, the melting of the methodological boundary that separates the criminologist from the research setting and those others who occupy it. In liquid ethnography, researchers move back and forth between investigation, involvement and activism, all the while reflexively accounting for their own emotions and effects as part of the research. Significantly, this methodological re-orientation is once again a professional and disciplinary reorientation as well, replacing the solid certainty of 'social scientist' or 'criminologist' with an uncertain mélange of roles and identities. As with the practice of *autoethnography* (Ferrell 2012b; Hallsworth 2013; Root et al. 2013), this confusion of roles and expectations – anathema to the conventional social scientist – offers a new generation of researchers profound methodological and scholarly possibilities, opening the research process to emergent experiences and alternative perspectives, and attuning it to the ambiguity and uncertainty of the world under study. Here liquid criminology comes full circle. Criminologists who are less likely than their predecessors to occupy stable careers and are less likely to define themselves by distinct institutional affiliation are able to convert their inconsistencies of status and identity into a new sort of methodological imagination, and a new, slippery sort of *verstehen* with those they seek to study.

The slab upturned, the beach beckons.

## References

Anderson, Nels (1923/1961) *The Hobo: The Sociology of the Homeless Man.* Chicago: University of Chicago Press.

——. (1940) *Men on the Move.* Chicago: University of Chicago Press.

Armstrong, Justin (2010) 'On the Possibility of Spectral Ethnography'. *Cultural Studies ⇔ Critical Methodologies*, 10(3): 243–50.

Brighenti, Andrea Mubi (ed.) (2013) *Urban Interstices.* Farnham: Ashgate.

Coles, Robert (1997) *Doing Documentary Work.* New York: Oxford University Press.

Ferrell, Jeff (2012a) 'Outline of a Criminology of Drift', in Steve Hall and Simon Winlow (eds), *New Directions in Criminological Theory.* London: Routledge, pp. 241–56.

——. (2012b) 'Autoethnography', in David Gadd, Susanne Karstedt and Steven Messner (eds), *The Sage Handbook of Criminological Research Methods.* London: Sage Publications, pp. 218–30.

——. (2014) 'Manifesto for a Criminology Beyond Method', in Michael Hviid Jacobsen (ed.), *The Poetics of Crime.* Farnham: Ashgate, pp. 285–302.

Ferrell, Jeff and Cecile Van de Voorde (2010) 'The Decisive Moment: Documentary Photography and Cultural Criminology', in Keith Hayward and Mike Presdee (eds), *Framing Crime: Cultural Criminology and the Image.* London: Routledge, pp. 36–52.

Ferrell, Jeff, Keith Hayward and Jock Young (2015) *Cultural Criminology: An Invitation*, 2nd edn. London: Sage Publications.

Garot, Robert (2010) *Who You Claim: Performing Gang Identity in School and on the Streets.* New York: New York University Press.

Hallsworth, Simon (2013) *The Gang and Beyond.* Basingstoke: Palgrave Macmillan.

Lange, Dorothea and Paul Taylor (1939/1969) *An American Exodus.* New Haven: Yale University Press.

Linnemann, Travis (2015) 'Capote's Ghosts: Violence, Media and the Spectre of Suspicion'. *British Journal of Criminology*, 55(3): 514–33.

London, Jack (1907) *The Road.* New York: Macmillan/Aegypan Press.

Miller, Russell (1997) *Magnum: Fifty Years at the Front Line of History.* New York: Grove.

Redmon, David (2015) *Beads, Bodies and Trash.* New York: Routledge.

Root, Carl, Jeff Ferrell and Wilson Palacios (2013) 'Brutal Serendipity: Criminological Verstehen and Victimization'. *Critical Criminology*, 21(2): 141–55.

Tunnell, Kenneth (2011) *Once upon a Place: The Fading of Community in Rural Kentucky.* Bloomington, IN: Xlibris.

Young, Jock (2004) 'Voodoo Criminology and the Numbers Game', in Jeff Ferrell, Keith Hayward, Wayne Morrison and Mike Presdee (eds), *Cultural Criminology Unleashed.* London: GlassHouse Press, pp. 13–27.

——. (2011) *The Criminological Imagination.* Cambridge: Polity Press.

# Index